PRAEGER LIBRARY OF U.S. GOVERNMENT DEPARTMENTS
AND AGENCIES

The National
Park Service

PRAEGER LIBRARY OF U.S. GOVERNMENT DEPARTMENTS
AND AGENCIES

Consulting Editors

ERNEST S. GRIFFITH

Former University Professor and Dean Emeritus, School of International Service, American University; former Director, Legislative Reference Service, Library of Congress; and author of *The American System of Government* and *The Modern Government in Action*

HUGH LANGDON ELSBREE

Former Chairman, Department of Political Science, Dartmouth College; former Managing Editor, *American Political Science Review;* former Director, Legislative Reference Service, Library of Congress

THE U.S. GOVERNMENT today is a maze of departments and agencies engaged in a worldwide range of programs and activities. Some departments are as old as the government itself; others are newly created or have been expanded or redirected by recent legislation. The books in this series describe the origin, development, function, methods, and structure of specific departments or agencies and explain how far their activities extend and how they relate to other branches of the government and to the public. All are written by authors with firsthand knowledge of their subjects.

The *Praeger Library of U.S. Government Departments and Agencies* is the only comprehensive, detailed source of such information. More than seventy titles are planned for the series; a list of those already published appears at the back of this volume. — THE EDITORS

The National Park Service

William C. Everhart

FOREWORD BY
GEORGE B. HARTZOG, JR.

PRAEGER PUBLISHERS
New York • Washington • London

This book is for

MARY, KIM, AND ROB

PRAEGER PUBLISHERS
111 Fourth Avenue, New York, N.Y. 10003, U.S.A.
5, Cromwell Place, London SW7 2JL, England

Published in the United States of America in 1972
by Praeger Publishers, Inc.

© 1972 by Praeger Publishers, Inc.

Library of Congress Catalog Card Number: 77–151951

This book is No. 31 in the series
Praeger Library of U.S. Government Departments and Agencies

Printed in the United States of America

Foreword

by GEORGE B. HARTZOG, JR.
Director, National Park Service

The publication of this book in 1972 is particularly timely, for it coincides with the celebration of the 100th anniversary of the establishment in 1872 of Yellowstone, the world's first national park. The development in this country of the national park idea was in many ways a natural outgrowth of the "pursuit of happiness" clause of the Declaration of Independence, for it initiated the policy of preserving superlative natural landscapes and cultural sites in public ownership for the benefit of all citizens.

In 1976 the United States will be celebrating its 200th anniversary, and without question one of the most critical issues of this nation's future will be to create a truly livable environment for all Americans. The two anniversaries are thus closely related, for national parks, in the broadest meaning of that term, constitute an indispensable element of a livable environment.

In the early stages of the park movement, the mission of the National Park Service was to manage the parks, and its activities did not extend beyond park boundaries. This book vividly records the broadening of this mission until today the Park Service can be considered a social institution, concerned

v

with human as well as scenic and wildlife values. The national parks, like life, are meant to be lived, and in parks we can better understand, or perceive, our place in the universe. The ultimate test of the national park idea is its ability to respond to the urgent needs of society.

You will find also that the future of the national parks is dependent upon the attitude which this nation takes toward its environment. For the parks are not perfect sanctuaries, isolated from the ecological dangers which threaten other localities. The pesticide residues that drain from Florida agricultural lands pass into the water system of Everglades National Park, where they menace the delicately balanced chain of life upon which all plants and wildlife in the park depend. The national parks can survive only if the quest for a quality environment is successful.

This book was written by a veteran Park Service interpreter, a fitting choice. Interpretation is the art of making the park experience meaningful, and through this significant activity the talents and experience of the Park Service organization are being mobilized in support of the environmental struggle.

A century ago, when the first national park was set aside, a frontier still existed in the West. There was no immediate need for such a national preserve, and few people were aware of the existence of Yellowstone. Now, a hundred years later, national parks are desperately needed, and our task is to ensure that the parks have a meaningful relevance to the daily lives of all of our citizens.

The National Park Service organization is small enough so that a good majority of its career employees know one another—and young enough so that some of the men who helped organize the new agency back in 1916 are still close associates. The greatest factor in binding these people into an intensely dedicated organization is the continuing opportunity that each individual has of contributing to the development of the national park concept.

We have not yet become, as an organization, all that we should be. Recognizing that the national parklands are superlative examples of the nation's natural, historic, and cultural resources, we are seeking a way to use these living standards of excellence in the national search for an environmental ethic.

John Gardner expressed this aspiration when he spoke of the ethical principles which must govern the relationship between man and his environment: "in touch with the land and living things, reverent, healing, renewing, committed to preserve, to enhance, to enjoy."

Preface

A number of men spent a grueling day a couple of summers ago slogging through the Toklat River in Mount McKinley National Park, risking chilblains or worse from extended immersion in icy water while searching in vain for a glimpse of an elusive wolf pack. Later that day, over a memorable slug of bourbon, one member of the party remarked that in Alaska most undertakings turn out to be adventures. The comment explains something of the attraction of working for the National Park Service. Although the ratio between adventures and paper shuffling seems to be increasingly weighted in behalf of the latter, there is still a measurable flavor of adventure to most Park Service assignments.

There is also present a degree of partisanship, for one tends to think of, say, the Grand Tetons as something more than a textbook example of glaciers at work. As a result, someone who writes a book about the Park Service, particularly while he is still, like the author, an active participant in the organization, has considerable difficulty maintaining a coolly dispassionate viewpoint, if he should happen to cherish such an approach. People who are responsible for the administration of the national parks inevitably have strong feelings about them. In the Park Service, the more easily aroused are generally referred to, not without affection, as "heavy breathers."

As will be evident to the reader, the author of this volume is, of course, not a heavy breather himself. But I have not passed up the opportunity to direct an occasional barb at the mumbo-jumbo workings of the federal bureaucracy or at the rarefied pronouncements of some conservationists.

Those interested in pursuing National Park Service history and policy matters further will find it profitable to consult the following sources, which I have found particularly valuable: the two biographies of the founding fathers of the Park Service—the fast-paced *Steve Mather of the National Parks*, by Robert Shankland, and *Wilderness Defender: Horace M. Albright and Conservation*, by the conservation historian Donald C. Swain—as well as *Our National Park Policy: A Critical History*, by John Ise, a scholarly compendium of most known facts about the scenic and archeological parks.

My perception of Park Service matters has been vastly heightened over the years by a rewarding association with Freeman Tilden, whose *Interpreting Our Heritage* and *The National Parks* are classic treatments by the wisest interpreter of our national parks and one of the most felicitous writers on the subject.

I acknowledge a substantial debt to many Park Service colleagues for the substance of this book and for reviewing portions of the manuscript. Hopefully the Director, George Hartzog, will not have second thoughts about his having taken the position that I should be entirely free to say what I thought. My organizationally appointed guardian, Joe Jensen, an engineer of rare sensitivity, was supportive well beyond prescribed limits. Jim Reid, that Alaska sourdough and *Merck's Manual* practitioner, kept me straight on matters ecological, and many of his delightful marginal notes were surreptitiously incorporated in the text. Administrative support services were in the competent hands of Mary Coyle Mapleleaf.

WILLIAM C. EVERHART

Reston, Virginia
January, 1972

Contents

CHART AND MAP

A section of photographs follows page 84.

The National
Park Service

I

In the Beginning

In the fall of 1914, Secretary of the Interior Franklin K. Lane was looking for a man who could administer the Department of the Interior's national parks. A former journalist and lawyer, Lane's approach to conservation said something about the climate of the times. He had announced that conservation problems were simply a matter of common sense on which men of good will, sitting around a table, could obviously reach agreement.

The Secretary had little to offer any candidate for the national parks job. The salary was a mere $2,750 a year, the problems were immense, and there was no staff. The thirteen national parks were being administered under loosely defined —if that—ground rules laid down by civilian and military superintendents acting under the even more capricious supervision of the various secretaries of the Interior, who generally had little time for the parks. Upon taking office Lane had declared, "If the railroads were conducted in the same manner as the national parks, no man would be brave enough to ride from Washington to Baltimore."

In the mail one morning Lane found a letter complaining about the national parks—hardly a rare item then or now. It

3

was signed "Stephen T. Mather." Lane knew Mather personally. They had attended the University of California together, and since college days Mather's career had been spectacular. He had become one of the giants of the borax industry, and now, at forty-seven, he was a millionaire and philanthropist, an outdoorsman who found escape from business pressures in wilderness camping trips.

Mather had recently visited Yosemite and Sequoia National Parks, and his letter described the deplorable conditions encountered: trails were almost impassable; cattle grazed inside the parks; and enterprising lumbermen had acquired some of the choicest sequoia groves on the intriguing premise that because the ground around them was soggy in the spring from melting snow, they qualified for cutting under the Swamp Land Act.

Mather's angry letter of protest to the Secretary of the Interior drew a quick and historic reply: "Dear Steve—If you don't like the way the national parks are being run, come on down to Washington and run them yourself."

It took considerable persuasion, but Mather finally agreed at least to go to Washington and talk the matter over with Lane. The Secretary made an eloquent appeal, pointing out that the unfortunate conditions Mather had observed were typical, that the parks desperately needed public and congressional support and the kind of leadership that Mather might provide.

Knowing that Mather had a free-wheeling style and anticipating that he would take little delight in exchanging this freedom for the numbing procedures of the federal bureaucracy, Lane introduced his personal aide, Horace Albright, a young lawyer of twenty-four, as a person who could serve as Mather's assistant and handle the red tape. Then the Secretary withdrew, and the two men sat down in Lane's spacious office to talk it over.

A Californian, Albright had come to Washington for a

year's experience. His time was up, he told Mather. He had a good job offer back in San Francisco and was planning to get married. Mather was equally reluctant to stay on in Washington. His wife was concerned for his well-being and felt he already had far too many interests going at the same time. But as they exchanged confidences, the two men agreed that someone must do battle for the parks, for both shared a profound love of the wild country. Mather's ingrained enthusiasm soon surfaced as he began to picture the contribution that could be made in establishing a first-class, professional organization to administer the parks. "I couldn't resist him," Albright later recalled.

In January, 1915, Stephen Tyng Mather was sworn in as assistant to the Secretary of the Interior. He began an association with Albright and the national parks that was to last for the rest of his life. Neither Mather nor Albright—nor the national parks—would ever be quite the same again.

Beginning a book on the National Park Service with the timeworn account of the arrival of its founding fathers probably vindicates a former assistant secretary of the Interior, who became so frustrated by steadfast Park Service insistence on maintaining its traditions and its identity within the Department that he publicly declared the bureau to be suffering from a bad case of "mystique." Too bad for his pique, and his no doubt unselfish intent—he added but one more choice anecdote to Park Service lore, and the mystique lives on.

For Mather and Albright did succeed. An organization to administer the national parks was established, and over the years it became a model for the world. The real story of the National Park Service is not a recounting of budgets or visitor statistics; it is primarily the story of people, highly motivated, who have been drawn to the Park Service because they wanted to work in and for the national parks. While not many of the park men who followed Mather could match his flamboyance, nearly all shared his idealism and his total commitment to the national park idea.

But the National Park Service, as a bureau of the Department of the Interior, did not come along until almost half a century after the first national park was set aside. In deference, then, to established protocol governing discussions of national park beginnings, the story must start with Yellowstone.

FOR THE BENEFIT AND ENJOYMENT OF THE PEOPLE

For the pioneer settlers who followed Lewis and Clark into the American West, wilderness was the cruel and dangerous enemy that had to be conquered, and there was no higher aspiration than to make the trackless wasteland blossom like a flower. In the course of his visit to the United States in 1831, Alexis de Tocqueville fulfilled a lifelong urge by traveling to Michigan to see primitive country. Men he encountered could comprehend neither his craving for wilderness nor his indifference to such traditional frontier pursuits as land speculation, timber-stealing from the public domain, and destruction of the American Indian in the name of progress and religion. Americans had a different set of values, their vision "fixed upon another sight . . . the march across these wilds, draining swamps, turning the course of rivers, peopling solitudes, and subduing nature."

The perceptive French observer knew that those farthest away from the wilderness treasured it the most. For those who lived on the frontier, the untouched lands seemed so incredibly vast that no practical man could conceive they might ever be exhausted. It was an era in which the exemplary virtues of rugged individualism and free enterprise were the foremost commandments of Manifest Destiny. On the frontier the climate was such that the pioneers railed against any government interference with their right to exploit freely whatever natural wonders they happened upon first. One of the earliest areas to attract such attention was the mysterious region lying at the headwaters of the Yellowstone River.

John Colter, the legendary mountain man, first brought back tales of the unbelievable phenomena encountered in his wilderness trek of 1807, and for the next sixty years prospectors and fur trappers, Jim Bridger among them, helped fill in the details. The accounts only strengthened general disbelief among sober citizens as to the actual existence of a land where the earth smoked and fumed from subterranean fires and exploding waterspouts. Not to mention streams so saturated with alum they had power to pucker distance itself.

In the fall of 1870 an expedition set out from Helena, in Montana Territory, to make the first official exploration of the Yellowstone country. Heading the party were General Henry D. Washburn, surveyor-general of the territory and former member of Congress, who had come to Montana with a wagon train in 1862 and had heard tales of Yellowstone direct from Jim Bridger; Nathaniel P. (later "National Park") Langford, writer, lecturer, and vigilante; and Lieutenant Gustavus C. Doane, who led a small cavalry troop as protection for the civilian party against the uncertain hospitality of the Crow and Blackfeet.

One of the most memorable experiences for expedition members, as for most park visitors today, took place shortly before the exploration ended. Following along the Firehole River, the party abruptly emerged from a dense lodgepole forest. Only a few hundred yards away, in an open valley marked by numerous wisps and clouds of vapor, a column of water and steam was shooting more than one hundred feet into the sky. With impeccable timing, the geyser, which the party named "Old Faithful," emerged from fable to become the symbol of Yellowstone.

The Washburn-Langford-Doane expedition marked the effective beginning of the effort to preserve Yellowstone. Articles and speeches by members of the party, along with the results of the scientific exploration of the following year, which was led by Dr. F. V. Hayden and included artist Thomas Moran and photographer William Jackson, helped generate widespread public interest. Doane reported to Congress:

As a country for sightseers, it is without parallel; as a field for scientific research, it promises great results; in the branches of geology, mineralogy, botany, zoology, and ornithology, it is probably the greatest laboratory that nature furnishes on the surface of the globe.

On March 1, 1872, President Ulysses S. Grant signed the Act establishing Yellowstone National Park, setting aside an enormous tract of 2 million acres "as a public park or pleasuring ground for the benefit and enjoyment of the people." The Act not only barred forever from commercial use the riches of timber, grass, water power, and minerals, it also established for the first time the policy of national ownership of superlative resources for the common good.

Considering the fact that to reach the borders of the new park would require a couple of weeks' tough travel by horseback from the nearest rail line, the possibility that many people would ever reach Yellowstone must have seemed extremely remote in 1872—particularly after the untimely death of a couple of early park visitors at the hands of Nez Percé warriors under Chief Joseph. Nevertheless the basic elements of the national park idea, as it is recognized today, were stated, or implicit, in the Act of 1872 and provided the guiding philosophy for all the parks that were to follow.

In fact, the whole idea of setting aside Yellowstone as the world's first national park seems today almost to smack of the miraculous. It was primarily the work of a handful of idealists—members of the several Yellowstone explorations who believed the scenic wonders should be shared by all and a few men of vision in Congress, including the senator who predicted that if government protection were not forthcoming some worthy member of the land-grabbing fraternity would "plant himself right across the only path that leads to these wonders, and charge every man that passes along between the gorges of these mountains a fee of a dollar or five dollars." These men were supported and given public attention by crusading publishers and conservationists. The pattern has really not changed much since 1872.

CONVERTING SCENERY INTO GOLD

By 1900 a few more national parks had been created, Yosemite, General Grant (later included in Kings Canyon), Mt. Rainier, and Sequoia. There was, however, no central organization to direct park matters, and each park was regarded as a separate entity. Establishment of a park was most often the result of local action led by a few concerned individuals to prevent despoiling, which, in the case of Yosemite, reached a scale disturbing to even the freewheeling spirit of the frontier. Although Yellowstone was the first federal park, Yosemite had an even earlier history as a state preserve, and there are some, mostly Californians, who claim that it all really began with Yosemite.

Forty-niners returning home empty-handed brought accounts of the grandeur of the valley they called Yo Semite and the fantastic size of the giant sequoias. Hustling to find a way to convert scenery into the gold that escaped them in the Mother Lode, one of the first of the California travel-boosting organizations stripped the unique "Mother of the Forest" sequoia tree in the Calaveras Grove to a height of 116 feet, exhibiting the bark shell as a carnival curiosity in Eastern cities and, in 1854, at the Crystal Palace in London.

James Russell Lowell was among those who damned the wanton destruction of the 3,000-year-old tree, and *Harper's Weekly* declared it had been cut and peeled "with as much neatness and industry as a troupe of jackals would display in cleaning the bones of a dead lion." Public interest in Yosemite picked up with Horace Greeley's personally publicized Western jaunt in 1859. After Mr. Greeley recovered from a bad case of saddle sores, he proclaimed Yosemite "the greatest marvel of the continent." In transferring the lands to California for administration in 1864 to prevent such idiotic depredations as bark stripping, Congress made it clear Yosemite was to be preserved for all citizens by stipulating that the land was ceded "upon the express conditions that the premises shall be held for public use, resort and recreation, shall be held inalienable for all time."

The original Yosemite preserve consisted only of the eight-mile-square valley and the Mariposa Grove of sequoias. Even before the cession, tourist operators and homesteaders had thrown together tourist accommodations. The Secretary of the Interior described the scene a hundred years ago: more than half the valley fenced with barbed wire, fields of grain under cultivation, fragile vegetation destroyed by the plow, the unenclosed portion of the valley reserved for grazing horses—with wildlife, if any, and visitors restricted to the narrow area between the fences and the valley walls.

In the spring of 1868, young John Muir first viewed the steep-walled valley of Yosemite, which was to become for him a personal sanctuary. His lyrical descriptions of the "mountains of light" and his pleas for legislation to enlarge the Yosemite reservation were influential in arousing support for the Yosemite Park Bill, which passed in 1890.

National park status did not immediately solve all of Yosemite's problems, for it needed most of all protection against the great bands of sheep, Muir's despised "hoofed locusts," which continued to use the Yosemite High Country meadows as summer range, cropping grass and wildflowers down to the roots. Leaving the mountains in the fall, sheepherders would set the forests on fire, burning out the tree cover so that in spring the sun could more quickly melt winter snows and provide earlier forage. When Congress got around to providing the first appropriations for Yosemite in 1898, men hired for the purpose drove thousands of sheep and cattle from the park.

While laudable and farsighted, early national park legislation could scarcely be viewed as extravagant. Setting aside parks from the public domain cost little or nothing, and no laws were included to protect the resources or to enforce regulations. Yellowstone at first received no appropriations, and, apparently deeming the honor sufficient reward, Congress provided the first superintendent with neither salary nor staff. The only penalty faced by poachers, who roamed almost at will, was eviction from the park. When a frustrated park superintendent, fearing extermination of the buffalo and elk herds, confiscated the weapons and outfits of a notorious gang of hunters, they brought suit for illegal seizure, and the attorney general held the act unwarranted and ordered the guns returned.

Unable to give the park or its wildlife needed protection, in 1886 the Secretary of the Interior turned to the Secretary of War for help, and that summer the First United States Cavalry relieved the civilian superintendent of his duties and began a thirty-year span of army control of Yellowstone National Park. As Captain Moses Harris and his troops jogged into the park, they passed wagonloads of logs being carted out. They encountered hunters camped by the rivers and saw tourists happily bringing out some of the first Yellowstone souvenirs—mineral specimens knocked off of the geyser and hot spring formations.

. . . AND OTHER OBJECTS OF HISTORIC OR SCIENTIFIC INTEREST

In 1906 the park idea was considerably broadened by two acts of Congress that indicated there could be other than wilderness values in national parks. Scattered throughout the magic lands of the American Southwest are thousands of cliff dwellings and pueblo sites, the remains of a proud Indian civilization whose occupants abandoned their homes centuries before the voyage of Columbus. By 1900 early settlers entering the Four Corners region were quick to discover that Indian artifacts had considerable market value. Inevitably, these priceless cultural remains, which had weathered the ages remarkably well in the dry desert climate, were favored by visits from greedy pothunters seeking maximum salable loot.

In the heyday of commercial looting that followed, probably no cliff dwelling was more thoroughly victimized than the largest and most famous, Cliff Palace, where vandals camped in the ruin broke down the ancient walls with blasting powder, and used thousand-year-old beams for firewood. Mesa Verde National Park in southwestern Colorado, established in 1906, preserved not only that incomparable green tableland slashed by deep, winding canyons, but gave protection also to the greatest collection of archeological ruins in the Southwest, including Cliff Palace.

Sponsored by Representative John F. Lacey, chairman of the House Public Lands Committee and an outstanding conservationist of his time, the Antiquities Act was passed in 1906. It proved one of the most significant pieces of park legislation ever enacted. Culminating the effort to preserve Indian sites, the bill gave legal protection against damaging or removing any historic object from the public lands of the United States. Perhaps of greater importance, the Antiquities Act empowered the President to proclaim as national monuments any lands owned or acquired by the federal government that contained historic landmarks, historic or prehistoric structures, and other objects of historic or scientific interest.

A perhaps unfortunate and lugubrious term, "national monument" originated in Europe, where unusual natural features were so described. Because of its funereal image, the name has been the source of much confusion and considerable hilarity, but frequent efforts to find a better title—beginning with the congressional debate on the bill—have regrettably failed. National monuments have been established to preserve caves, forts, canyons, battlefields, glaciers, birthplaces of famous men, and sand dunes. A substantial number of the areas of the national park system have been established under the Antiquities Act, and before his term expired President Theodore Roosevelt had proclaimed the first eighteen national monuments. Administration of the monuments was left to whichever federal department had jurisdiction over the land.

A Case of Sentimental Nonsense

As the nation moved into the twentieth century, there were signs of a changing attitude toward natural resources. The census of 1890 had sounded America's earliest environmental warning, announcing that for the first time in its history the country no longer had a frontier—a term long synonymous with abundance and prosperity. The continent was finally conquered but, as people were beginning to realize, at a terrible cost. Hundreds of millions of tons of coal and hundreds of millions of barrels of oil were wasted each year by inefficient and criminally reckless methods of mining and drilling. One suspects that William Jennings Bryan was speaking for a good portion of the electorate when, in response to business tycoon J. P. Morgan's fatuous observation, "America is good enough for me," he said, "Whenever he doesn't like it, he can give it back to us."

Theodore Roosevelt's love for the out of doors, coupled with his ranching experience in the Dakotas, engendered his deep concern for the nation's resources. The first President to make conservation a national goal, Roosevelt in 1908 convened a Conference on Conservation, at the White House, that brought together one of the most distinguished assemblages of national leaders ever gathered in this country, including almost all members of the Cabinet and the Supreme Court, the heads of more than seventy societies, and the governors of thirty-four states. President Roosevelt opened the proceedings with a disturbing declaration: "It seems to me time for the country to take account of its natural resources, and to inquire how long they are likely to last."

A small group of park enthusiasts had been trying for some years to convince Congress of the need to establish an organization to administer the national parks and monuments. Their leader was the vigorous president of the American Civic Association, J. Horace McFarland, whose wide conservation interests ranged from rose culture to photography and whose organization was the most effective supporter of the parks during this critical period. His address to the Conservation Conference anticipated by fifty years the present concern for environmental quality. Declaring that the national parks, "all too few in number and extent," must be absolutely inviolate and that the scenic value of all the public lands "must be jealously guarded," he asserted, "We have for a century, Mr. Chairman, stood actually, if not ostensibly, for an uglier America; let us here and now resolve . . . to stand openly and solidly for a more beautiful . . . America."

Establishment of the early parks, during an era when exploitation of the country's resources was the watchword, was a concession to a zealous minority of wilderness lovers. Congress never contemplated there would be a *system* of national parks, properly organized. There was little coordination of policy and no continuity of personnel. And so the parks came along, one by one, created out of what seemed endless public domain, each the work of a relatively few men who saw the need and waited until the political climate was right.

In 1912 President William Howard Taft sent Congress a special message that began, "I earnestly recommend the establishment of a Bureau of National Parks." Taft declared that the lack of support and scattered administration of the parks and monuments among several federal departments threatened their survival; if they were to be given the kind of protection and provided the facilities that would enable people to use and enjoy them, a much more unified and professional administration must be developed. "The first step," said Taft, "is the establishment of a responsible bureau."

Those national parks and monuments already established were receiving little more than custodial care because the great struggle within the conservation movement between the preservationists and the utilitarians was just getting under way. At the moment those supporting the preservation of scenery for its own sake were in the distinct minority. The utilitarians, headed by Gifford Pinchot, who believed the public lands should be managed for many purposes under a plan for balanced use, were in command. Pinchot was Theodore Roosevelt's Chief Forester and, as the President's most trusted adviser in conservation matters, was a powerful influence in the creation of the conservation movement in this country.

The utilitarians saw the dangers of unplanned and uncontrolled exploitation of the nation's resources. They held that scientific efficiency was necessary to achieve full utilization of timber, grasslands, irrigation sites, mineral deposits, and hydroelectric power. Their approach was practical, and, because national parks were not considered practical, a savage battle was drawn between the two factions over Hetch Hetchy. To national park people, the struggle over Hetch Hetchy is only slightly less significant in American history than the furore raised by the Teapot Dome scandal or the Sacco and Vanzetti affair.

About 1900 the city of San Francisco, in looking for a

source of electric power and a future water supply, selected as the best possible dam site the Hetch Hetchy Valley on the Tuolumne River in Yosemite National Park. Selection of the site by city politicians may or may not have been influenced by the fact that, while other sites inspected would cost a great deal of money to acquire, the Yosemite site on federal land would cost the city nothing. The valley itself was incredibly lovely—it was known as the Tuolumne Yosemite —but beyond the destruction of the valley itself the case rested on the integrity of all national parks. The resulting controversy raged for almost fifteen years and involved five secretaries of the Interior—three of whom opposed the sorry project and two of whom, one regrets to add, did not.

John Muir and the Sierra Club, which he founded in 1892 and which had already won its spurs as an outfit with considerable backbone willing to scrap with anyone, led the fight against the dam. Pinchot was for the dam, saying: "I will stand ready to render any assistance in my power." His conservation philosophy did not encompass preservation of nonutilitarian park scenery, which he grandly termed "sentimental nonsense."

The Hetch Hetchy Dam Bill finally passed Congress in 1913. During the debate the chairman of the House Public Lands Committee spoke for the utilitarians and for his era:

When it comes to weighing the highest conservation, on the one hand, of water for domestic use against the preservation of a rocky, craggy canyon, allowing 200,000 gallons of water daily to run idly to the sea, doing no one any good, there is nothing that will appeal to a thoughtful brain of a commonsense, practical man.

Muir had perhaps the final word when he took consolation in the fact that, finally, "the conscience of the whole country has been aroused from sleep." Despite the ever continuing attempts by the dam-building brotherhood to blast its way into the parks, most recently into Dinosaur and Grand Canyon, Hetch Hetchy was and is the only dam ever to be built in a national park.

PARK SERVICE BILL SIGNED

Marking a turning point in the fortunes of the national parks was the arrival on duty of Stephen T. Mather in January, 1915, as special assistant to the Secretary of the Interior. While the cause an agency represents is truly of primary importance in the legislative process, it also happens that in the Washington hierarchy only those agencies with a strong and recognized constituency and plenty of friends in high places get the kind of congressional support that the national parks so badly needed in 1915. Mather's credentials for the job of selling the parks were hard to beat.

Physically, he commanded attention in any group, with broad shoulders, prematurely white hair, and a strong, handsome face. He was everyone's friend, a born promoter with inexhaustible steam, but wholly incapable of deceit, and was described as a practical idealist of the live-wire type. He was also a confirmed disciple of the wilderness, ever since he had climbed Mt. Rainier with fellow Sierra Club members in 1905. A colleague described the Mather approach: "Something about his eyes and the way his face changed color when he talked. If he was out to make a convert, the subject never knew what hit him."

The immediate job that faced Mather was one to tax even a former supersalesman for Twenty Mule Team Borax. Most important was getting passage of the bill to establish a new parks bureau, following which the new bureau would have to be organized and staffed. Substantial increases in funding would have to be obtained for the thirty-one existing national parks and monuments; a nationwide publicity campaign was needed to get the general public interested in parks; concessioners must be stimulated to make vast improvements in hotels, camps, and other facilities; Congress must be persuaded to establish new parks, defeat substandard park bills, and protect existing parks from commercial raids. It wouldn't take more than a year, Mather predicted.

He began, typically, like a whirlwind, first sponsoring a national parks conference in California that brought together superintendents, concessioners, travel people, and congressmen to discuss park needs. He opened Yellowstone to automobiles for the first time as a stimulus to park travel, despite the argument that mixing horse-drawn and motor-powered vehicles would be murderous. To governors and mayors, civic associations and travel clubs, Mather preached on the theme that, if properly promoted, national parks could bring in tourist gold. Having spent five years on the *New York Sun*, Mather had a well-developed talent for public relations, an untilled field for the national parks. As his publicity and promotional schemes multiplied, he hit upon a real winner— one that every succeeding Director has used. He invited influential persons into the parks to receive their blessings.

Mather's successful string of mountain trips began that summer of 1915 when he gathered a distinguished party of politicians, publishers, businessmen, writers, and conservationists for a back-country camping expedition into California's Sierra Nevada. In addition to Mather and Albright, the party included such well-known figures as Burton Holmes, the noted travel lecturer of lantern slide memory; Henry Fairfield Osborne, president of the American Museum of Natural History; Emerson Hough, author of *The Covered Wagon*; Frederick H. Gillett of Massachusetts, later Speaker of the House; and Gilbert Grosvenor, editor of *National Geographic*.

Among the first to appreciate the persuasive elements of a junket, Mather wisely chose not to subject his Eastern visitors to excessive privations. The lavish arrangements, for which he personally paid the bill, included a new sleeping bag and air mattress for each pioneer, an abundant supply of fresh fruits and vegetables, and Tie Sing—whose selection as camp cook was a stroke of genius. "An Oriental dream," exclaimed one guest, recalling the meals that, accompanied by freshly baked bread and rolls and served on a white linen tablecloth, unfailingly provided a perfect ending to each day's journey. Saddlesore and weary, the two dozen "Big Men," who had eaten freshly caught trout under stately sequoias, returned to civilization after two weeks with unmistakable signs of having picked up that incurable national park fever. With such inspired methods, a small army of friends of the Park Service was recruited over the years by Mather.

After this initial mountain trip, Mather and Albright set out to review field operations, crisscrossing most of the West by railroad, switching to automobiles and traversing primitive roads as they visited Crater Lake and Mt. Rainier. They helped promote national park status for Mt. Olympus National Monument (it took twenty-three years and one of the epic conservation battles before Olympic National Park was finally established), and joined in the dedication of Rocky Mountain National Park. From Denver they traveled by train to Cody, Wyoming, then wallowed along by automobile in a driving rain into Yellowstone and on to Glacier. Ignoring local advice they mounted horses and set off over Gunsight Pass in heavy snow, spending two nights in back-country chalets while crossing the Rocky Mountains west to east.

Soon after returning to Washington they found the year they had pledged to the parks was almost gone. Both had set a killing pace—Mather alone had traveled 30,000 miles—and significant progress had been made. But a Park Service Bill had not been passed, so they agreed to pledge another year.

Legislation was again introduced in 1916; similar bills

had been advanced in almost every session of Congress since 1900. In previous years, a distressing obstacle was the fact that no more than a scattered few members of Congress could have spoken on the subject of national parks for as long as five minutes, even allowing for the usual digressions. But Mather was now on a first-name basis with well-placed congressmen. He had extensive lobbying help from conservation organizations, and he encouraged national magazines to muster their readers. The popular *Saturday Evening Post* joined the campaign; *National Geographic* devoted an entire issue to the nation's scenic wonders; the railroads paid for a handsome *National Parks Portfolio* book, which a corps of volunteers from the General Federation of Women's Clubs addressed and mailed free to a quarter of a million people. It was a well-organized and vigorously executed legislative drive.

Still, progress was slow; 1916 was a Presidential election year, and Congress adjourned twice for the Democratic and Republican conventions. Despairing of any action, Mather left Washington to lead yet another contingent of dignitaries into the mountains, but in late August the bill finally passed. With only one day left before Mather would have completed his camping trip, Albright set out to give his chief a well-earned surprise. By adroit footwork, he shepherded the bill from the Capitol to the White House for a signature by President Woodrow Wilson the same evening.

When Mather and his party arrived at the Palace Hotel in Visalia, California, the following day, a telegram awaited him. "Park Service bill signed nine o'clock last night. Have pen used by President in signing for you."

The office of the Director of the National Park Service, in which the telegram and pen are today displayed as treasured mementos, could, without much discomfort, contain the entire staff that the Act provided for: a Director at $4,500, an assistant director at $2,500, a chief clerk at $2,000, a draftsman at $1,800, a messenger at $600, and as many more employees as Mather desired—so long as the total expenditures for the new organization did not exceed $19,500 for the year. Just slightly more generous in its treatment of the parks, Congress allowed a half million dollars for operations. It was a tiny organization and a meager budget to administer seventeen national parks and twenty-two national monuments.

The genius of the bill, however, was contained in the enduring statement of national park purpose, never improved upon, largely the work of the noted landscape architect Frederick Law Olmstead, Jr.:

To conserve the scenery and the natural and historic objects and the wildlife therein and to provide for the enjoyment of the same in such manner and by such means as will leave them unimpaired for the enjoyment of future generations.

II
The New Bureau

Establishment of the new bureau coincided with the entry of the United States into World War I. Not only was fiscal support curtailed, but, in a spirit of wartime sacrifice, the new agency was faced with demands that resources "locked up" in the parks be made available for the war effort. Eager to have his Department on the firing line, Secretary Lane proposed that all of Yosemite except the valley be opened for pasturing sheep.

Immensely stirred by Lane's loyal instincts, cattle and sheep patriots exerted heavy pressure on the Park Service, and newspapers regretfully decided that, while "wild posies" were beautiful, they were not as vital as mutton. Eventually some grazing was permitted in several of the parks, but the short duration of U.S. participation in the war prevented serious damage.

In exchange for this wartime concession, the Park Service offered an equally patriotic suggestion—that army detachments in the parks be released for more meaningful activities in France. Getting the troops out would markedly improve the administrative chaos that Mather faced. Although exclusive control of Yellowstone supposedly rested with the Secretary of the Interior, the superintendent was an army officer appointed by the Secretary of War, as was the case in Yosemite, Sequoia, and General Grant. Yet Mount Rainier and Crater Lake had army engineers for road-building, who were answerable to the War Department but had civilian superintendents.

The Park Service argued that the cavalry troops had outlived their original purpose of driving off commercial poachers and, presumably, putting down local insurrections. Instead, they occupied their days in less military exploits of fighting forest fires and enlightening park visitors. Army occupation had given many parks a first-class road system and provided badly needed protection during the early days, but in 1918 the cavalry troops were finally withdrawn. The Corps of Engineers, which has always displayed a staying power and a political infrastructure unknown to other agencies, chose to relinquish its last park bastions the following year.

THE MATHER ERA

The first decade of the National Park Service was the most formative period. It was a time of rapid growth and development, building an efficient and devoted organization almost from scratch, making the parks known to millions of people, overcoming congressional inertia and public indifference, fighting off vested interests on all sides. By coincidence, it was also an era of accelerated economic prosperity for the nation, and the spectacular arrival of the automobile—a sign of the times—both promoted popular support for the parks and ultimately brought them to a desperate crossroads.

Not all that was achieved during these hectic years was due to Director Stephen Mather, certainly, yet he happened to have the kind of personality that brought to a focus in himself, at the opportune time, all the aspects of the park movement. Able men outside the Park Service provided equally invaluable contributions: a dozen or more members of Congress worked unceasingly to bring in new parks and provide necessary funds; the ever watchful and increasingly influential conservation organizations did much to help formulate park policy and beat off the exploiters; a large number of magazines and newspapers featured stories on the parks; and often, in the absence of congressional appropriations, the responsive philanthropy of private citizens was decisive. The Rockefeller and Mellon families literally gave national parks to the nation.

Railroads had provided the first access to many parks, and the railroad companies built the great hotels, some of which still survive. While automobiles strayed into the parks at a remarkably early date—1908 in the case of Mount Rainier— the roads were narrow and steep. High and hideous, but efficient, the Model T made summer holidays in remote parts of the country a reality for many families. In 1924, the year Henry Ford turned out No. 10,000,000 in his unending line of black tin lizzies, there were only twelve miles of paved roads in all of the national parks.

Mather was a person who went along with progress, taking delight that the automobile would enable a great many more people to enjoy the parks, having confidence they would be converted into certified park boosters. Increased travel would also establish a demand for additional accommodations; except for the railroad hotels, which catered to a favored class of travelers, facilities were scarce and primitive. The concessioners, by instinct and experience on the conservative side, were reluctant to invest until visible signs of prosperity appeared. Encountering resistance from a Yosemite concessioner who agonized over the suggestion that he replace his converted army barracks with a new hotel, Mather exclaimed, "Why, look at those cars! There must be close to two hundred of them. Where's your imagination, man? Some day there'll be a thousand!" By 1928, Yosemite counted 130,000.

An urgent need of the Park Service was to develop a capable and professional ranger force. At his first national parks conference Mather had been disappointed with the caliber of the superintendents, many of whom were politically appointed lightweights, unmoved by his idealism. Rangers and superintendents were not under civil service, and predictably the parks were crippled by vigorous application of the spoils system. When a new administration took office in Washington the faces of new superintendents appeared in the parks, for appointments to many jobs were prerogatives of local congressmen. A story is told, which has the ring of truth, that one such ranger appointee in Glacier National Park had to be assigned patrol duty along the railroad tracks so that he wouldn't get lost in the woods.

Postponing entry into civil service, the Park Service thoroughly cleaned house. It unloaded misfits and shifted jobs around and was highly successful in finding good men, many of whom were attracted from other agencies. Fortunately, from its beginnings, the Park Service has been able to attract a different type of individual. A group of men from unlikely backgrounds have somehow been assembled who combine a cultivated disregard for standard operating procedures with an unorthodox ability to get the job done. For the special flavor that such men have imparted to the agency, the Park Service has been grateful—generally. One who came along in the early days was unusual, even for the Park Service.

A tall, redheaded pilot in the U.S. Air Service, Colonel John White turned up in the Washington office shortly after the 1918 Armistice, willing to take any job available in the parks. Told there was no position suitable for a colonel, White replied, "Never mind the 'colonel,'" and quickly settled for one of the two ranger vacancies in Grand Canyon National Park at $100 a month and no keep.

British-born, White had set out as a soldier of fortune in

his teens, picking up a war wound fighting with the Greeks against the Turks in Macedonia. Making, as they say, a separate peace, he promptly joined the gold rush to Alaska's Klondike but ended up tending bar before signing on, in Seattle, with an army regiment bound for the Philippines during the Spanish-American War. He survived some bloody uprisings and made colonel. When World War I broke out, he went to Europe with the Red Cross and, after American entry, returned to the United States and received a commission in the Signal Corps. Somehow, he felt disoriented in America, learned to fly on his own time, and made it to France as a pilot.

After the war, White found that the variety and freedom of duty in the parks fitted his life style to a T: he served in several parks as superintendent, collaborated in writing a standard work on the giant sequoias, and by the time of his retirement after thirty years of eventful service had become a regional director.

Another critical problem that faced the young agency was the efforts on the part of reclamation and irrigation advocates to utilize the parks "to assure to man the use of neglected resources." Seventeen pages of the Park Service annual report for 1920, under the heading "A Crisis in National Conservation," were required to list such threats. Legislation had been introduced to construct in Yellowstone a series of dams, canals, and reservoirs that would flood vast stretches of the park for the purpose of supplying Idaho potato farmers with more water. Noting that the contour map of the Geological Survey showed the character of the country to be swampy, the Bureau of Reclamation had approved the proposal.

It was a close call. The bill passed the Senate and was on the unanimous-consent calendar of the House. All of the strength that the American Civic Association, the Sierra Club, the Boone and Crockett Club, and the National Parks Association applied could not budge Secretary of the Interior

Lane, who had endorsed the legislation and had ordered the Park Service to prepare a favorable report on the bill.

The previous year in his annual report, Director Mather had publicly condemned the project as a "desecration of the people's playground for the benefit of a few individuals or corporations," and he appealed that all such commercial exploitation of the national parks be denied by Congress. "Is there not some place in this great nation of ours," Mather asked, "where lakes can be preserved in their natural state; where we and all generations to follow us can enjoy the beauty and charm of mountain waters in the midst of primeval forests?" The timely resignation of Lane and the immediate reversal of his decision by the succeeding Secretary of the Interior blocked the legislation and established a precedent in favor of the parks. It also released Mather and Albright from their agreement to resign rather than to support the legislation.

The Mather era ended abruptly in November, 1928, when Stephen Mather suffered a paralytic stroke, an ironic fate. As "Steve Mather of the National Parks," he had become a well-known public figure. Among thousands of tributes, one that may best reflect Mather's accomplishments and the stature of the Park Service came from John D. Rockefeller, Jr., who wanted "to give myself as a citizen of the United States the pleasure of telling you of my admiration and appreciation of what you have done in building up the parks and the park service during the years of your leadership of that department. . . . There is perhaps no other department in the national government run on so high a plane and so wholly in the interest of the public which it serves."

Mather's epitaph was spoken in Congress: "There will never come an end to the good that he has done." Undoubtedly the many staunch companions of his numerous mountain expeditions would have agreed, even perhaps those who first learned of Mather's high-voltage energy and his delight in practical jokes when awakened at the crack of dawn by the melancholy hiss of the air mattress deflating beneath them.

HISTORY AS WELL AS SCENERY

Mather was succeeded by his close associate, Horace Albright, who in 1919 had become, at twenty-nine, the first civilian superintendent of Yellowstone since the army took over in 1886. The Park Service was well past its infancy and had grown to an organization administering twenty-one national parks and thirty-three national monuments, with 2.6 million annual visitors and a budget of $9 million. As field director under Mather, Albright had been an able and tireless administrator whose attractive personality had created a wide circle of friends, a great many of whom happened to be in Congress.

Albright was particularly fortunate that his four-year span as Director coincided with the terms of Secretary of the Interior Ray Lyman Wilbur and President Herbert Hoover. Wilbur had served on the California State Park Commission, and Hoover was a past president of the National Parks Association. Albright realized that the frenetic and rather unstructured operations of the agency's first decade must give way to a more organized approach to administering the parks, but he had no intention of marking time.

A longtime history buff, Albright could get excited about historic places, particularly when there was a possibility of their being administered by the Park Service. Responsibility for historical monuments, memorials, and assorted sites was scattered among government agencies. Civil War battlefields, with their frequently eccentric monumentation, had been set aside as a result of the spirited nostalgia of the veterans, and the sites were therefore administered by the War Department for want of more enlightened stewardship. In the first annual report of the Park Service in 1917, Acting Director

Albright had wondered, somewhat pointedly, "whether these [military] parks should not . . . be administered as a part of the National Park System."

The conservation movement had not yet accepted the mission of historic preservation (one sometimes wonders if it ever will), and in those days there was little more than ceremonial respect for historic sites, excluding perhaps the concern of doughty antiquarians and the unflagging interest of the Daughters of the Confederacy. Many in the Park Service held that the American heritage was made up in equal parts of the land and the deeds of the people, and that it was just as important to preserve historic places as it was to set aside places of unique natural beauty. Both were necessary components of a true conservation philosophy. There was an accompanying belief, totally selfless, that it simply made practical sense to include all parks, whether historical or scenic, in one bureau—namely, the National Park Service. The fact that the historical parks were east of the Mississippi River and that expansion by the Park Service into the more heavily populated East would make its programs better known and give the organization a nationwide image was not overlooked.

The celebration of the 200th anniversary of the birth of George Washington, in 1932, provided a rare opportunity. As a part of the nationwide observance, the Wakefield Memorial Association, a private organization headed by the great-great-grandniece of General Washington, had acquired one hundred acres of the original Wakefield plantation. Unable to raise, in time for the anniversary, the funds needed to complete the reconstruction of the house in which Washington was born, the Wakefield ladies went to the Park Service for help.

Judging that the climate was highly favorable for positive action and that Congress would hardly choose the bicentennial year to turn its back on Washington, Albright converted the Wakefield appeal into a legislative proposal. Fittingly, there was little opposition to this well-timed tribute to the Father of his Country, and in 1930 Congress established the George Washington Birthplace National Monument, pledging funds to rebuild the original house. It marked the entry of the National Park Service into the field of historic preservation.

The Washington precedent paved the way for adding another historical park to the system the same year. The massive restoration project at Williamsburg, begun several years earlier, was beginning to focus attention on the need to preserve the nearby Jamestown Island and the Yorktown battlefield sites. While one could scarcely expect the federal treasury to compete with the resources Rockefeller was allotting to Williamsburg, still it seemed a not unreasonable argument that Jamestown, site of the first English colony in America, and Yorktown, scene of the triumphant conclusion of the American Revolution, were about as worthy of preservation as the colonial capital of Virginia.

Reminded once again of the glories of the American past by such stalwart advocates as the Association for the Preservation of Virginia Antiquities, and Governor Harry Byrd, Congress established the Colonial National Monument in 1930, which included the surrender field at Yorktown, with the remains of its forts and redoubts, and Jamestown Island, the two to be linked by a parkway passing through Williamsburg.

But the great leap forward came shortly after Franklin D. Roosevelt took office in 1933. By executive order nearly 50 historical sites were transferred to the National Park Service from the several administering agencies, most of them in the departments of War and Agriculture. At one stroke of the President's pen the number of areas in the national park system was almost doubled. Included were 11 national military parks, 10 battlefield sites, 11 national cemeteries, and 10 national monuments.

The decision indicated a recognition of the maturing of the National Park Service as an agency capable of operating all federal parks. It also constituted a significant evolution of the national park idea, for joining such illustrious wilderness names as Grand Canyon, Yosemite, and Mt. McKinley were equally famous names from the American past: Antietam, Fort McHenry, and Gettysburg.

NEW DIRECTIONS UNDER THE NEW DEAL

As the country plunged deeply into the Great Depression of the 1930's, it seemed likely the expansion days of the Park Service were ended. Yet many of the New Deal emergency relief programs were conservation-oriented, for there was general agreement that the nation's plight could be traced in part to the ruinous waste of natural resources and that massive efforts would be required if the land were to recover from generations of abuse.

Perhaps remembering his concerns of thirty years earlier, when he served as chairman of the Forest, Fish, and Game Committee of the New York State Senate, President Franklin D. Roosevelt soon proved himself another—and equally effective—conservation Roosevelt. He was particularly committed to the Civilian Conservation Corps philosophy of conserving both the jobless youth and the nation's resources, and before his first day as President ended, he had scrawled out and signed an organizational plan, noting, "I want personally to check the location, scope etc. of the camps, size, work to be done, etc.—FDR."

Within three months 1,000 camps were in operation with more than 300,000 young men at work, mostly in the national forests and parks. All work done on parklands, whether federal, state, or municipal, was under the supervision of the Park Service, a program of considerable scope that reached into almost every section of the country. CCC camps were established in almost every national park, which enabled the areas to catch up on their backlog of needed projects: campgrounds, buildings, trails, and bridges were built, utility systems installed, roads constructed or improved, historic buildings and battlefields restored, and visitor-use facilities improved.

In the seven hectic years from 1933 to 1940 the Park Service received $220 million for projects funded from a variety of emergency relief projects. The Public Works Administration provided $50 million for land acquisition and construction of facilities; the Emergency Relief Administration gave $28 million for recreation demonstration areas in which the Park Service converted unused lands near cities, developing nearly fifty recreation areas that were later conveyed to the states; and the Civilian Conservation Corps provided $130 million for operating 650 camps and alone required the Park Service during the peak of the program to employ more than 7,000 employees—greater than the total permanent employment of the Park Service in 1972.

It was to be a long, long time before the organization would see that kind of money again or be heading at top speed in so many directions at once. Division and branch chiefs carried responsibilities that on occasion rivaled those of the Director only a few years earlier. Both field and central office employees moved up to higher classifications and better salaries, accelerating the development of a bureau capable of responding to new directions and executing large-scale projects. One of the casualties of the frenzied pace was the Director, Arno B. Cammerer, a workhorse administrator who had been able to take less than two weeks' leave in five years and who was forced to step down in 1940 when his health failed.

To cope with the new work load, and as the final mark of having achieved big-league status in the federal bureaucracy, the Park Service decentralized its administration, establishing four regional offices—each a small-scale replica of the Washington office. The Park Service also received an invaluable transfusion of talent. Because the Depression greatly reduced job opportunities for men in a variety of professions, an exceptional group of highly qualified people went into government service during the 1930's. The Park Service got its full share.

The intellectual ferment and the barrage of social and political legislation characteristic of the New Deal resulted in a succession of congressional acts that expanded and transformed the original mission given the Park Service in 1916. The Historic Sites Act of 1935, which established a national policy of preserving historic places, designated the Park Service as the responsible agency. The Park, Parkway, and Recreation Study Act of 1936 marked the beginning on a national scale of an attempt to plan for the outdoor recreation needs of the entire country. The Park Service carried out a nationwide inventory of outdoor recreation needs while at the same time conducting a national survey of historic sites and structures under the Historic Sites Act. The providing of technical planning assistance to state and local park agencies became a major activity.

Other legislation introduced a number of new kinds of parks into the national park system, continuing the evolution of the original national park idea of preserving wilderness areas into a considerably broader concept, in response to contemporary social needs: the Blue Ridge Parkway, the first of the national parkways, which now extends for 500 miles along the crest of the Blue Ridge Mountains connecting Shenandoah National Park with Great Smoky Mountains National Park; Lake Mead, the first of the national recreation areas, followed by other lakes created by the giant multipurpose dams; Cape Hatteras, the first national seashore, to be followed by a dozen national seashores and lakeshores along the Atlantic, Gulf, and Pacific coasts and the Great Lakes.

MISSION 66

Pearl Harbor brought to a sudden end twenty-five years of almost unbroken growth for the Park Service. With the American declaration of war the Park Service entered upon a bleak period of decline, which lasted through World War II and its aftermath and on through the Korean war and its aftermath, until nearly fifteen years later a leading conservationist shocked a good part of the country when he bitterly advised, "If we cannot protect the parks and decently care for visitors, let us close the national parks."

During World War II, travel was a first casualty to rationing; by 1943 the number of Park Service employees had dropped to less than 2,000, and to make room for more important war functions in Washington, D.C., the central headquarters of the agency was moved to Chicago. Travel to the parks immediately picked up after the war ended, reaching a record 22 million visitors in 1946, but the austere wartime budget, which had dropped from $21 million in 1940 to $5 million during the war, rose only slowly. A pattern was being set; while the number of visitors increased, funds to maintain and staff the parks trailed far behind.

In 1940, for the first and only time, the Secretary of the Interior had looked beyond the career ranks of the Park Service to pick a Director. He selected a good one. Newton B. Drury had been head of the Save-the-Redwoods League for twenty years, but he arrived in difficult times. In 1949 he issued a blunt warning, "The Dilemma of Our Parks," describing the critical situation that existed: roads and trails wearing out, too few campgrounds, museums or accommodations, too small a staff to protect the resources. The statistics were ominous. Almost ten years had passed without significant maintenance of facilities, and as a result of this neglect, repair and replacement of buildings, utility systems, roads, and trails would require $321 million. The total operating budget for 1949 was barely $14 million.

The outbreak of the Korean war in 1950 doomed hoped-for relief, as all nondefense agency appropriations were cut back, but the phenomenal demand for outdoor recreation continued to accelerate, and by 1954 the parks were absorbing 54 million visitors a year, with a level of staff and the run-down facilities designed for the 17 million visitors in 1940.

As a result, working conditions in the parks were enough to tax even the legendary devotion and enthusiasm of the rangers, who daily witnessed the erosion of the parks. Their own working conditions seemed a test of their commitment; 60 per cent lived in one-bedroom houses or worse—Civilian Conservation Corps barracks built of tarpaper in 1934 and intended to last no more than five years, old warehouses, or cook shacks built of slabs. It was at this point that Bernard De Voto, the highly combative historian and probably the first conservationist in half a century to command a national audience, published his scathing denunciation in *Harper's Magazine* in 1953. The only alternative was to close the parks, De Voto declared, since neither the people nor the Congress seemed concerned that "so much of the priceless heritage which the Service must safeguard for the United States is beginning to go to hell."

Less choleric, but no less stern, a *New York Times* editorial observed that the national park system could not be maintained unless granted funds "to preserve it from present deterioration and future ruin." Everything was insufficient—accommodations, facilities, staff, the protection of the parks themselves. "In fact, just about everything concerning the parks is inadequate except their magnificent scenic or historic values and the dedication of the men and women of the National Park Service, whose morale remains, on the whole, unshaken despite the shabby treatment sometimes accorded them."

Conrad L. Wirth had become Director in 1951, following a less-than-one-year incumbency of Arthur E. Demaray. By training a landscape architect and by instinct a planner, he had entered the Park Service in 1931 and had carried a heavy load, including the Civilian Conservation Corps program during the 1930's. Possessing an easy, outgoing personality and a practical knowledge of how things get done in Washington, Wirth saw that the awesome task facing the Park Service could not be tackled on a piecemeal, how-can-we-get-more-money-this-year basis. He saw the need—and foresaw the political attractiveness—of putting the whole want list into a single package, and the Park Service thereby became one of the first agencies in government to apply a systems approach: the objectives defined, the cost identified, the target dates for completion of every project assigned.

Selection of a name is of course recognized as the most important decision in any large-scale enterprise, and here Wirth struck pure gold. In 1966 the Park Service would be celebrating its fiftieth anniversary. What a God-given target to shoot for! Why not produce a ten-year program, which would begin in 1956, aimed to bring every park up to standard by 1966—and call it MISSION 66?

A special committee was activated and worked for a year under wraps, putting the plan together. In actual fact, the entire organization went into action, regional office and park staffs developing individual project plans and supplying cost estimates for each park. Morale rose steadily as mouth-watering details were passed along that old grapevine. In Washington, the park packages were reviewed every weekend, until the total plan, containing the management and budget requirements for each of 180 parks, had been completed. And yet, the final tab seemed far beyond the limits of reality for those who had been on short rations for so long. The total MISSION 66 program was projected at $800 million. That the actual expenditure would pass $1 billion was not realized until much later.

At a special meeting of President Dwight D. Eisenhower

and his Cabinet in early 1956, the Park Service presented the MISSION 66 program. The documentation of the plight of the parks had powerful impact, and the President responded by pledging the unqualified support of his Administration. In the jubilant victory celebration following the unprecedented audience with the President, it was generally agreed that the color slide showing a long line of visitors seeking relief in front of a battered old outhouse may have struck the most sympathetic note. Shown the need and the total cost, and with something nice in the package for every member of the House and Senate with a park in his district, Congress bought MISSION 66 completely and gave it a warm reception at budget-hearing time throughout the ten-year cycle.

For the national park system MISSION 66 brought rejuvenation. Worn-out facilities were rehabilitated or replaced and new ones added. More than 2,000 new houses were built for employees. The concessioners responded by upgrading and expanding their facilities. But the program involved more than construction. There was a rejuvenation also in the spirit of the Park Service people. Substantial increases in staff provided for badly needed protection activities and permitted resumption of many lapsed interpretive and visitor-services programs. More than 130 new visitor centers were constructed, museums and information centers serving as focal points for visitor information and interpretation. Two training centers were established, at Grand Canyon and Harpers Ferry, which provided handsome physical plants for one of the most extensive training programs in government.

THE NATIONAL PARKS IN A WORLD OF CHANGE

Midway through MISSION 66, the decade of the 1960's opened, with a new concern for environmental problems evident. As the destruction of the American landscape and the pollution of its air and waters moved to front-page prominence, the new Secretary of the Interior, Stewart L. Udall, became the articulate voice of environmental preservation, and he made no effort to disguise the fact that his first two loves within the Department were Indian affairs and the national parks.

Upon the retirement of Wirth in 1964, George B. Hartzog, Jr., was named seventh Director of the Park Service. Leaving the Washington office in 1955 to acquire field experience, he returned in 1963 as associate director. Trained in the law, and possessing unerring political instincts, Hartzog has proved to be one of the most resourceful agency heads in government. Coming to office at a time of furious activity in matters involving the parks, Hartzog has fought their cause with formidable skill, employing a management style that most closely resembles a three-ring circus. With a zest for combat that has generally confounded combinations, public and private, that have designs on the parks, he is, among all the Directors, the closest to Mather in style. And he faces, no one would deny, the most difficult job.

Any meaningful account of the National Park Service in the 1960's would require more space than this capsule account permits. Such landmark pieces of legislation as the Land and Water Conservation Fund Act and the Wilderness Act in 1964, the Historic Preservation Act in 1966, and the Wild and Scenic Rivers Act in 1968 added substantially to the responsibilities of the Park Service—and immeasurably to the complexity of management. Who, at the beginning of the decade, would have foreseen the need to establish an Office of Urban Affairs, or that the location of a significant number of parks and recreation areas in and near major cities would make the Park Service the operator of the largest urban park system in the country? The National Park Service has become big business, and ecologists and environmentalists and wilderness travelers alone cannot quite handle the myriad programming, budgeting, legislative, planning, and construction activities required to administer some 284 parks and an annual budget in the vicinity of $300 million.

In the early days of the Park Service the objective was relatively clear-cut: how to provide sufficient facilities and encourage enough people to visit the parks and thereby ensure that the exciting new concept of setting aside great nature preserves for the benefit and enjoyment of the people would ultimately succeed.

Yet today, ironically, the picture is reversed, and the objectives are no longer clear-cut. The facilities were provided and the people did come (in 1971 more than 180 million), but now the question is how, or perhaps whether, in the face of such an overwhelming tide of visitors the national parks can survive and continue to provide the incomparable benefit of enriching the mind and spirit of those who have come to the parks to leave behind the noise and congestion of their daily lives.

Preparing in 1969 for his briefing of the newly appointed Secretary of the Interior, Walter J. Hickel, and taking a long look into the future, Director Hartzog defined the problem in one sentence: How can we make the national parks relevant in a world of rapid change?

The last of the Mather men have retired, but as this book was in preparation Horace Albright, the one-time "Duke of Yellowstone," completed his annual inspection trip to his favorite park and both Director Hartzog and Jack Anderson, the park superintendent, soon received notice, at some length, that Albright and indeed all retiring employees retain the inalienable right to suggest ways of improving the operations of the National Park Service.

Upon his retirement in 1933, Albright gave his colleagues one final admonition: "Do not let the Service become 'just another Government bureau.' Keep it youthful, vigorous, clean and strong." While the organizational structure never seems to be quite right (will they *ever* stop tinkering!), and

God knows there have never been enough people and money, if the former assistant secretary is still interested, the mystique and the traditions survive. Mather's biographer described the Park Service job rather accurately when he concluded that "men and women are working, planning, maneuvering, doing everything humanly possible to save and protect America's great natural wonders. It is a grinding and often heartbreaking job, but few jobs are worthier."

III
Organization

The basic unit of the Park Service organization is the park staff, and the assignment of responsibilities among employees reflects the essential functions: protection of the park and the visitor, a program of visitor services and interpretation, maintenance and upkeep of facilities, and administrative support services.

The minimum staff for any park is five permanent employees: a superintendent, responsible for the management of the area; a ranger, who may be a naturalist, historian, or archeologist and who provides the professional knowledge required for protection and interpretation of the area; a guide or other technician responsible for information and interpretive activities; an administrative officer who handles fiscal, personnel, property, and procurement matters; and a maintenance man responsible for needed cleaning and repair of buildings, roads, trails, and campgrounds. This basic staff is increased during the travel season by seasonal help, particularly in the interpretation, protection, and maintenance activities.

When several relatively small parks are located within a compact geographical area, they are consolidated into "clusters" under a general superintendent, in order that expertise can be shared and administrative overhead can be reduced. The Navajo Lands cluster in Arizona and New Mexico, which includes Canyon de Chelly National Monument, Hubbell Trading Post National Historic Site, and Navajo National Monument, also brings together parks that have similar historic themes and that have close relationships with the Navajo people.

A large park may have up to one hundred or more permanent and several hundred seasonal employees. Rather than a single administrative officer, the superintendent will have an administrative division, which includes branches of budget and finance, personnel, and property and procurement.

Administering a large park, or a cluster group, is a complex operation, and the superintendent requires professional counsel and assistance in a variety of fields. He has on his staff as many of the following disciplines as the situation requires: a naturalist, historian, or archeologist; a landscape architect, an architect, or a historical architect; an engineer of the civil, mechanical, electrical, or sanitary variety; a museum curator.

The practice is to compare the authority of the superintendent with that of the captain of a ship, a not wholly implausible comparison, although the claim is advanced more frequently in the regional and Washington offices than by the superintendents, who are occasionally reminded that a navy also happens to be provided with admirals. Still, the job of park superintendent is generally regarded as the best assignment in the Park Service.

THE REGIONAL OFFICE: A TOUCH OF SCHIZOPHRENIA

On the next higher level of authority are the regional offices, each of which is responsible for the coordination and supervision of up to fifty parks. Headquarters for the regions are in Philadelphia (Northeast), Atlanta (Southeast, including Puerto Rico and the Virgin Islands), Omaha (Midwest), Santa Fe (Southwest), San Francisco (Western, including Hawaii), and Seattle (Pacific Northwest, including Alaska). National Capital Parks, which intermittently achieves regional status, administers the parks, memorials, and parkways of Washington, D.C., along with several areas in nearby Virginia and Maryland.

The regional offices provide the instrument through which the Director can communicate with the 284 field areas, and vice versa. Because of the far-flung nature of the national park system, it is physically impossible for Washington office staff members to visit more than a relatively few parks each year, and it is the function of the regional office to maintain a close working relationship with the individual parks. The regional director is expected to be thoroughly knowledgeable about all of the parks and most of the employees in his region.

The precise workings of a regional office in any organization, public or private, has long defied explanation by even the least obtuse of the organization and management practitioners. The staff organization of a Park Service regional office is somewhat more comprehensible. It contains the professional people who can advise, and comfort, their counterparts in the parks on almost all matters that might arise. In particular, the regional office provides technical expertise to the small parks that do not have similar staff capabilities. Staff people in the larger parks generally recognize no source of experience or intelligence comparable to their own.

From the point of view of the regional office personnel, it must often seem that their humble position, like that of the governor of North Carolina, lies between two mountains of conceit. The conceit of the park staff is its conviction, apparently resulting from divine inspiration, that no one else even remotely understands what the park's problem is all about. The conceit of the Washington office is a tendency to presume that its policy directives come from Mount Sinai. Dodging the flak and succoring the casualties, the regional office becomes quite adept at translating Holy Writ, and thereby insures that Park Service policy is implemented with intelligent respect for the individual differences that exist in the parks.

The regional director, as the Director's designated representative in the field, wields most of the Director's authority and takes credit for all Park Service exploits in his region, the good with the bad. Maintaining sanity in a regional office requires steering a middle course between the Washington office—which is consistently spurring the parks on to greater glory—and the parks—none of which, to hear them tell it, appears to be adequately staffed or funded. It's simply remarkable how much good work gets done under such supposedly trying conditions.

THE WASHINGTON OFFICE: DELUSIONS OF GRANDEUR

The first corridor on the third floor of the Department of the Interior building is occupied by the Directorate of the Park Service and is aptly nicknamed "The Hall of Heroes," for along the hallway are the Director's principal staff advisers, including his three deputy directors. To his lieutenants the Director delegates—when he remembers—as many as possible of his responsibilities, retaining only those which are not transferrable: relationships with members of Congress, including key legislative matters; determination of budget and fiscal allocations; public and ceremonial appearances and membership on an excessive number of commissions; critical personnel selections, including all superintendents; remarkably frequent meetings with the regional directors in the field; and all matters of concern to the Secretary of the Interior.

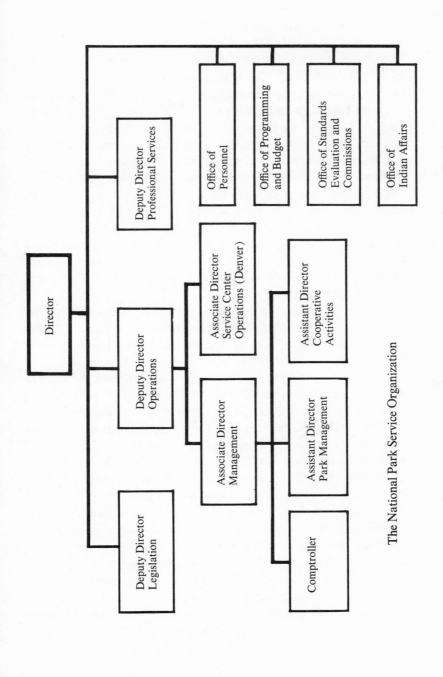

The National Park Service Organization

The deputy director for Operations is responsible for day-to-day operations of the National Park Service. To a considerable degree, his responsibility is to run the parks. The regional directors report to him. Two associate directors—for Service Center Operations and for Park Management—and the Office of the Comptroller report to him, and most Park Service operational matters pass over his desk.

The deputy director for Legislation handles those undertakings that lead to congressional legislation, and the spinoff that results. His office is the contact point for all relationships on Capitol Hill, and the Park Service generates more congressional mail than any other bureau in the Department. Along with this delicately explosive responsibility, he has the Office of Information, which almost rules out boredom as an occupational hazard.

The deputy director for Professional Services directs the creative, scientific, and historic preservation activities of the Park Service and is responsible for achieving highly professional results in these fields.

There are four other offices that, in addition to the deputy directors, report to the Director and whose close relationship suggests the importance given to their responsibilities.

Early in his administration, the present Director replaced a five-foot shelf of administrative manuals, which he felt were a burden on creativity and an obstacle to innovation, with three booklets outlining policy direction for each of the three categories of parks—natural, historical, and recreational. In addition, standards of performance were established for all activities and for all major positions in the Park Service, in order that every employee should know what is expected of his position and his program. The Office of Standards, Evaluation, and Commissions is responsible for these program and position standards.

In the development of his annual budget, the Director determines the direction and extent of the Park Service effort.

The Office of Programming and Budget is responsible for the intricacies of putting together a budget, moving it through the incomprehensible maze of the budget cycle, overseeing its expenditures, and finding ways—hopefully legal—for the Director to meet unexpected financial needs.

Breaking somewhat with tradition in the federal government, the Park Service does not join personnel and fiscal matters together in the Washington office under the general heading of Administration. The Office of Personnel is responsible for the effective use of human resources—recruiting, training, selection for transfer and promotion—and the Director and regional directors maintain a close working relationship with this key office.

The fourth activity reporting to the Director is the Office of Indian Programs. Heading the office at present is Ben Reifel, an Indian who was a career employee of the Bureau of Indian Affairs before his election to the House of Representatives, where he served on the Interior and Insular Affairs Committee. With a number of national park areas located within or in the neighborhood of Indian reservations, the Park Service is re-evaluating its own policies in areas involving Indian history and relationships. It is also exploring ways in which assistance might be provided to the Indian people, in planning recreational developments on tribal lands, and in training Indian people for park-type employment.

THE NATIONAL PARK SYSTEM

This book is about the National Park Service, not the national park system. There is an important difference. Books about the national parks or about individual parks are numerous. Despite good intentions, a great many of the books, like films, seem destined to end up as travelogues. Some do succeed in conveying something of the sheer beauty and immensity of the parks. There are, however, few books about the National Park Service, and this is as it should be, for the parks are the important element. While the organization is charged with preserving priceless lands and objects, it did not, after all, invent the national parks.

The 284 parks that make up the national park system include an incredible variety of scenic and historic entities. They range from Federal Hall National Memorial, where George Washington was inaugurated President of the United States in 1789, located on busy Wall Street in downtown New York City, to the vast solitude of Katmai National Monument in Alaska, made famous by a National Geographic Society exploring party as the "Valley of Ten Thousand Smokes," following the volcanic eruption of 1912. Although one of the largest units in the national park system, Katmai has fewer visitors each year than the number of people passing Federal Hall during the morning rush hour.

The greatest confusion in coming to an understanding of the national park system has been caused by the apparent delight, or perhaps whimsey, displayed by Congress in creating ever new titles for the parks that it adds to the national park system. A congressman introducing a bill to add still another Civil War battlefield to the nearly twenty already enshrined can choose from the following titles: National Military Park, National Historical Park, National Battlefield, National Battlefield Site, National Historic Site, and so on. There are so many titles that Park Service people cannot begin to remember them and simply refer to all of them as "parks." Obviously it would be too simple a solution to call them all parks officially, although efforts to simplify the nomenclature have helped somewhat. But if one is referring to Kennesaw Mountain, he just has to get out the directory and look it up, finding that it is a National Battlefield Park.

A listing of all of the parks under the twenty-one separate titles appears in Appendix II. A helpful publication, *National Parks and Landmarks,* which gives a short description and pertinent data on each park, and which includes also the Registered Historic and Natural Landmarks, is available through the Government Printing Office.

Of equal interest in describing the content of the national park system is the difference between use of the title "national park" and "national monument." Originally, the distinction was technical. National parks can be established only by the Congress, whereas, under the Antiquities Act of 1906, national monuments can be established on federal lands by Presidential proclamation. The early national monuments were relatively small and generally included unique geological features or archeological sites. But the Antiquities Act was soon interpreted much more liberally, and many national monuments have been vast in size. Glacier Bay in Alaska, at just under 3 million acres (almost one and one-half the size of Yellowstone) is the largest area in the national park system.

There is, however, one important reason for establishing national monuments rather than national parks. With few exceptions, the national parks are free from any commerical exploitation. Some national monuments qualify in every way for national park status, except that under present mining laws, claims can still be filed.

The practical effect of this situation was made clear on a recent Park Service field trip to Glacier Bay, a national monument eminently worthy of national park status, which, incidentally, would probably receive the highest number of votes if a poll were taken within the Park Service to determine which park contains the most spectacular and remote wilderness. Drifting along quietly in a ranger patrol boat and with good cause believing themselves about as far from civilization as one can get these days, members of the Park Service party were startled by the sudden appearance of a helicopter and watched with barely restrained fury as the chopper landed and a mineral exploration party unloaded.

About one-third of the present thirty-six national parks were originally established as national monuments, many changing their status when it was possible to eliminate commercial uses. Death Valley National Monument, deserving of national park status in terms of its scenic beauty, still has more than four thousand patented mining claims within its boundaries, and under present laws prospectors can still stake claims, despite the fact that no minerals have been found in extractable quantities for a great many years.

In 1972, the predicted number of visits to the national park system will be 212 million, a staggering figure. The five most visited parks are Chickamauga and Chattanooga National Military Park in Georgia and Tennessee, with more than 15 million; the Blue Ridge Parkway in Virginia and North Carolina, with 14 million; the Natchez Trace Parkway in Tennessee, Alabama, and Mississippi, with 13 million; Colonial National Historical Park in Virginia (which includes the parkway linking Yorktown and Jamestown with Colonial Williamsburg), with 10 million; and Great Smoky Mountains National Park in North Carolina and Tennessee, with 7.5 million. All either are parkways or have major highways running through the park area.

SERVICE CENTERS AND TRAINING CENTERS

In carrying out its professional activities, the Park Service has made a clear separation between management, which determines what services are required, and the professional staff, which decides how the problem will be solved. The arrangement is not unlike that between an architectural firm and a client. In the case of the Park Service, the client is generally the park superintendent, who needs a facility constructed, perhaps a campground. It is the function of management to determine the campground need, its size, and its type and to program the funds for construction. It is the function of the professional staff to design and construct the campground according to this program.

In actual practice, the division of responsibility is not that distinct, nor can it be. The original decision to build the campground is made at the master plan level; the master plan is produced by the professional staff but approved by the regional director. The design of the campground is done by the professional staff but also must be approved by the regional director. Design proceeds freely but with the understanding that it must solve the problem in a manner satisfactory to the needs of management.

The Denver Service Center has a staff of several hundred people: architects, landscape architects, civil, electrical, and sanitary engineers, planners, historians, archeologists, ecologists, historical architects, appraisers, land and water rights specialists, and construction supervisors, all supported by administrative, fiscal, and program staffs. The Harpers Ferry Center is a specialized service center of about one hundred people concerned with the design and production of publications, museum exhibits, graphics, and audiovisual programs.

There are three training centers, in which a considerable variety of courses are offered throughout the year. In Grand Canyon, the Albright Training Center provides an orientation course for new uniformed employees who report directly for this training experience before receiving their initial park assignment. The Mather Training Center at Harpers Ferry gives emphasis to the training of park interpreters, and the National Capital Training Center concentrates on the training of recruits for U.S. Park Police and provides law enforcement training for the ranger force. The employee, with the consent of management, selects and applies for the courses he believes will be most helpful to his career needs.

PROMOTION AND TRANSFER

The Park Service does go "outside" on occasion to fill key positions, but for the most part outside recruitment is infrequent and largely restricted to more specialized jobs, such as the fourteen computer programmers now employed—gainfully, it is hoped. But as a general rule, positions except those at entrance levels are filled by the transfer and promotion of career Park Service employees. The need to staff new parks and the accumulation by the Park Service in recent years of additional program responsibilities have accelerated job openings, and, for those who qualify, opportunities to transfer are fairly frequent.

The Park Service abides by the policy that it is better for the employee and for the Park Service if he moves every few years and gets exposed to other park situations, rather than allowing his roots to go down and thereby become a "homesteader," a potential ailment in the more attractive park locations. As a result, to move up in grade it is necessary to move out, a fact that produces high mobility for Park Service employees.

Another contribution to upward mobility is the musical-chairs exercise initiated by the departure of, say, a regional director. This often sets in motion a half-dozen or more transfers: the regional director's slot is filled by the superintendent of a major park, whose slot is filled by a Washington office division chief, whose slot is filled by another park superintendent, whose slot is filled by a chief ranger . . . and so it goes. A real problem has been created in recent years by the need to make frequent transfers, which often does not allow a ranger or a superintendent time to acquire a thorough knowledge of the park or even the people within his responsibility. Nevertheless, this suggests the kind of career ladder by which most Park Service employees advance.

The Annual Budget and Other Matters

For the 1972 fiscal year the National Park Service budget will be in the vicinity of $300 million. Of this total, $75 million is for management, protection, and administrative work; $57 million for the maintenance of roads, trails, and buildings; $46 million for construction of new roads, trails, and parkways; $40 million for construction of new buildings, utilities, and pollution abatement systems; $8 million for historic preservation, including grants to the states and to the National Trust for Historic Preservation; and $3 million from donations for specific purposes.

As a method of speeding up the acquisition of recreation lands, Congress in 1965 passed the Land and Water Conservation Fund Act. This fund is supported by moneys received from the sale of excess federal property, from the tax on motorboat fuel, from offshore oil reserves, and from sale of the "Golden Eagle" passport, which admits the holder to all federal recreation areas, including the national parks. Sixty per cent of the fund goes to the states on a matching basis, with 40 per cent going to the National Park Service, Forest Service, and Bureau of Sport Fisheries and Wildlife. For the 1972 fiscal year, the fund will provide a total of $300 million, of which the Park Service will receive about $70 million for land acquisition.

As an indication of the remarkable expansion in the programs of the National Park Service in recent years, the total operating budget for fiscal year 1956, the last year before the beginning of the Mission 66 program, which brought the Park Service into the modern era, was less than $50 million.

There has always been an ironclad restriction against any federal agency keeping the funds that it takes in as a part of its operations. All fees collected at park entrance stations are covered in the miscellaneous receipts of the U.S. Treasury. This is a prudent policy on the part of Congress, which prefers an arrangement under which each agency is required to justify its request for operating funds annually. If an agency had another source of funding, it could carry out its own programs free from congressional restriction.

Early park visitors needed good publications and maps, which were seldom available, and in response to this demand, coupled with the prohibition against the government entering into business, "cooperating associations" were developed, beginning in the 1920's. Most parks have these associations, which are incorporated under the laws of the state. They are operated by a board of directors, which includes both Park Service employees and private citizens. Their primary activity is selling interpretive items such as books, maps, and scientific or historical studies that contribute to the visitor's appreciation of the park.

Whatever income is realized from these sales must be contributed to projects that help the Park Service carry out its visitor services responsibilities. The nearly 190 history and natural history associations now in operation have contributed more than $2.5 million to aid the Park Service, making possible an extensive publication program ranging from trail guides to illustrated handbooks to children's coloring books to scholarly studies, financing employees to demonstrate crafts, funding research, purchasing audiovisual equipment, and making many other valuable contributions.

The present development of the National Park Service would not have been possible without the timely intervention, often on a substantial scale, of private philanthropy. The Rockefeller and Mellon foundations have, at the eleventh hour on countless occasions, stepped forward to save the day. Recognizing the need of the Park Service for a means of receiving and using private donations, Congress established the National Park Foundation, which has proved of invaluable assistance. The foundation picks up options on critical tracts of land until congressional funds are forthcoming and sponsors new programs, such as the highly successful experiment in environmental education. The foundation, with a charter from Congress, mobilizes the resources made available by private citizens for the national parks.

Under the Volunteers in Parks Act, the National Park Service is authorized to pay the incidental expenses—transportation, uniforms, and subsistence—for volunteers who serve without salary. Senior citizens, housewives, students, or anyone wishing to serve can help visitors better understand and enjoy the parks by demonstrating crafts, by working in period costumes, or by aiding rangers in surveying wildlife or carrying out study projects.

Established by law, the Advisory Board on National Parks, Historic Sites, Buildings, and Monuments is composed of distinguished private citizens from professions associated with the concerns of the national parks. The Advisory Board, through its frequent field reviews and associations with employees, has become a respected part of Park Service operations and is perhaps the most important link in providing the public with an opportunity to contribute to the formation of national policy. Meeting twice a year and making at least one extensive field trip annually, it serves as a kind of board of directors, advising the Secretary of the Interior on all matters affecting the parks. After serving terms on the Advisory Board, members are invited to serve on the Advisory Council, in which they enjoy all privileges except that of voting, sharing with the new members their considerable experience in park matters.

As a means of obtaining citizen participation in the development of new parks, particularly those in areas where private land holdings require complex acquisition policies, Congress has authorized establishment of park advisory commissions, which review plans and make appropriate recommendations to the Secretary. These commissions ensure that local views will be considered during the planning process; they are equally helpful in communicating to the nearby communities the purposes and objectives of national parks. The Independence National Historical Park Advisory Commission, created in 1948, and the Cape Cod National Seashore Advisory Commission, created in 1961, are outstanding examples of this approach.

IV
Functions of the Park Service

When it created the National Park Service in 1916, Congress defined its purpose: "The Service thus established shall promote and regulate the use of the federal areas known as national parks, monuments, and reservations." The management of the areas that make up the national park system remains today the primary mission of the Park Service. The considerable complexities involved in balancing preservation with use in the management of the parks is the subject of Chapter V.

The ultimate purposes for which parks are managed have spiritual overtones. To some degree, each of the bountiful elements of the parks—plant or tree or bird, historic building or artifact, seashell or pot shard—helps a person to find his place in the universe. The function of a national park might be considered as contributing insight into those sovereign questions that human knowledge derived from practical experience finds so difficult to answer: Who are we, where are we, and why?

As the conservation movement gained momentum and scope after 1916, Congress recognized the need to initiate a number of needed programs related to the purposes of the national parks. In a series of legislative acts, the National Park Service was assigned conservation responsibilities beyond the limits of the national park system, and management of these collective programs expanded considerably the original mission and constitutes the second major function of the Park Service.

There is one general misconception about the national parks that should be corrected: the belief, much too prevalent, that the national park system consists only of large wilderness tracts, most if not all of which are located in the big-sky country of the West.

Quite a few people who enter the Park Service as historians, and who wear the same Stetson hat as the park ranger, get fed up with answering the question "But what does a historian do in the National Park Service?" The answer to this question is that the national park system contains more than twice as many historical parks than parks of the scenic variety and employs many more historians and archeologists than it does naturalists. True, all wearers of the green uniform are rangers, but that does not mean they are all looking for forest fires or renegade bears.

Although several federal agencies—the Forest Service, the Bureau of Sport Fisheries and Wildlife, the Bureau of Land Management—administer outdoor recreation areas, only the Park Service administers historical properties. It is in this area that in recent years the Park Service has received its most extensive program responsibilities; the Secretary of the Interior has been authorized to provide national leadership in the field of historic preservation.

MANAGEMENT OF NATURAL AND HISTORICAL RESOURCES—AND PEOPLE

Suggesting that both resources and people must be "managed" in a national park is a seeming contradiction. Ideally, both should be free from constraints or manipulation, but a nation of 200 million people exerts considerably more pressure on its national park system than did a nation of 100 million people a few generations ago. A sensitive concern for the integrity and the perpetuation of park resources, whether a natural ecosystem or a historic site, is a fundamental obligation of management.

In 1962 the Secretary of the Interior appointed an Advisory Board on Wildlife Management, composed of leading scientists and conservationists, to develop an over-all policy for managing wildlife resources in the national park. The board, headed by Dr. Starker Leopold, of the University of California, observed that parks should represent "the mood of wild America"; yet, because of complex factors that have had greater or lesser influences on their resources, the parks "do not necessarily represent primitive America."

It was the opinion of the board that the basic purpose of national parks is to preserve places that have been undisturbed by the processes of civilization. Where ecological changes have occurred, the Park Service should seek to recreate the conditions that existed at the time of the discovery of the New World by Europeans. Granting that the implications of this objective were stupendous, and since the ecological competence to achieve the goal did not then exist, the board concluded that "A national park should represent a vignette of primitive America."

Management of this kind can only be based upon knowledge that comes from research, not enough of which has ever been done in the parks, although the program has been expanded considerably in recent years. Each park involves an ecosystem of interrelated plants, animals, and habitat; glaciers advance and retreat; disease kills off a forest; the ecological time clock cannot be turned back.

Corrective action for some interruptions in the natural cycles may seem obvious: restoration of a meadow invaded by trees; introduction of bighorn sheep into a desert area from which they have disappeared; protection or restoration of a falling water table that threatens to radically change the vegetative cover; control of surplus deer populations that are destroying their range.

How to effect these changes, how to supply the missing elements of the biological whole without introducing new and even more destructive influences, are delicate problems indeed to which some fifty biologists who work in the parks are continually seeking solutions. Research can be disquieting for management. It may indicate that a road has interfered with drainage or that a campground has been placed on the travel route of grizzlies. Lacking staff or funds to engage in pure research and to follow wherever the data might lead, the Park Service research program works to provide management, in the person of the regional directors and park superintendents, with answers to pressing day-to-day problems.

An additional function of national parks is to serve as outdoor laboratories in which the uninterrupted operation of natural laws can be studied to the best advantage. These areas also serve as a refuge for plant and animal species, a kind of biological bank in which a reserve can exist and from which species that have been exterminated elsewhere can be protected and studied.

Historic and archeological (or prehistoric) resources present an entirely different management problem. Buildings deteriorate if not protected, the figures who once lived and made history are gone, and, unlike the goal of management in the natural parks, the historical event cannot be restaged. In part, the objective is to recreate the setting as accurately as possible and then to find ways to put life into the scene.

The Park Service carries out an extensive research program in the historical parks, one that requires the combined talents of historians, archeologists, architectural historians, and curators. At some sites, there may be no visible remains, and research programs have uncovered some remarkable evidence: on Roanoke Island, North Carolina, the oldest identifiable structure in this country, an earthwork fort built by Sir Walter Raleigh's colonists in 1587; at Fort Vancouver, Washington, artifacts from the Hudson's Bay Company; beneath an alley in downtown Philadelphia, foundations and household articles from the home built by Ben Franklin.

In general, the Park Service avoids reconstruction of buildings, except those of outstanding importance and then only if sufficient data are found to make the reconstruction accurate. The policy followed is that it is better to preserve than repair, better to repair than restore, better to restore than reconstruct. Restoration of historic buildings can be an exceedingly expensive and long-drawn-out process and may require combing archives in many countries. Actual restoration work may also require the expertise of craftsmen no longer available. Finding an Englishman who knew how to sew reeds together to construct a seventeenth-century thatched roof was essential to the rebuilding of the glass-blowing "factory" at Jamestown.

For the Gettysburg Battlefield in Pennsylvania, a historic base map has been prepared that not only indicates the extent of tree cover and agricultural land but identifies just what crop was being grown in each field at the time of the battle. For the excavation of Wetherill Mesa in Mesa Verde National Park, the Institute of Arctic and Alpine Research installed environmental measurement stations. Because native vegetation is regarded as one of the best expressions of the totality of a climate, plant studies were carried out along with studies of fossil pollen and tree rings in the surviving roof timbers—all contributing to the more conventional research on shards, tools, and weapons and other evidences uncovered by the excavations.

That people management is a function of Park Service administration was illustrated strikingly during the summer

)71, when some forty young men and women casually removed their clothes and proceeded to gambol in Yellowstone's Firehole River. Rangers are learning to cool it these days, and, equally casually, the ranger called to the scene issued no ultimatums but sat down on the bank to rap. Eventually agreeing that, while the act was innocently intended, the stage was probably ill chosen, the young people split the scene. The ranger presumably went back to the less intriguing routine of dealing with people who would never think of undressing in public places but somehow consider it a constitutional right to feed Hershey bars to the bears.

Particularly in recent years, law enforcement has become an even more significant function of the park ranger force. The need to record crime statistics for the national parks is highly regrettable, but petty thefts, vandalism, and other minor offenses are on the increase, and the day has almost passed when a camper could leave gear unguarded without fear of loss. Crimes against property—burglaries, larcenies, automobile thefts—have jumped from just over 2,000 in 1966 to nearly 6,000 in 1970. There were an additional 8,000 arrests for such offenses as drunkenness, weapons violations, and drug use.

The use of drugs is becoming an increasingly difficult part of law-enforcement work in the parks. Drug offenses rose from 10 in 1966 to 563 in 1970, and this figure obviously is only an indication of the scope of the total problem. In addition to serving as naturalist, fire fighter, and wildlife management specialist, the ranger is being asked to take on the responsibilities of a policeman—and sociologist—as well.

The ranger's role in protecting visitors from larceny is accepted; more controversial is the degree to which the Park Service should shield the visitor from potential dangers inherent in the park itself—a role discussed in detail in Chapter VI.

INTERPRETATION

A remark made by President James A. Garfield, that his ideal college would consist of a log in the forest, with a student at one end and Mark Hopkins at the other, aptly describes the original concept of education, or "interpretation," in the national parks. Hopkins, an American educator and president of Williams College, would have been a good park interpreter; he felt no great need to follow the traditional academic approach to teaching, and, while he had not read widely, he thought deeply.

Interpretation is considered to be the most important function of the National Park Service, at least by those gifted employees who have devoted their careers to an activity that the Park Service can take credit for pioneering. It is not education, although it was originally so called, but a distinctive refinement of—and one is tempted to say an improvement on—the classroom variety of the learning process. Its origination, shortly after the Park Service was established, supplied an essential ingredient required if people were to appreciate the meaning of national parks.

Indignities suffered by early travelers in the parks were not limited to barbaric cuisine and rude accommodations. Information about wildlife or natural features could be obtained only from the spiels of itinerant stage drivers or the shameless concoctions of hotel guides. The chance visit of a Californian to Switzerland ended the sacrilege.

Dr. Charles M. Goethe observed in one of the Swiss Alpine cantons that groups of tourists were being led on nature hikes by informed guides, learning firsthand of the interrelationship between plants and animals—an experience the tourists were obviously enjoying. Dr. Goethe transplanted this type of adventure to Lake Tahoe in the summer of 1919, with trained naturalists laying out trails and conducting evening lectures. One evening Director Stephen Mather happened along and quickly decided this was precisely what the national parks needed.

Mather moved the program to Yosemite the following year, and it was an instant success. The guided walks drew throngs of interested visitors, and the evening campfire lectures drew more than twenty-five thousand people that first summer. Park museums quickly followed, made possible by grants from the Laura Spelman Rockefeller Fund, in Yosemite, Yellowstone, Grand Canyon, and Mesa Verde. Several are still going strong; more than three hundred visitor centers and museums have followed the original experiment.

Interpretation is today an accepted activity of state and municipal parks and of most museums. Colonial Williamsburg in Virginia has a director of interpretation. Just as schools can no longer afford the one-to-one ratio of Mark Hopkins and a schoolboy on opposite ends of a log, the Park Service and most other organizations have had to turn to modern means of communication. Motion pictures, publications, and museums augment the personal approach. Still, park visitors, particularly family groups, will be missing a rare experience if they pass up the opportunity to join a guided walk, whether the subject is a coastal tide pool or the Oregon Trail.

The word "interpretation" came gradually to replace the term "education," in part no doubt to avoid any suggestion that the modest appetite for knowledge that the average visitor carries with him while on vacation would be promptly submerged in a tide of completely accurate but exquisitely boring facts. But interpretation also seemed a better term to describe the function of dealing with subjects that for most people were unfamiliar—geology, biology, botany. It was almost like learning a new language. The process of translating this language, the language of the earth, suggested the term "interpretation."

Freeman Tilden, who turned from a successful career as

an essayist and playwright to an even more distinguished association with the National Park Service, during which he both refined and defined the art of interpretation, concluded, in his *Interpreting Our Heritage,* that interpretation is an "educational activity which aims to reveal meanings and relationships through the use of original objects, by firsthand experience, and by illustrative media, rather than simply to communicate factual information."

This approach is important. It lacks the stiffness of formal instruction; it is not forced upon anyone. The visitor can take it or leave it. The immediacy of the site is crucial, for a classroom lecture on geology is one thing, but listening to a description—while seated before the observation window in the Yavapai Point Museum—of how the Grand Canyon was formed is quite another.

In some parks, such as Everglades in Florida, the problem for the interpreter is quite different, and perhaps more difficult, yet critical to visitor appreciation of the park. To the casual tourist the Everglades is a flat, uninspiring landscape, not more than a few feet above sea level at its highest point, an endless expanse of saw grass bending with the breeze. But, for the interpreter, it is a wonderland, where the regenerative powers of sun and water nourish a food chain whose delicate balance is unmatched elsewhere on the continent. It has beauty, but not the kind which announces its presence boldly, as does the grandeur of Mt. Rainier; there is little that the travel people would call spectacular, except perhaps the sunsets. But the interpreter's task at Everglades, or in any park, is to fulfill the charge of Charles Darwin: "We must see with the eye of the mind." Interpretation, concludes Freeman Tilden, is "mindsight."

When historical parks were added to the national park system, interpretation was even more important to visitor understanding. From Little Round Top, the battlefield of Gettysburg is little more than a pleasant view of agricultural fields stretching off toward the South Mountains until an interpreter vividly recalls the scene on the afternoon of the second day of battle, when Hood's Texas Brigades formed in the woods beyond Devil's Den, sunlight glinting on bayonet tips, and launched the savage attack that almost turned the Union left flank.

For certain needs a film—or a publication, or a museum—may be more effective than personal interpretation. Faced with the problem of conveying the life of Booker T. Washington, and lacking any of the actual possessions associated with his early life, the Park Service film maker commissioned an artist to depict the events of Washington's life, using a collage art technique. Through the materials that the young Washington knew, burlap and rough board, cotton fibers and dried wildflowers, an evocative interpretive film was produced.

Highly sophisticated graphic design or multimedia audiovisual programs are not always appropriate to the subject. Along the Blue Ridge Parkway there is a classic interpretive sign, which marks a pioneer cabin standing in the midst of a clearing in a hollow. Could a description of human experience be more vividly conveyed than by these thirty-seven perfectly chosen words?

> HERE LIVED HARRISON CAUDILL AND HIS
> WIFE JESSIE, WHO RAISED A FAMILY OF
> SIXTEEN IN THIS ONE ROOM DWELLING,
> SEVEN MILES BY TOTE TRAIL TO THE
> ABSHER ROAD AND YET ANOTHER SEVEN
> MILES TO THE NEAREST STORE.

Environmental Interpretation

In conjunction with its quickened response to the recreation needs of urban communities, the Park Service has sought appropriate ways in which it might support the national concern for improving environmental quality. A likely possibility has been through interpretation, which in the past was largely restricted to programs carried out inside the parks and whose subject content was likely to be focused upon park resources. It was decided that Park Service experience might best be utilized in helping the education community seek methods of introducing an environmental approach to classroom instruction.

Experience thus far has suggested the desirability of restructuring the entire interpretive program of the Park Service, and this has taken place. Two experimental projects tested nationwide have been particularly effective. National Environmental Education Development (NEED), funded by the National Park Foundation, is designing teaching materials and a program of studies and experiences for children from kindergarten through high school, to enrich the existing curricula with environmental concepts. As a part of the NEED experiment, school classes, including pupils from inner-city environments, have spent a week in a natural area, some of which were in national parks.

When one observes the reaction of a school group from a disadvantaged sector of New York City who were spending their field trip at Fire Island National Seashore and later reads the reports of the "quiet hour," a period in which each child goes off completely by himself to the spot he likes best and looks for beauty in the world around him, one better comprehends the need to make such experiences a less rare part of the lives of urban children, for whom Yellowstone is about as remote as Hadley Rille.

School teachers have participated in pilot studies to show that ecological values can be made an effective part of all classroom subjects—math and science, art and history, music and social studies. A number of states have conducted NEED workshops for their administrative and teaching staffs, and manuals covering all grades have been published.

Not only are almost all school systems without a facility

that would serve as a nature camp, most lack even a small preserve close enough for day use. Although park areas in their entirety constitute outdoor laboratories, the relatively few Park Service interpreters could hardly serve the needs of the school population of the entire country. But to help school systems use the parks for study purposes, the Park Service has designated nearly one hundred Environmental Study Areas within the parks, which the schools use under teacher direction with the help of a handbook guide prepared for the Park Service by the National Education Association. The Environmental Study Area concept has considerably broadened the capacity of the smaller historical areas to participate in the environmental movement.

Writing in the *National Parks and Conservation Magazine* in 1970, Darwin Lambert reported upon his visit to an Environmental Study Area in Shenandoah National Park, Virginia, with a class of children. Lambert, who had known the first Park Service Director Stephen Mather, and who had followed the development of interpretation from its origins, observed that the new directions of Park Service interpretation represented "a momentum-gathering, lastingly significant change, not merely in the parks' long-established educational-interpretive program but in man's understanding of his basic situation."

Planning and Designing a National Park

Precisely how the Park Service will carry out its function of administering the national parks is largely determined by the planning activity, one of the major divisions of Park Service operations. In developing its approach to planning, the National Park Service has been guided by two precepts: (1) that no action will take place until a comprehensive plan has been prepared, and (2) that planning requires a multi-discipline approach.

Master planning, which began in the 1920's to ensure that development in the parks would take place with a sensitivity for environmental concerns, precedes the establishment of a park. In advance of legislation, a detailed master plan is prepared, designating boundaries, identifying development sites, and providing estimates for land acquisition and visitor-use facilities.

A master plan is prepared for every park in the system and is periodically revised and updated. It might be described as temporary but enduring. The primary objectives—the protection of the resources and enlargement of the nature of the visitor experience—tend to continue. The means by which these goals will be achieved may well change. The Going-to-the-Sun highway, through Glacier National Park in Montana, is now under study by a master plan team. It is quite possible a recommendation will be made that, at some not too distant point, this road will no longer be open to private automobiles during the heavy travel season; people will be transferred to another transportation system, which will preserve and improve the experience.

By the Wilderness Act of 1964, the Park Service is required to review all roadless areas that are 5,000 acres or more in size for appropriate inclusion in the National Wilderness Preservation System and to make specific boundary recommendations to the President for submission to the Congress. There are nearly sixty parks scheduled for wilderness study. Once these wilderness areas have been approved, in which no man-made intrusions are permitted, they are inviolate and their status and use cannot be changed without approval of the Congress.

Master planning includes classification of all lands within a park, following the system prescribed by the Bureau of Outdoor Recreation. There are six classifications: Class I lands are for high-density use, such as visitor accommodations; Class II, for general outdoor recreation of less intensity; Class III designates natural environment areas, not so spectacular as those in the remaining three classifications but as buffer zones essential to the preservation of natural lands or to the setting of historical areas; Class IV contains the most fragile and precious natural features, such as Old Faithful geyser; Class V is wilderness; Class VI lands have the historic structures or sites for which historical parks were established. Through zoning, the use of park lands is identified and restricted, to the end that park visitors seeking different kinds of experiences are accommodated, but with care for protection of the resources.

In some combination, according to the need, a planning team is assembled to carry out the various planning tasks, whether they involve a new area study proposal, a master plan for an existing park whose present plan may be ten years old, or a wilderness designation. Teams vary in size and composition, depending upon whether the area has historical, recreational, urban, or natural values primarily. A typical master plan team engaged in a national park study might be headed by a landscape architect and include an ecologist, a sociologist, an interpretive planner, an architect, the superintendent of the park backed up by his staff, and such other members or consultants as the situation requires.

In a special 1968 issue devoted to the subject of Graphic Design of the Human Environment, *Print* magazine declared:

> Of all government agencies, the National Park Service has been concerned the longest with environmental design, but then, the Park Service is hardly a johnny-come-lately to the problem of improving the human environment, having been concerned with just that since its inception 52 years ago.

Probably more than most federal agencies, the Park Service has an enormous equity in the field of design. The Smithsonian Institution has more extensive museum collections but is not involved in a large-scale architectural design program; the United States Information Service produces more films annually but has no comparable publication program; the General Services Administration, which handles design and construction for most government agencies, a staggering enterprise, is not involved in developing an extensive network of national parkways. Additionally, the Park Service produces such sophisticated programs as "Sound and Light" and the presentation of modern drama at Ford's Theater in Washington, D.C., and in 1971 began symphony, ballet, and popular concerts at Wolf Trap (just outside the District of Columbia), the first national park for the performing arts.

For the 1972 fiscal year the Park Service received $46 million for construction of buildings, utility systems, and related structures and $40 million for roads and trails. The design of these facilities is handled primarily by the design staff in the Denver Service Center and by contract with private architectural firms. Architectural design is as controversial inside the national parks as elsewhere, perhaps more so. An architectural theme is developed as part of the master plan and the Park Service operates on the premise that all design, whether for an information sign or a museum building, must complement the environment in which it is placed.

This does not mean an attempt to create an antique setting by using Old English script on a wormy cypress signboard. Good designers are not imitating old-time styles, and while those who cry for a return to log-cabin architecture are entitled to their opinion, the Park Service holds to the philosophy that everything that is built in the parks should aspire toward the highest level of design excellence.

Some of the finest architects in the United States have done buildings for the parks that have received national recognition: Eero Saarinen for the Gateway Arch in St. Louis, Richard Neutra for the Gettysburg Visitor Center, and Ulrich Franzen for the Interpretive Design Center at Harpers Ferry. For sustaining a superior quality of design throughout the MISSION 66 program, the American Institute of Architects awarded the Park Service a Special Citation Award, and its *Journal* reported upon the distinction with an article entitled "Our Park Service Serves Architecture Well."

Design of museum publication and audiovisual programs is carried out in close association with the architectural activity. About 20 million colorful and informative "minifolders" and interpretive booklets are produced each year. If collected together in one place, the components of the Museum of the Park Service would occupy more than fifty acres, a group of exhibits and furnished historic rooms one football field wide, extending for almost three miles. The largest single museum complex in the country, it contains more than 10,000 museum and wayside exhibits. The collection of historical objects, comprising more than 3 million individual specimens, ranges from the silver inkstand used in the signing of the Declaration of Independence to Franklin D. Roosevelt's wheelchair at Hyde Park, New York.

URBAN PROGRAMS

The accelerated urbanization of the United States has helped emphasize the relatively wide gap that separates the largest population centers from most of the national parks. A considerable gap, both economic and geographic, separates a large portion of the city dwellers in the East from the national parks of the West. Operating an extensive urban park system, with substantial park areas located in Baltimore, Philadelphia, New York, St. Louis, and an entire complex in Washington, D.C., the Park Service has attempted in recent years to make these aesthetically pleasing green spaces more responsive to the recreation needs of city people.

Several years ago an Office of Urban Affairs was established to restructure, and reorient, the agency's programs. The bright and sprightly "Summer-in-the-Parks" program, initiated in 1968, has revitalized the parks of Washington, D.C. Surprise bus trips for children are offered daily, fashion shows and rock bands tour the downtown parks, and a variety of recreational activities are provided for all age groups. Utilizing park areas within the city, the Richmond (Virginia) Battlefield Park has proved that historical parks need not be untouchable shrines by creating a lively summer fun entertainment for children called "Sum Fun."

Two gigantic "Gateway" park proposals, now awaiting congressional action, would vastly expand the urban function of the Park Service. The project in New York would encompass lands surrounding New York Harbor, providing extensive beach lands within an hour or two of 10 million people. A similar project has been proposed to include lands at the entrance to San Francisco's Golden Gate, but the areas included are largely under the administration of the military, as are key land parcels in New York. Acquiring land for park purposes from the military is uniformly regarded by the Pentagon as a threat to national security, which is a tough rap to beat.

Urban parks are no longer confined to city boundaries. A seashore park within a few hours' drive of a major city is an urban park and must be planned accordingly. The National Recreation Area to be created by the Tocks Island Dam (if indeed it will be built), is located midway between New York City and Philadelphia at the Delaware Water Gap, within two hours' drive of more than 20 million people. It is anticipated that one of its half-dozen major developed areas could serve as many people as an entire national park.

Urban needs have strongly influenced the philosophy of what kinds of parks should be administered by the National

Park Service. The original concept was that parks are where you find them. Both President Lyndon Johnson and President Richard Nixon have enunciated a policy that the time has come to take a different view and to give priority to establishing parks where people might have the best chance of using them.

SERVICE FUNCTIONS BEYOND THE PARKS: HISTORIC PRESERVATION

The preceding sections of this chapter have summarized, perhaps too briefly, the functions of the Park Service in administering the parks. A second functional responsibility is to carry out a group of wide-ranging activities that go far beyond the primary mission of operating the national park system in supporting the over-all conservation movement. The Historic Sites Act of 1935 authorized the Park Service to discharge the federal responsibility in the field of historic preservation, and under this and succeeding authorities, the Park Service has conducted a number of programs that seek to preserve the significant remnants of the national heritage.

National Survey of Historic Sites

An interesting project, begun in the 1930's, has been concerned with locating and evaluating all of the important historic sites in the United States and selecting those that possess national significance. Supported by state and local agencies and by professional historians, architects, and archeologists, the National Survey of Historic Sites and Buildings has identified nearly one thousand sites in all of the states, Puerto Rico, the Virgin Islands, and the Canal Zone. These sites collectively illustrate the total history of the country, beginning with the earliest occupation by man.

When approved by the Secretary of the Interior, sites so

identified are designated National Historic Landmarks, and owners applying for the certificate and bronze plaque agree to cooperate in preserving the site. Landmark recognition is a form of protection; it calls attention to the importance of the site in national history, it encourages preservation support, and it entitles owners to technical advice from federal preservation experts.

In their scholarly inquiry into all segments of American history, Park Service historians who have conducted the surveys have displayed a refreshing lack of pedantry when interpreting the solemn guidelines established to ensure that only earthshaking events and heroic leaders meet the test of national significance. The San Francisco cable cars have met the test, as has the Anheuser-Busch Brewery in St. Louis and the winter quarters of Ringling Brothers Circus, the Jack London Ranch, and Ernest Hemingway's Key West retreat, and those two Chicago tributes to the creative arts and modern technology—Frank Lloyd Wright's Robie House and the First Nuclear Reactor site in Stagg Field.

Scientific areas, which meet the qualifications for Natural Landmarks, are designated in the same way, and unusual geological phenomena such as Grants Lava Flow in New Mexico, the John Day Fossil Beds in Oregon, and Reelfoot Lake in Tennessee have qualified for Landmark status. A new category, Environmental Education Landmarks, was recently established to recognize outstanding programs in the field of environmental education.

Historic American Buildings Survey

Recognizing that all old buildings cannot be saved but that the total loss of a style of architecture is comparable to the extinction of a bird or animal species, a companion program to the National Survey of Historic Sites survey got under way during the 1930's to record with measured drawings and photographs the diverse building styles of America's past—public and private, ornate and restrained, grandiose and inconspicuous. The Historic American Buildings Survey, carried out with the cooperation of the American Institute of Architects and the Library of Congress, now constitutes one of the largest collections of its kind in the world, a remarkably complete record of nearly fifteen thousand buildings.

The survey materials deposited in the Library of Congress include nearly 80,000 individual photographs and precise measured drawings, along with architectural and historical documentation, photogrammetry, and maps. Copies of these records are available from the Library of Congress Division of Prints and Photographs. When St. Michael's Cathedral in Sitka, Alaska, burned to the ground in 1966 and the decision was made by church officials to reconstruct what had been the outstanding surviving structure of Russian occupation of Alaska, survey drawings and photographs provided the needed plans.

The actual work of the Historic American Buildings Survey program is done by summer teams consisting largely of architectural students under faculty direction. About fifty organizations—historical and preservation groups, foundations, and educational institutions—participate each year with the Park Service, usually on a shared-fund basis.

Historic American Engineering Record

The Historic American Engineering Record was begun in 1969, in cooperation with the American Society of Civil Engineers and the Library of Congress, to document that particular American engineering genius that has produced waterworks, bridges, canals, and tunnels. The Engineering Survey is carried out also by field teams, who photograph and record achievements from railroad viaducts to suspension bridges.

INTER-AGENCY ARCHEOLOGICAL SALVAGE PROGRAM

The threatened loss of a well-known historic house or architectural landmark is often highly publicized. Occasionally, although not often enough, this helps to prevent its destruction. Underneath the ground, buried and unseen, evidences of occupation by prehistoric American Indians are found almost everywhere throughout the country in the form of ruins, campsites, shell middens, or mounds. In these sites are found the priceless records of Indian life—broken pottery, stone implements, and weapons.

Unless prior excavations are carried out, the flooding of entire river valleys by dams, the barren swaths cut by interstate highways, or gas and oil pipelines can destroy archeological sites of major importance. Responsibility for the recovery of archeological remains in federal reservoir areas and in other places where construction activity threatens archeological sites is a Park Service responsibility; the Service sponsors the Inter-Agency Archeological Salvage Program, which oversees much of the archeological salvage work done in the United States. It coordinates research and allocates funds to qualified agencies and institutions that carry out the actual salvage work. More than 2,000 contracts have been awarded, resulting in the recovery of many millions of artifacts and the publication of more than 2,500 articles and books.

One of the most ambitious projects in this field has been the Missouri River Basin study. After World War II, when the Bureau of Reclamation and the Army Corps of Engineers reactivated their visionary enterprises to dam the rivers of America (1,400 square miles along the Missouri River alone), a significant part of the country's cultural heritage was threatened with destruction. The National Park Service and the Smithsonian Institution joined hands and have administered an immense salvage operation in advance of dam construction.

Of the eight hundred sites identified in the middle Missouri alone, more than ninety were excavated, with the field work done largely by universities receiving funds and technical direction from the Park Service. A rare discovery was made in 1968 of the steamer *Bertrand,* which sank during the Civil War in a section of the Missouri that is now a part of the DeSoto Wildlife Refuge in Nebraska. When excavated, the river boat was found to be almost intact, a storehouse of nineteenth-century Americana. The textiles and toys, the stomach bitters and liquors, the kerosene lamps and farm implements thus recovered constitute one of the most valuable historical finds on record.

Historic Preservation Act of 1966

Passage of the National Historic Preservation Act of 1966 brought national policy on conservation matters into better balance. On the federal level, conservation programs had been largely concerned with natural resources—soil and water, the forests, and outdoor recreation areas. Although the Historic Sites Act of 1935 had emphasized the desirability of preserving historic places, legal protection and financial assistance were provided only for sites within the national park system. The new Act broadly expanded federal support.

One powerful tool is the National Register of Historic Places, a listing of all historical sites and buildings nominated by the individual states. The National Register is maintained by the Park Service, which accepts state nominations meeting the criteria. Properties on the National Register, which eventually may include as many as 100,000 sites, are given special protection against destruction by any project in which federal funds or other actions are involved, including highway construction, urban renewal projects, and dam building —projects which in the past have relentlessly destroyed countless historical sites.

The Act specifies that all federal agencies must review the effect of such undertakings "on any district, site, building, structure, or object that is included in the National Register." The newly created Advisory Council on Historic Preservation, composed of federal department heads, the Chairman of the National Trust for Historic Preservation, and citizens appointed by the President, provides a high-level forum to represent the public interest and to advise the President and the Congress on the desirability of proceeding with projects that threaten historical values. The Director of the National Park Service is the executive director of the council.

Through congressional appropriations, the Historic Preservation Act also authorizes the Park Service to administer a grants-in-aid program to the states and to the National Trust for Historic Preservation, on a matching basis. The state grants may be used to conduct inventories of historic sites and to acquire and restore individual properties. New York State alone estimates that it has thirty thousand worthy historical properties. To be eligible, a site must be listed on the National Register, and its preservation must be consistent with a state-wide plan for historic preservation that has been approved by the Secretary of the Interior.

V

Preservation and/or Use

When it established the National Park Service in 1916, Congress defined the fundamental purpose of national parks in simple language: that scenery, the natural and historic objects, and the wildlife were to be conserved and that these resources were to be made available for people to enjoy.

Since the day the Act was passed, two all-pervasive elements, "preservation" and "use," have been involved in every decision, small or large, that has ever affected the parks. No facility for public use, no policy of resource management, no proposal of any kind has been advanced but that park people have pondered and examined—and argued—just how best to respect the demanding requirements of preservation and use. The issue is never clear-cut. A decision is never finally reached without reaffirmation of the axiom that truth is indeed hard to come by.

The instruction to preserve the parks unimpaired, while at the same time providing needed facilities for public use, seems on first encounter to be ambiguous, perhaps even meaningless, as a guideline. Certainly, a road cannot be constructed within a park without doing damage to the park scene, and the framers of the enabling legislation understood this well.

They came to a better solution than attempting to spell out precisely how much is enough and what constitutes too much. By defining only the spirit in which the parks are to be managed and the ultimate purpose for which parks are set aside, they ensured that with every decision affecting the parks the process must begin again, each proposal thoughtfully appraised in the light of experience, the changing nature of park use, and the possible effect of each action upon the resources.

As might be expected from decisions reached by this process, controversies will arise. When the battle lines are being formed, two camps can be identified. On the one side are the preservationists, for whom the word "unimpaired" is the key and who counsel purity in all things. They hold that parks are established primarily to protect wilderness, that one best sees wilderness on foot with his gear on his back. Whether the word "preserve," which was not used in the legislation, is a faithful translation of the word "conserve" is of such philosophical consequence that reams have been written on the subject. There has been name-calling. Some say the term preservation should be applied only to paintings or artifacts, not to dynamic, constantly evolving ecosystems, although this observation could also start a fist fight.

On the other side are a mixed assortment of individuals and organizations who do not regard the parks as shrines but rather as places to have fun. They enjoy the scenery fully but tend to believe cabins and hotels are preferable to sleeping on the ground. Generally supportive in their own way of protective measures in the parks, they see no inconsistency in development of the parks for appropriate recreational pursuits.

Preservation and use policies within the National Park Service are in a sense only a restatement or a refinement of the basic schism responsible for most of the controversies within the conservation movement, the utilitarians vs. the preservationists. Conflicts among conservationists are frequently as bitter as between conservationists and the parties they try to restrain—or reform. A tree can be claimed by the Forest Service as lumber or by the Park Service as scenery; a river by the Bureau of Reclamation for electricity or by the Park Service for recreation. Because neither tree nor river can serve both demands at the same time, epic battles are generated on the national level. (With less publicity, but no less fervor, they are generated also within the National Park Service.)

The national parks arouse powerful concerns and deep commitments from many people who are pledged to their protection. There are incessant skirmishes over preservation and use issues in the conservation magazines; one almost suspects an occasional recourse to the tactic as a tried and true remedy against apathy in the ranks.

Probably at the crux of the eternal dialogue between Park Service administration and a considerable body of conservationists is that the conservationist, unencumbered politically, economically, or philosophically, looks at park problems and decides what *should* be. The Park Service, exceedingly encumbered, and not excluding ingrown habits and the inherent tendency endemic in government toward self-preservation, examines the park problem and decides what *can* be. Or, more simply, many conservationists have the good fortune to live in the best of all possible worlds while the Director and staff of the Park Service live in this one.

The National Park Service is not, however, free to operate the parks according to its own preferred policies. The bill establishing Assateague Island National Seashore specifies that a road shall be constructed the length of the sand spit. Conservationists who believe a road would destroy the character of the island call upon the Park Service to ignore the provision, but this is a matter of law, not Park Service policy.

If the establishing legislation for a park obligates the

Park Service to actions that it deems injurious to park purposes, the Director can (and has the responsibility to) present his case to Congress in order that it might be reconsidered. With the passage of the Environmental Policy Act of 1969, the Director has an even broader obligation to review all developments the Park Service intends to carry out in the parks and to report upon those that will have a significant impact on the environment.

Whether the Director is being offered advice by the Gettysburg Travel Council, which once petitioned him not to allow the park to erect signs guiding visitors to its information center, thereby avoiding local cultural attractions; or whether the Wilderness Society is charging that his well-known promotion of motor nature trails shows an open disregard for wilderness values, the Director is reminded that people certainly approach the parks from different angles. One thoughtful observer of the conflicting demands of preservation and use believes that it simply constitutes an always tough job, for the perfect solution is never truly attainable.

We may agree that it is a counsel of perfection, for even the discreet use of a wilderness area cannot help being in some degree an impairment. But why split hairs about it? The intent of Congress was high and good, and the very difficulty of fulfilling the injunction has been one of the fruitful challenges that has reached down through the personnel of the National Park Service to the loneliest laborer in the most remote spot.

A Seeming Contradiction

The increasing congestion in many parks is a seeming contradiction. Are not national parks supposed to offer solitude for people trying to get away from the concentrations of people and automobiles and the confusion of the cities? Back in the 1920's the historian James Truslow Adams expressed irritation when, after a number of years' absence, he returned to a favorite beach on the tip of Long Island, only to find himself sharing its "solitude" with several thousand fellow Americans. Granting that there was no reason why a privileged few should enjoy Montauk Point, Adams observed that, theoretically at least, there was no reason why many thousands of people could not enjoy the beach area at the same time. But theory, Adams concluded, had nothing to do with it; the crowded beach and the adjoining highlands did not offer the rare experience that he had previously enjoyed. "The point is that by the mere fact that eight thousand people tried to enjoy the solitude and beauty of Montauk at one time, the solitude and beauty evaporated. What the many got was something entirely different from what the few had got."

Considering the awesome responsibility of judging whether it is better to preserve a superlative experience for the few, or a less grand experience for great numbers of people, Adams concluded—as have countless park people—that "Which of these, for the whole human race for generations to come, might be the better, would baffle the mathematics of even an Einstein to figure out."

Adams responded as most people would who prefer solitude, although solitude itself has many meanings according to the differing requirements of individuals. Some people find escape and solitude on a crowded beach, while for others the spell is broken when they see a trail of footprints along the shore. Crossing Great Smoky Mountains, even in bumper-to-bumper traffic, is as sublime an experience for a person who rarely gets to the mountains as hiking down the Bright Angel Trail in Grand Canyon is for another—and changing places would be about as traumatic for both as trying to agree on a definition of preservation and use.

PARK PLANNING

Understandably, in its early years the Park Service emphasized the "use" side of management, promoting travel and

Members of the Hayden Survey party—scientists who explored Yellowstone during the summer of 1871, a year before it was established as the first U.S. national park. The Survey was accompanied by William Jackson, whose photographs were among the first to acquaint the public with the wonders of Yellowstone.

Between 1886 and 1918, the army administered Yellowstone. This young cavalry trooper, heading into Yellowstone's back country, is equipped for any emergency with rifle, fly rod, and creel. The year is 1903.

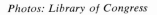

SOME EARLY VISITORS TO THE NATIONAL PARKS

Above: An army guide
explains the plumbing of a
Yellowstone geyser, 1903.

Right: A venturesome party
heads down the Grand
Canyon's Bright Angel Trail,
1908.

Below: A campground scene
in Yellowstone, 1924.

Photos: Library of Congress

More than 650 Civilian Conservation Corps camps were operated by the National Park Service during the 1930's. The "CCC boys" built roads, set up trails and campgrounds, and restored historic sites. *Photo: National Archives*

Left: Not a new species of elk but a snappy park ranger ready for patrol duty in 1941. *Right:* Mounted Park Service rangers are still very much in evidence in Yosemite. *Photos: National Park Service*

NATIONAL PARK SERVICE INTERPRETERS IN ACTION

Above: A naturalist explains the Teton fault action, which created the Teton Range in Wyoming. *Lower left:* A ranger at Virgin Islands National Park discusses marine life. *Lower right:* Not an airline stewardess but an archeologist in the new women's Park Service uniform. *Photos: National Park Service*

Rangers in other uniforms—the living-history program. *Left:* A break during production of a period film at Fort Frederica National Monument, Georgia. *Right:* Demonstrating Civil War life at Harpers Ferry, West Virginia.

Photos: National Park Service

An exhibit specialist prepares a diorama of the building of the Chesapeake and Ohio Canal at the Park Service Harpers Ferry Center.

Above: Archeologists uncover the walls of the Spanish mission at Tumacacori National Monument, Arizona.

Right: A Park Service curator assembles the pieces of an archeological jigsaw puzzle.

Below: Examples of Indian craftsmanship excavated from Mug House in Mesa Verde National Park, Colorado, and restored by Park Service personnel.

Photos: National Park Service

The steamer *Bertrand* sank during the Civil War in a section of the Missouri River that is now part of the DeSoto Wildlife Refuge in Nebraska. Excavated in 1968–69 under the Inter-Agency Archeological Salvage Program, this river steamer yielded up one of the most valuable finds of intact Americana on record—from toys to stomach bitters.   *Photo: Nebraska State Historical Society*

The old and the new.

Above: The new visitors' center at Gettysburg National Military Park, Pennsylvania.

Left: A Historic American Buildings Survey crew prepares measured drawings of Independence Hall, Philadelphia.

Photos: National Park Service

DIRECTORS OF THE NATIONAL PARK SERVICE

Stephen T. Maher, first Director from 1916 to 1928.

Horace M. Albright, Director from 1929 to 1933.

George B. Hartzog, Jr., whose administration began in 1964.

Photos: National Park Service

beginning to provide the roads and accommodations that were totally lacking. By the early 1920's a field engineering division had been established in Portland, Oregon, to supervise construction of roads, trails, buildings, and water and sewage systems. It was realized at the time that construction in the national parks presented an entirely different problem from construction elsewhere and that equally important in the process of providing facilities was an office sensitive both to the kind of development permissible and to the impact that it might have on the park scene.

The answer was a division of landscape architecture, probably unique at that time in the federal government. To the landscape architects was assigned responsibility for determining how far and in what manner facilities would be permitted to intrude. Engineers prepared their development schemes, but landscape architects determined how the campground should be sited for minimal encroachment or how close to a mountain meadow the road should be located. In all planning and construction of physical improvements in the parks, the strictest landscape control was exercised.

Emphasizing the importance of planning as the most effective method of minimizing the impact of use on the park environment, the Park Service began in 1926 to prepare documents for each park—determining the limit of development and marking out the areas to be preserved as wilderness—which soon evolved into the preparation of master plans. Through the technique of classifying, or zoning, all lands within a park, the various kinds of uses are separated, and each group of visitors has the opportunity to enjoy its preferred kind of use, unless that happens to involve bowling alleys or motion-picture theaters.

Even with the care taken to locate developments where they will do the least damage, however, some effects are impossible to predict, as evidenced in Carlsbad Caverns National Park in southeastern New Mexico. At Carlsbad the visitor center and the extensive parking lot constructed some years ago act as a waterproof seal, preventing natural seepage of ground water down through the caves, the process that helped create the formation. Electric lights are required to guide people through the caves, and, while they are turned off immediately when the tour has passed, the lights have permitted the growth of algae and other green plants. Because sufficient funds were lacking to air-condition the visitor center when it was constructed, the building is cooled by air drawn from the underground caverns, which has a warming-drying effect. Because of the widespread use of pesticides and herbicides nearby, the number of bats leaving the cavern entrance every night—one of the remarkable features of the park—may be steadily decreasing. While the effects of these influences are small and can be identified only by scientists, and while research is being carried out to find ways of reducing the impact, the experience is informative. Even in national parks where actions are taken with the most elaborate care, tinkering with ecological events has unforeseen results.

Up for review at this writing is the problem of a small developed area in a major national park, and the situation is both typical and informative. For many years a delightful, little-known retreat, it has achieved an inevitable popularity. As a result, the sanitary facilities are overtaxed, water is scarce, and the overnight accommodations are inadequate to meet the demand. The area used for sewage treatment is restricted, and enlargement would be destructive. More people require more water, but if the needed water is taken from the few springs in the area, the natural vegetation and the animals that depend upon this supply will suffer. If more cabins and parking areas are provided, more land will be occupied and the remote and unspoiled character of the basin, its greatest charm, will be endangered. Further development is obviously not a preferred option.

But neither is maintaining the status quo. Because of

accelerating prices and wage rates, the small size of the concessioner's development now makes the operation uneconomical; to make a profit, and this is necessary if the concessioner is to stay in business and provide service, he must expand— more cabins, more employee housing, more parking, and upgraded sewage and water systems. In countless similar situations, the wisdom of Solomon is a requirement for park planners.

Encroachments and intrusions are not a problem only of the natural and wilderness areas of the national park system. Historical areas face problems that are little different. Two projects presently under way, one in downtown Philadelphia at Independence Hall and the other two thousand miles away at Yellowstone, seek to correct identical problems of resource damage caused by overuse.

In Yellowstone, a bypass road is being built around the Old Faithful geyser basin so that the main automobile traffic flow does not pass close to the venerable geyser, threatening damage both to its plumbing and to its beauty. At Independence Hall, steel I-beams are being inserted into the floors to enable the building to withstand the pounding of pedestrian traffic.

At Yellowstone, existing structures and activities are being withdrawn from the vicinity of Old Faithful, in order that visitors can better enjoy the scene in relative peace and quiet. Because of the almost impossible congestion in Independence Hall, it is now necessary to move the Liberty Bell into new quarters where it can be viewed and appreciated by people without the present crowding and confusion.

CARRYING CAPACITY OF A PARK

Setting aside wilderness in national parks gives protection from exploitation yet at the same time, by calling national attention to a scarce recreational commodity, exposes the wilderness to increased use. Since the automobile first enabled city dwellers to seek out more remote places, the amount of solitude per seeker began to dwindle, and the journey grew longer. As the competition to find quality outdoor recreation has intensified, the increasing scarcity of wild places makes each that much more desirable.

In Grand Teton National Park, Wyoming, one of the more delightful experiences available is floating down the Snake River on a raft. Although not far removed from the road, the meandering Snake has cut deeply into the outwash alluvial plain, and, as one drifts silently past abundant wildlife, he has the impression of being deep in the wilderness. Only a few years ago the number of rafts on the river was negligible, but the word was passed and float operators multiplied. Now more than sixty thousand people make the trip each summer. The rafts are often within sight of one another, and a Park Service litter patrol is required to police the waters and pick up trash.

Deciding whether it is better to allow six thousand people to have a superlative experience on the Snake River or to allow sixty thousand to carry on a more gregarious activity is the kind of decision over which James Truslow Adams agonized. But determining how many constitute too much is only part of the riddle of the Snake, which is a river and cannot, like a road, be resurfaced. It has an ecological capacity, beyond which the impact of use begins to alter the ecology of the river and its life.

Some people, most perhaps, are fully satisfied to enjoy the wilderness along the park roads, with modest explorations from the comfort and safety of their automobile. Breathing the winesap air of the high mountain valleys, viewing fantastic vistas, and enjoying a total change of scenery is enough. As they see it, by staying to the road they do no damage to the wilderness that they too want to preserve.

But the wilderness-lover is unlikely to conclude that roads, which he abhors, may be the saving of the wilderness. More probably he would say that mass use must be considered incompatible with the concept of solitude, that when the Park Service speaks of "development" in terms of providing roads, trails, or campgrounds, it is not truly developing in the sense of adding values but rather is diluting the quality of the wilderness.

Psychologists have noted that the love of wilderness can in some individuals be traced to a longing to get away from his fellow man, as much as an urge to get to some primitive scenery. It is an interesting phenomenon that those who speak with disdain of the "hordes" of park visitors somehow are able to use the same facilities without being part of the horde. Few who argue for restricting park use will also volunteer to be among those excluded from the quota.

The historical preservationists, from whose world all but antiquarian minutiae seems to have been excluded, and the backpackers who lament the stultifying existence of organized campgrounds, are entitled to their religions and can always find their particular kind of enjoyment in the parks. There are also those sensible people who agree that old buildings are terrific, in proper doses, and that a day of wilderness-hiking is beyond compare—if topped off by a hot shower and the tinkle of ice cubes.

For some time park planners have been trying to find a handle to the problem of determining the "carrying capacity" of a park, upon which all planning for park use could be based. The suggestion is frequently made that parks should be operated like theaters, where one buys a ticket in advance, and, when all tickets are sold, the management announces the house is full. The problem is to develop an equitable formula for determining when parks are "full." The capacity of a historic house can be measured, the optimum number of people a naturalist can lead is known, but these are the more quantifiable aspects. All campsites in a park may be occupied, but what constitutes "full" occupancy of the road and trail systems or the museums and scenic overlooks? And must all be "full" simultaneously?

Attempting to explore such an approach, the Park Service contracted with a private consulting firm to undertake a carrying-capacity study for Rocky Mountain National Park. The study produced more questions than answers. Even within selected park activities that seemed measurable, the range of attitudes and preferences confounded the scientists and their questionnaires.

Some people, for example, go camping to "get away," but others enjoy camping as a means of "getting together." It was observed that in one campground, as the number of campers began to drop off sharply after Labor Day, those remaining tended to gather more closely together, rather than taking the opportunity to gain more solitude. Until recently, while the campgrounds in Yosemite Valley were deluged, the campgrounds available in the High Country beyond the valley were never completely filled.

As in all known human activities, people tend to complicate things. Some park visitors have a high tolerance for the presence of fellow human beings, others have remarkably little. Only a few years after automobiles were to be seen in numbers in the parks, a noted landscape architect grumpily announced that the only difference between Yosemite and Los Angeles was that Yosemite had trees and no traffic lights while the city had traffic lights and no trees.

Because of the many interests and preferences involved, the Park Service seeks to bring the general public into the process of determining preservation and use policies. Private citizens are sometimes invited to serve on master plan teams or to act as consultants to the team. Upon its completion and before approval every park master plan is presented for review and discussion at a public meeting. This procedure, which gives the public and the press opportunity to enter into a dialogue with the Park Service over any phase of the plan, is intended to make the administration of the national parks responsive to the public, which owns and uses the parks.

Some years ago, before publication of *The Greening of America* made him a controversial prophet, Charles A. Reich published for the Center for the Study of Democratic Institutions a report entitled "Bureaucracy and the Forests." Holding that any government agency is following a perilous course when it decides it knows what is best for people, Reich declared, "In a democracy the 'public interest' has no objective meaning except insofar as the people have defined it; the question cannot be what is 'best' for the people, but what the people, adequately informed, decide they want."

The key proviso of this thoughtful analysis is obviously that people be "well informed" before making their decisions, and this is one of the reasons for holding open hearings on park master plans. One of the inherent problems of these hearings is that they are held in the locale of the park, where sentiment and interests may not be representative of the public at large. Recommendations received are, however, advisory, and the procedure is not meant to suggest that park-planning matters are best solved by a majority vote, particularly in matters where the heart and the pocketbook might be in conflict with one another. And it is remarkable how opinions change over the years, as social, and economic, factors that affect individual attitudes also change.

When the question of whether to allow automobiles into Yellowstone was being studied in 1915, the park concessioners were much against the proposal. Having a large investment in carriages, horses, and a string of corrals, they were hardly interested in allowing the visitor to bring his own transportation into the park. Soon, however, they were operating a profitable line of tour buses. Some fifty years later, another Yellowstone transportation study was made, this time provoked by owners of neighboring motels, service stations, and restaurants, who called upon their congressional delegation to have the Park Service use snowplows to open park roads during the winter to inject a little life into the off-season tourist business.

Estimating the cost per car at considerably more than $10, the Park Service was noticeably reluctant to accept this sample of public opinion, but time, and the promise to "study the matter further," are aces back-to-back in the hands of bureaucrats. Within a few years the snowmobile craze was under way, and with the machines restricted to the park road system, the gateway town of West Yellowstone has become almost as bustling in mid-winter as it is in mid-summer, and the clamor for plowing the roads is heard no longer. Meanwhile, the daily count of snowmobiles into Old Faithful is reaching several hundred, complaints against the incredible noise level of the little monsters are mounting, and the Park Service may be due to make yet another study of transportation in Yellowstone.

PARKS ARE FOR PEOPLE

Alexis de Tocqueville rightly predicted that in America many would demand what in other lands had been reserved for the few. Parks, whether national, state, or municipal, are one of the best expressions of this ideal. Long ago it was decided—and time has strengthened the belief—that parks are not for any special interest groups, neither the scientist nor the fisherman, the affluent nor the disadvantaged, the wilderness-enthusiast nor the man in a hurry. All of the people buy the parks, pay the not inconsiderable costs of operation, and through their elected representatives determine park policy: the scholar and the scientist, the Civil War buff and the bird watcher, the lonely hiker and the antiquarian, the hopeful cameraman and the hard-pressed but indomitable father of four.

Almost no one would deny that parks have been set aside for people's enjoyment, even though amid the din a wistful voice may sometimes be heard observing that the country might do well to set aside a particularly fine example of primitive America, with its wildlife, forests, and geologic evidence, for its own sake, a kind of ecological Fort Knox, never to be seen but its carefully guarded treasure bringing comfort to all mankind.

If it is granted that parks are set aside for people's enjoyment, then a phrase used by the Park Service, although not much heard recently—"Parks are for People"—would seem to be a self-evident truism. But the expression is in some quarters received with suspicion and dismay, and it has been the subject of acrimonious debate by those who regard it as a threat, a platitude, or worse. In his eloquent account of life as a Park Service employee at Arches National Monument in eastern Utah, Edward Abbey views the maxim as a public relations slogan, "which decoded means that parks are for people-in-automobiles." Let them walk, says the acerbic park ranger in Abbey's *Desert Solitaire*, "or ride horses, bicycles, mules, wild pigs—anything—but keep the automobiles and the motorcycles and all their motorized relatives out."

Another source of unending controversy is the word "recreation." What *is* recreation and what *kind* of recreation is justified in a national park? The word itself is so broad that it defies definition. Before being adopted—and adapted—as a national goal, recreation was a lovely word admirably describing a worthy ideal, to recreate and find new purpose.

Parks can provide only a limited amount of recreational space for the ever increasing numbers of recreationists, and some activities are more space-devouring than others. At thirty miles an hour, the power-boat addict consumes many times as much space as a more sane person who idles along quietly in a canoe, seeing, hearing, experiencing. John Ruskin must have anticipated the automobile when he said of the coming of the steam engine: "There was always more in the world than a man could see, walked he ever so slowly. He will see no more by going fast, for his glory is not in going, but in being."

The problem of what constitutes justifiable and appropriate recreation is fought with equal fervor in historical parks. The restoration of Ford's Theater, scene of Lincoln's assassination, created a spirited intramural dispute when the proposal was first made that, rather than serving as an exhibit, the theater should be used for live performances. Architectural historians, who often seem to prefer bricks and mortar to flesh and blood, argued the building was sacred to the memory of Abraham Lincoln, although it is all a reconstruction, except for three exterior walls. Observing a thrilling, captivating performance of "Trumpets of the Lord," one suspects this is much more the way historic buildings should be treated, rather than embalming them as lifeless shrines.

THE PROBLEM OF ROADS

Perhaps no decisions have been more difficult to reach than those involving the complex question of how best to transport people through the parks. Whether a small historic site of a few acres, or a park covering a million acres, the location and extent of the road system is probably the most important single factor affecting use and preservation values. With all but a small fraction of visitors arriving in automobiles, the way in which the park is experienced is largely determined by the way roads are located, designed, and constructed.

Road construction probably causes more damage to park resources than any other kind of development. Roads often pass through rugged country, so that construction can require blasting a roadbed out of solid rock. On such terrain and in desert country, the scar may never heal. The road itself can to some extent interrupt drainage, impede the natural movement of wildlife, and cause the growth of exotic vegetation in the disturbed ground.

Some of the great and bitter conservation battles have been fought over road construction in the parks, and almost always the conservationists have lined up against the Park Service. The reconstruction of the Tioga Road in Yosemite National Park was a classic battle.

The result of a silver mining rush to the Tioga district within the present Yosemite National Park, the Tioga Road was built in 1883 by Chinese labor in the employ of the Great Sierra Consolidated Silver Mining Company. The company soon failed, and the hastily constructed fifty-six–mile road built to freight machinery, supplies, and ore in horse-drawn wagons soon disintegrated.

Looking for a way to encourage travel to Yosemite when he took over the direction of the national parks, Stephen Mather decided to buy the Tioga Road, still privately owned; and in 1915, by soliciting from friends and interested organizations, including the Sierra Club, he raised half the purchase price of $15,500 and paid the remainder himself. Occasional improvements were made to the roadbed, but by the time of the post World War II boom in travel, the road was swamped. Too narrow, too winding, too steep, it became a frustrating bottleneck, with long lines of automobiles inching along when flatlanders, unaccustomed to mountain driving, froze at the wheel.

What to do? The Tioga Road is crucial to Yosemite access, for it links the several entrances on the west side of the Sierra Nevada with the single entrance for visitors approaching Yosemite from the east. The already impossible conditions could only get worse; reluctantly, the Park Service decided to rebuild the road to modern standards and in the late 1950's began work on the last twenty-one miles.

As viewed by many conservationists, this section of the

road meant unforgivable destruction of one of the most fragile sections of Yosemite's High Country, particularly at Tenaya Lake, a noble sight, where bulldozers blasted through areas of glacially polished granite. The Sierra Club led the attack. The Director of the Park Service personally inspected the road location, and construction was halted on several occasions to seek alternative locations and to lessen the impact, but no one would argue that painful damage resulted.

The completed Tioga Road has provided park visitors with an opportunity to drive through one of the most inspiring sections of any national park. But this pleasure has been bought for a price. In one of many stinging rebukes in the Sierra Club *Bulletin*, it was pointed out that, while a few generations would restore the trees, only another ice age would restore the wilderness, some portions of which were "destroyed for the duration of this civilization."

A decade later, the Park Service faced a similar problem in Mesa Verde National Park in Colorado. The principal ruins in Mesa Verde are found on Chapin Mesa, and, as the number of visitors increased, restrictions on access to the ruins were imposed to protect the cliff dwellings. Eventually only guided trips through the ruins were permitted. As the processions became too unwieldy, the size of the groups had to be reduced, and finally only those who obtained tickets in advance could take the tours.

To relieve the overcrowding at Chapin Mesa, the Park Service decided to excavate a series of cliff dwellings on Wetherill Mesa. Aided by a grant from the National Geographic Society, a five-year program was carried out, resulting in the uncovering of Long House, Mug House, and Step House, whose size and remains rival those of Cliff Palace and Spruce Tree House on Chapin Mesa.

The final phase of the work was to provide access to Wetherill Mesa. Archeologists had used an antiquated seventeen-mile Jeep road, which passenger vehicles could not navigate. Funds for a new road were programmed, specifications were prepared by the Bureau of Public Roads, which designs and supervises construction for major park roads, and construction had just begun when the road was brought to the attention of the Park Service Director.

As is their habit, the Bureau of Public Roads engineers had designed a high-standard highway, with minimum grades and wide, sweeping curves. Where the existing road topped the successive mesas, providing breathtaking 360-degree views before dipping down to climb the next mesa, the new design would avoid both extremes. By benching heavily into the sides of the mesas, and piling fill up to forty feet deep in the canyons between, the road would be nicely leveled out— with devastating impact on the landscape.

The Director immediately canceled the contract and ordered that the new road should stick to the existing road location, with only minimal improvement of the steep grades and sharp turns. Later he was to conclude that he had made the right decision but for the wrong reason. He had canceled the original design in order to avoid a major road scar, but more important was the impact that a high-standard road would have had upon the visitor's experience at Wetherill Mesa. In a relatively few years, would Wetherill not be suffering the same congestion that it had been planned to avoid?

The low-standard road to Wetherill Mesa will not attract all visitors; those preferring a quick trip will still go to Chapin Mesa. At Wetherill visitors will leave their cars behind in a parking area; they will be encouraged to walk to the ruins, but a minibus transportation system will also be available. The Wetherill experience will be a much different experience from that of Chapin Mesa, if the Park Service belief is correct that *how* one sees a park is sometimes as important as *what* one sees.

Out of the Wetherill Mesa exercise came a thorough study of national park roads by a special task force, which developed new standards for park roads: national parks cannot continue indefinitely to accommodate every person who wants to drive his automobile through the parks; if the parks are to retain their distinctive character, the numbers of people and their means of access will have to be controlled; in seeking solutions to park access, new roads should be considered the last resort.

"A park road is not one that merely conforms to standards of technical road-building excellence," the task force report concluded. "Preserving the integrity of the landscape, respecting ecological processes, insuring a fully rewarding visitor experience—these are the elements which dictate the means of visitor access and the development of design standards."

As a final control, a new policy was adopted that no road can now be built in a national park until it has been reviewed and approved on the ground by the Park Service's chief scientist and the chief of interpretation, which is a way of saying that park roads are much too important to be left in the hands of engineers. As one who served as a member of the road standards study, as well as being a member of the team that has racked up plenty of mileage, on foot, reviewing proposed road construction, the writer can attest to the care with which road decisions are made by the National Park Service.

VI
The Matter of Protection

For most visitors, the national parks seem to be the last sanctuary of unspoiled wilderness, untouched by the progress of civilization; the giant sequoia groves, for example, present a timeless scene unchanged by passing centuries. The ecologist, however, would disagree that even the oldest parks are "pure," while many of the more recently established parks and monuments have been subjected to various degrees of logging, mining, agriculture, and livestock-grazing in the period before the area was set aside. More than half of Great Smoky Mountains National Park had been cut over before its establishment, and relatively little of Shenandoah National Park contains virgin timber.

Protecting the Forest

Through inadvertence and the less scientific management of years gone by, or by the carelessness of visitors, exotic vegetation and plant diseases have been introduced in the national parks. Pack animals entering the park leave behind in their droppings seeds that bear strange fruits. The beloved burro, companion of countless gold prospectors, escaped into the wild and now roams many of the arid parks as a feral animal, competing for water and grass with the native wildlife. The wolf has almost totally disappeared, the mountain lion is seldom seen, and the mighty grizzly bear can now be found only in the northern Rocky Mountain parks in the U.S. and Canada and in Alaska.

There was never any doubt, however, that protection of the forests and the wildlife therein was from the beginning a major objective of park management. It seemed an eminently logical decision, for fire killed trees just as surely as hunters killed animals. As quickly as the parks were staffed, rangers endeavored to protect the forests against fire. It was known that fire had always been a natural element in the life of the forest. Lightning from a summer thunderstorm can set off a dozen or even several dozen fires, most of which do little damage and are restricted to a single tree or a small area but on occasion can develop into a roaring forest fire.

Less well known was the effect that fire suppression could have on the forest environment. Rather than keeping out a destructive force, the policy eliminated, to some degree, an environmental factor needed to regenerate certain plant species. In some places where fire had previously swept through the forest, with the resulting new growth providing food for wildlife, heavy thickets of trees developed. The policy of "overprotection" could therefore alter the numbers and kinds of, and the relationship between, plants and wildlife.

The sequoia trees* have been almost impervious to fire because their thick bark acts as an effective insulating material, but they too were given protection. Before being protected in national parks, the sequoia groves had experienced lightning-caused fires every fifteen or twenty years.

---

*There are two species of sequoias, or "redwood" trees, in the United States. *Sequoia gigantea,* the "Giant Sequoia," is found on the western slopes of the Sierra Nevada and, while not so tall, is considerably greater in circumference and older than *Sequoia sempervirens,* which grows in the coastal fog zone of California and southern Oregon.

The result of protection has been the accumulation on the forest floor of thick layers of combustible materials, made up of dead limbs, twigs, and needles. Should a fire start now it might become so intense as to penetrate the insulating protection of the bark and could become a crown fire, sweeping through trees that have withstood natural fires for thousands of years. While successfully protecting the great trees against little fires, the protection policy created the distinct possibility of a major, damaging fire. Without fires, the sequoia forest could be doomed, for if the sequoia seeds are to germinate, the mineral soil must be exposed to the sun by fires that have burned away the ground cover. In a sense, elimination of fire is the equivalent of manipulating park resources, although fire suppression is more easily justified to protect the rain forests of Olympic National Park or the fragile vegetation of desert parks and other areas where fire is rare and recovery requires many generations.

Under the most tightly supervised conditions (probably accompanied by silent incantations), rangers are setting fires experimentally in several parks. After the first year of controlled burning in Sequoia National Park, 6,000 sequoia seedlings sprouted. In Everglades National Park in Florida, there is a more extensive use of controlled burning, particularly in the pinelands, to reduce unnatural competition from the hardwoods that natural fires had formerly kept under control.

It should be noted that fire suppression was adopted as standard policy by the Park Service because of several practical considerations. Allowing natural fires to burn would necessitate a difficult task of determining which fires are due to natural causes and which are the result of human factors. It would be of scant comfort to park visitors, viewing only the blackened stubs of a once mighty forest, to be told by a ranger that they were viewing a perfectly natural process, indeed one to be encouraged, and that within only a few hundred years, barring another such conflagration, the trees would be bigger and healthier than ever. One can also contemplate only with the most painful of emotions the widespread consequences sure to follow if a forest fire, allowed to burn freely within the park, should cross the boundary and burn down a neighboring town. And, finally, there is that problem of what to do about Smokey the Bear.

PROTECTING THE WILDLIFE

Park administrators have encountered problems in protecting wildlife that were hardly anticipated by the framers of the Yellowstone Act. Believing that people who reached the remote park would have to depend upon fish and game for food, the Act barred only "wanton destruction" of animals. Regulations permitted hunting "for recreation, or to supply food for visitors or actual residents," and when one considers that Yellowstone was established four years before the Battle of the Little Bighorn, it is apparent that supply lines were at best uncertain. As a result, in the early years of Yellowstone, hunters provided meat for the camps and hotels, and even a superintendent observed "hunting in the Park was excellent sport, and the only recreation I enjoyed during the season."

One of the reasons for bringing the cavalry into Yellowstone in 1886 was to protect wildlife from commercial poaching. By this time the once great herds of buffalo (more accurately bison), which had once numbered as many as 60 million, had been nearly exterminated by the demon hide hunters, and substantial fortunes were made from the sale of tongues alone, at 25 cents each, leaving the half-ton carcass to rot. A scientific expedition in 1886 could locate only 540 buffalo in all of the West, most of which were in Yellowstone, and the number continued to dwindle.

The soldiers did an outstanding job, but the park was vast and the greedy poachers were incredibly bold and took a heavy toll of the herds. With buffalo heads—now rare and worth several hundred dollars—anyone who could avoid the cavalry troops was assured a good living selling hides and heads to the taxidermists in Livingstone and Billings.

In 1894 a notorious poacher was caught in the act of skinning out a buffalo by a civilian scout and a cavalry trooper. The number of dead animals nearby indicated he lacked only a little more time to clean out the entire herd. Fate, it has been observed, often seems to intervene for the parks at critical times, and just by chance the well-known outdoorsman-writer Emerson Hough was in Yellowstone on assignment from *Field and Stream*. The poacher proudly told Hough he had killed eighty buffalo in the park, a number then estimated to be one-fourth of all the wild bison left in America.

The general public had developed a striking sentimental attachment for the buffalo, now that he was on the verge of extinction, and the article Hough wrote, which dramatically joined together the eagle and the buffalo as the twin symbols of America's national glory, helped Americans realize for the first time that they owned a national park and that it was worth preserving. Two months after the incident Congress passed an "Act to Protect the Birds and Animals in Yellowstone National Park," which provided a code of laws giving protection to all wildlife and stiff penalties for offenders. The Lacey Bill, another conservation milestone for Representative John Lacey of Iowa, became a model for subsequent park legislation.

Although popular sentiment began to support the idea that parks should be wildlife preserves in which animals could live in complete protection from human interference, public opinion quickly separated the animals into the good and the bad. The "bad" animals naturally were the predators— coyotes, wolves, bobcats, bears, mountain lions. They were evil because they murderously preyed upon the "good" animals—elk, deer, buffalo, and antelope. But then it is interesting to ponder that all the "good" animals happened to be those man liked to eat. Since most of the Western parks are located in what might be termed the grazing sphere of influence, park wildlife populations were substantially influenced by programs that the grazing fraternity demanded and that federal agencies carried out by poison, traps, and bounty hunters, to wipe out the predators and eliminate any threats to lambs and calves. The programs continue, and the near disappearance of the once numerous prairie-dog towns is but one casualty of this effort, although the wise coyote seems somehow able to survive.

But the predator was not always safe even within the national parks, one must sadly admit. As recently as 1918, a distinguished naturalist, writing on the wildlife of Glacier National Park in Montana, expressed the prevailing view when he captioned a photograph of two dead mountain lions: "Picture of two cougars that will kill no more game. The only good mountain lions are those gathered in by hunters and trappers." Although Adolph Murie's *The Wolves of Mt. McKinley* is a classic wildlife study, published in 1944, it did not immediately stop the killing of wolves in the face of the argument that the park was set aside to protect Dall sheep, which the wolves killed.

At first, given double protection from hunters and predators, the Yellowstone elk herds increased. Under natural conditions the park provides adequate summer range in its meadows and forests, but the heavy winter snowfall forces the herds down to lower elevations. The northern elk herd traditionally roamed beyond the park boundary to lower and more sheltered ranges. But as the region was settled, these lowland pastures were converted to farming and livestock production, which along with ever increasing pressure from hunters forced the elk to winter within the park, on a limited range that provided only a fraction of the food required. Inevitably during the winter of 1919–20, there was a massive die-off from starvation, a tragic fate for animals in a wildlife preserve.

The Yellowstone herds were, however, almost the last remnant of this large native deer, which was once plentiful from the eastern forests to the Rocky Mountains. Beginning in 1892, a few elk were shipped to the Washington, D.C., zoo and to other zoos throughout the country to save the elk from extinction. Since then more than 10,000 have been live-trapped and shipped from Yellowstone to thirty-nine states. With few exceptions, the blood of Yellowstone elk is in every existing herd in the United States.

Neither live-trapping within the park nor public hunting outside the park was adequate to reduce the elk population to the carrying capacity of the range. In the mid-1930's, and as a last resort, park rangers armed with rifles began a selective reduction of the herds. The program was successful in bringing down the elk population to a healthy level; but when the herd built up again in the 1960's, the reduction program of shooting and live-trapping resulted in an explosive public controversy concerning the management of wildlife in the national parks. The reduction program is no longer used, and wildlife biologists now believe that elk and other wildlife populations can reach a balance, if man is willing to give them the opportunity. The northern Yellowstone elk herd is being given that opportunity through a cooperative program involving the Montana State Fish and Game Department, the Forest Service, and the Park Service.

One of the anomalies in the wildlife protection policies of the Park Service is that, while animals are protected, fish are not, but then fishing is traditional. Doubtless someone may be able to explain why hunting wildlife is bad and hunting fish is good. The only rational explanation one can offer is the sign hanging in the office of the deputy director of the National Park Service: *"But We've Always Done It This Way in Yellowstone."*

PROTECTING THE VISITOR

Although development of an appropriate policy for perpetuating the forests and wildlife poses a difficult enough management problem for the Park Service, protecting the park visitor can be equally baffling. In more recent years the question has been raised whether it is better to protect the animals from the people or the people from the animals, in particular, the grizzly bear.

The grizzly best symbolizes the once limitless wilderness, and for those fortunate enough to have seen him in the wild, he is the grandest animal remaining from primitive America. Andy Russell gave a classic description in his *Grizzly Country*:

> The animal that impresses me most, the one I find myself liking more and more, is the grizzly. No sight encountered in the wilds is quite so stirring as those massive, clawed tracks pressed into mud or snow. No sight is quite so impressive as that of the great bear stalking across some mountain slope with the fur of his silvery robe rippling over his mighty muscles. His is a dignity and power matched by no other in the North American wilderness. To share a mountain with him for awhile is a privilege and an adventure like no other.

Aptly named *Ursus horribilis*, the grizzly once roamed from the Mississippi River to the Pacific Ocean. Outside of Canada and Alaska, he can now be found only in the mountainous parts of Montana, Idaho, and Wyoming, centering on Glacier and Yellowstone National Parks. The last sighting of a grizzly in California, except on the state flag, was in 1922.

In strength and ferocity, the grizzly has competition from few other animals. Preferring to avoid contact with humans, the grizzly demands large wilderness areas for its habitat; within this habitat, however, the bear will defend its young, its food, and its territory against any intruder, and on rare occasions will attack man. Since the combination of people and wilderness is most often found in the national parks, grizzly encounters generally occur there.

None of the above refers to the black bear, smaller and with a much better disposition than the grizzly. He is a traditional hustler along the park roads who, unfortunately for park visitors, has racked up a fairly high score of bites and scratches. Black bear injuries are all too common, the result of mass insanity on the part of visitors who insist upon feeding the bears or on occasion even posing for a family portrait with the mother and her cubs.

About 1920 the first person was killed by a grizzly in a national park when a tourist of uncertain intentions chased a cub up a tree near the present Canyon Village in Yellowstone. The mother stormed up, ripping out the man's breastbone and one lung, and from these wounds he died a few days later. Still, in the almost one-hundred-year history of the eleven Canadian and American national parks that have grizzly populations, only five persons have been killed out of some 150 million visitors.

In the fifty-seven-year history of Glacier National Park, no person had ever been killed by a grizzly bear. Then, during a single night in the summer of 1967, two nineteen-year-old girls, in separate incidents twenty miles apart—an almost unbelievable coincidence—were seized in their sleeping bags by grizzlies and mauled to death. The stark tragedies, which occurred in the back country of Glacier, aroused national concern over the safety of people in the parks. Magazines and newspapers raised, and answered, the question whether parks are for people or for grizzlies.

There was considerable public support for the argument that, if grizzlies are indeed a potential danger, they should be eliminated from the national parks. Advancing the thesis that geysers, mud pots, and hot springs are unique features of Yellowstone, but that grizzlies are not, one scientist proposed that "if it seems important to preserve the grizzly, there are other habitats." The bears can be moved to other places, he argued, but Old Faithful cannot. Long before, the renowned ecologist Aldo Leopold had responded to a similar proposal that grizzlies be deported: "Relegating the grizzlies to Alaska is about like relegating happiness to heaven; one may never get there."

In part, the bear problem is a pollution problem, the pollution being garbage. National parks that have a daily population of twenty thousand people create the same amount of garbage and trash as does a city of twenty thousand residents. Garbage disposal is therefore a sizable and expensive job, and in all parks with bear populations the Park Service has launched a major campaign to install bear-proof garbage cans, to clean up the campgrounds and roadsides, and to require hikers to pack their garbage out of the back country.

While the debate over the grizzly was raging, the *Christian Science Monitor* was conducting a survey of reader attitudes toward the national parks and asked the question whether grizzlies should be eliminated. Only 104 out of nearly 3,500 responses favored this action, while 97 per cent voted for retaining the grizzly.

A gallant endorsement of this attitude came soon afterwards from a man with a more personal interest in the outcome of the debate. Early in 1968, a visiting Canadian schoolteacher was attempting to photograph a grizzly family at close range when the mother attacked. Fortunately, he escaped with only twenty-nine stitches. "The thing that makes me very unhappy about the whole incident," he later declared, "is my fear that this will only add fuel to the fire

for those people who advocate the destruction of the grizzly
to make our national parks safe." Pointing out the animal
was simply protecting her young, that her attack was therefore justified, and that he bore the bear no malice, he concluded: "The only thing that will prevent me from hiking
in the wilderness again is the eventual destruction of that
wilderness itself, and when anyone advocates the destruction
of the grizzlies they are in essence advocating the destruction
of true wilderness. Let us pray that this never happens."

Jack Olsen, in his *Night of the Grizzlies*, is more pessi-
mistic:

> After the next such rondeau of death in Glacier Park, the grizzly
> will almost certainly be banished into Canada, and thence per-
> haps into Alaska to live out his last years as a species, and all the
> goodwill and understanding in the world, all the good intentions
> and pious proclamations, will not alter his eventual fate.

The whole area of what constitutes reasonable safety
precautions in a national park came under considerable
attack in Yellowstone in 1970, following the tragic death of
a nine-year-old boy who wandered from the boardwalk and
fell into a hot spring in the Old Faithful geyser basin. If the
function of a national park is, as the Wildlife Management
Advisory Board concluded, to preserve a "vignette of primitive America," then certain potentially dangerous situations
—rivers, hot springs, mountains, wildlife—must exist. The
canyon rims in Zion, Bryce, and Grand Canyon, as well as
the trails that wind down into the canyons, are a potential
hazard. Whether they should be lined with chain link fence
is another matter.

Safety is, to a considerable degree, an attitude; witness the
high incidence of accidents in the home. Seeking to make the
visitor more aware of safety requirements in the parks, the
Park Service printed and distributed to all parties entering

Yellowstone in 1971 a special safety brochure, calling attention to the kinds of dangers that might be encountered. It was printed on bright red paper with the single word DANGER on the cover. Early in the summer a couple, who, like other visitors, were in possession of the safety brochure, sighted a buffalo lying down near the road. The husband photographed the wife in front of the buffalo, then gave her the camera to duplicate the pose. Aroused, the buffalo charged and killed the man. It was the only known death caused by a buffalo in Yellowstone's history.

In 1970, there were 165 fatalities out of 167 million visitors, and the ratio of one death per one million visitors has remained fairly constant. The leading cause of accidental deaths was motor vehicle accidents (75), followed by drownings (50), and falls (18); these accounted for almost 90 per cent of the fatalities.

A rather surprising number of people engage in mountain climbing in the parks, some of whom obviously should not. Driving from Yellowstone to Grand Teton in the summer of 1971, the author picked up a young couple, college students, and was alternately amused and dismayed by their plans to climb "the Grand," the tallest of the Teton peaks. Otherwise intelligent, they not only lacked rudimentary equipment but were nonplussed to find that a considerable amount of snow and ice remains up on top throughout the year. They doubtless respected the advice received from the ranger to whom they were directed.

One of the most physically arduous and demanding climbs in the United States is Mount Rainier, but more than 16,000 made the attempt in the 1960's and 10,000 were successful. In 1970, out of 2,250 attempts, 1,300 were successful. But inevitably, there are climbing accidents. Five people fell to their death in Grand Teton during 1971, and when this happens, ranger rescue teams must bring out the victims, which can be the most dangerous kind of mountaineering.

Secretary of the Interior Rogers C. B. Morton witnessed and provided support to one such rescue during an inspection trip to Rocky Mountain National Park in Colorado in 1971. An experienced climber had fallen while attempting the sheer East Face of Long's Peak, a famous and difficult ascent. The park's mountain rescue team of eight men had the arduous task of bringing down the badly injured man, who was hanging from his rope. One husky ranger backpacked the climber singlehandedly, rappelling down to "Broadway," a ledge running across the sheer face. From this point, the entire party was needed to lower the Stokes stretcher down the remainder of the rock face, float it across a small lake, and carry it to a place where the helicopter dispatched by Secretary Morton could evacuate the injured climber.

VII
Concessions

Stephen Mather, first Director of the National Park Service, was a practical man who once explained the basic reason for having concessions in the national parks: "Scenery is a hollow enjoyment to a tourist who sets out in the morning after an indigestible breakfast and a fitful sleep on an impossible bed."

Things have not changed much in the jet age. For most people, a national park visit is a leisure activity that achieves its greatest potential when all creature comforts have been taken care of. Some people have difficulty finding inspiration in the wonders of nature before being assured that a hotel room awaits them. The person in search of a restroom will seldom pause to ask the ranger, "What kind of bird is that?"

When it established Yellowstone, Congress gave some evidence of understanding that facilities for people's comfort would have to be provided, that these developments were essential to the purpose of the park, and that in all likelihood providing the public with these essential services would be a source of considerable trouble. The Act specified that "The Secretary may, at his discretion, grant leases for building purposes, for terms not exceeding ten years, of small parcels of ground, at such places in said park as shall require the erection of buildings for the accommodation of visitors."

This vaguely worded sentence, which constituted the only legislative direction for a good many years, contributed heavily to the confusion that followed. The door was left open for private enterprise, but Congress did not so specify or even demand. Whether a concessioner* was to be closely regulated, whether his profits were to be unlimited, or whether the laws of the market place were to prevail, were matters that the wording of the legislation ignored.

Although the earliest tourists came to see the scenery in the parks, most of them did not come prepared—unlike mountain men—to stay the winter and live off the country. They needed a roof over their heads and food that, while not resembling home cooking, would at least stay down. Incredibly, even before the first national parks were established, the spirit of enterprise prevailed and "hotels" began to make their appearance.

A posse of Californians calling themselves the Mariposa Battalion discovered Yosemite Valley in 1851 while attempting to discourage the local Indians from standing in the way of the exploitation of their lands by the gold-seekers. Before the end of the decade, crude accommodations had been constructed and a toll trail that led into the valley from the Merced River. In 1864, the year Yosemite was ceded to California, one of the hotels was acquired by James Hutchings, a dreamy, literary Englishman. In his delightfully written biography of Mather, Robert Shankland provides an account of life in the Hutchings House, which serves as an engaging introduction to concession history.

Perhaps in keeping with native British reticence, the sexes were separated in the Hutchings House, men on the first

*Although the person operating a concession franchise in a recreation area is generally called a "concessionaire," Park Service terminology is "concessioner."

floor, women on the second. Unable to withstand the entreaties of the married couples, Hutchings eventually partitioned off bedrooms with cheesecloth. Famous for its view of Yosemite Falls, the hotel now had much to offer "shadow watchers and interpreters of muffled woodnotes." Embarrassed by these nightly magic lantern shows on the cheesecloth walls, Hutchings set up a sawmill to build partitions, thereby giving employment to another literate dreamer, John Muir.

A couple of so-called hotels had appeared in Yellowstone in 1871, the year before the park was established, one being described by the Secretary of the Interior as an "earth-roofed log house in the ravine flanking the Mammoth Hot Springs." Within a few years saddle and pack horses could be rented at Mammoth, and a tour boat was operating on Yellowstone Lake. By 1891, there was a steamer on the lake that could carry 125 passengers. By 1880, stage lines were carrying visitors into Old Faithful and camping companies were offering accommodations of sorts in several areas of the park, although the superintendent reported there was not a hotel worthy of the name.

THE FREE ENTERPRISE ERA

During early days in Yellowstone, concession operations constituted a problem that was going to be around for a long time. One larcenous group of entrepreneurs, casting around for a way to eliminate troublesome competition, somehow obtained a lease on seven parcels of land, each a mile square. Having effectively expropriated all of the key visitor attractions in the park, they began chopping down trees to build their hotels. Because of this, Congress gave a little more thought to the matter and further refined concession policies: leases were to run for ten years and be limited to ten acres; they could not include important scenic features and must be a quarter mile away (even in the 1880's this seemed an excessive walk, and the distance was soon cut in half); and there were to be no "exclusive privileges." That powerful spoilsman from Montana, Senator Thomas J. Walsh, declared, "All who desire to operate concessions of any kind in Yellowstone National Park should be permitted to do so."

The senator's pronouncement was in keeping with the prevailing tradition of the frontier, but the Secretary of the Interior was more interested in the public's getting a fair deal. He believed the choice involved either the selection of one well-financed and responsible concessioner who would assume responsibility for the entire operation or granting leases to several smaller, and possibly less stable or less reliable, individuals. However, Congress declared that competition was the only answer.

The following description of the operations of competing Yellowstone camp companies in the ensuing period of free competition suggests the level on which business was conducted: "They jammed into the areas authorized for permanent camps, creating an eyesore and a nuisance near the natural curiosities. They lurked at the railroad stations and attacked the tourists stepping down from the trains with the most objectionable kind of amusement-park barker's routine." Unsuspecting tourists soon "found themselves wrapped up and delivered before they had got their legs untangled." In one camp twenty cases of ptomaine poisoning were reported in one day.

Fortunately for the national parks and their clients, the early development of the parks came at a time when the major railroads were completing their cross-country railroad systems, and they saw the parks as a way to expand their Eastern passenger market. First, however, it would be necessary to provide attractive accommodations. With some misgivings, the railroads entered the hotel business as concessioners: the Great Northern in Glacier National Park; the Northern Pacific in Yellowstone; the Union Pacific in Zion,

Bryce Canyon, and the North Rim of Grand Canyon National Parks; and the Santa Fe on the South Rim of the Grand Canyon. The railroads delivered most of the visitors to the parks, and in one year the Glacier Hotel registered as guests more than half the 6,250 tourists who entered Glacier.

Not only did the railroads build the first decent accommodations in the parks, they created architectural monuments that are among the most stately resort hotels in American history. Among several still in operation, Old Faithful Inn, built in 1903, stands unrivaled as the most distinctive example of log-cabin baroque in the world—designed, it is claimed, by an architect who had not yet completely recovered from a monumental scuffle with John Barleycorn.

Within the parks, transportation depended upon horse and wagon. Before 1900, concessioners in Yellowstone were responsible for the presence of more than 700 horses and nearly 250 stage coaches, surreys, and spring wagons of the two- and four-horse varieties. The Grand Loop road system in Yellowstone, which now accommodates, just barely, more than 2 million visitors annually, was built as a wagon road shortly after 1900. The major visitor-use and hotel areas of today were then located an easy day's ride from each other.

The era of railroad transportation left its mark on the parks. When visitors came by rail, they tended to be well-heeled and remained for several weeks. With the coming of the automobile age, people began to dart in and out of the parks as it suited their fancy, and the big hotels built for the railroad trade began to reflect a new life style. Sun porches became snack bars, and busy souvenir shops occupied the once placid lounges and card rooms. The cabins and motel units that mushroomed around the hotels absorbed most of the traffic.

Yosemite's experience with competition among many concessioners paralleled that of Yellowstone. In 1906, when California finally ceded Yosemite Valley back to the federal government to be a part of Yosemite National Park, there were twenty-seven concessioners operating in the valley. When Stephen Mather became Director in 1916, he saw that competition had bred chaos, and the result was damaging both to the park and to the public. Although a successful businessman, his solution was to eliminate competition and to license a prime concessioner in each park.

In Yosemite, the move ended wasteful duplication of services and eliminated incessant wrangling. The leases of the worst offenders were terminated, most of the eyesore attractions were eliminated, and the amount of parkland in the valley occupied by concessions was substantially reduced. Although the resulting explosion almost blasted Mather out of his job, he managed to survive the political repercussions.

With exceptions where necessary, the new policy, in effect by the mid-1920's, awarded the contract to one principal concessioner who was responsible for providing the full range of services, some of which might not be expected to show a profit. By converting from open competition to a single operator, the Park Service accepted the responsibility of protecting both the concessioner and the public. From this decision, the development of a strong and responsible concession system began.

A Modern Concession Operation

A good example of the modern concessioner is the Fred Harvey Company, which operates on the South Rim of the Grand Canyon. (Although only fifteen air miles from the North Rim, by road it is more than 200, and because of logistical difficulties and travel patterns a different concessioner operates on the North Rim.) Originally, the Harvey Company, with its justly celebrated Harvey girls, was in partnership with the Santa Fe Railroad in Grand Canyon, providing only the food services. In 1954 Harvey took over the entire contract.

The Harvey concession includes the monumental El Tovar Hotel, the Bright Angel Lodge and its complex of cabins and stores, the Yavapai Lodge complex of motel units, and the Phantom Ranch camp at the bottom of the Canyon along the Colorado River. About one hundred mules are stabled for the trips into the Canyon. The company operates several stores and curio shops.

The South Rim of the Canyon, at lower elevation than the North Rim, is open the year round, enabling the Harvey Company to keep a part of its facilities open all year and thereby to maintain the nucleus of its operating staff. During the peak summer season Harvey has about 700 employees, with a permanent staff of about 300 people.

Because the concessioner supplies the facilities and services used by a large portion of the public, people visiting Grand Canyon, or any of the parks with major concessions, have extensive encounters with dining-room waitresses, hotel bell-hops, service-station attendants, mule wranglers, and other service personnel, all of whom are assumed by the visitor to be employees of the park. Explaining this confusion to Congress, an assistant secretary of the Interior noted:

Visitors instinctively equate concession operations with the directly governmental operations. Applicants for jobs with concessioners write the park superintendent; complaints regarding service almost always come to the Department, many times in circumstances which indicate the complainant honestly believes he has been unfairly dealt with by a government servant; rangers are confused with bellmen, and vice versa; and people sometimes feel they have to be a hotel guest in order to hear the naturalist's lectures.

In 1969, there were 232 individual concessioners, operating in seventy-five areas of the national park system. The concessioners had gross sales of $83 million and during the year made new capital investments of $8.5 million. The following table shows the principal sources of concessioner gross income during 1969:

	Thousands of dollars
Food	$18,100
Rooms	14,200
Souvenirs	11,300
General merchandise	8,300
Service stations	6,200
Miscellaneous—other	3,340
Boat transportation	2,240
Bus transportation	2,236
Liquor	2,213
Marina services	2,025
Photographic supplies	1,800
Bathhouse	1,531
Saddle horses	1,047

There were twelve concession companies with sales for 1969 of more than $1 million, the largest recording a gross of almost $13 million. These companies accounted for more than 70 per cent of the total sales volume. Nearly sixty companies, however, had total annual sales of less than $5,000. In view of common opinion that national park concessioners make money hand over fist, a particularly significant figure is their percentage of profit. In 1953, a good business year, some 170 concessioners, doing a gross business of $32 million, had an average return of 6.9 per cent. In 1969, although their business nearly tripled, the average return was down to 3.8 per cent on gross income.

Probably the most characteristic feature of the concession operation is the uniformly attractive and pleasant employees, male and female, who make up the bulk of the work force. A pretty college girl, who carries on a running conversation while she serves the meal and never seems to be thrown off stride by incessant attempts at humor over her home town (which no one has ever heard of), adds considerable flavor to the meal and to the park experience for most visitors.

Each concession develops its own distinctive traditions from the nature of the park in which it is located and the region from which it draws most of its employees. At Yellowstone the "Christmas Party," held in late August shortly before the end of the season, with its colorful decorations and exchange of gifts, has been a highlight of the park social season for many years.

The only reason for licensing a business concern to operate a concession in a national park is to provide a service that is needed by the public. The only way the concessioner can stay in business and provide the service is to make a profit.

The Park Service insists, as it presses the concessioner for improved or expanded services, that of course it appreciates the fact that the concessioner's operation must be profitable. The concessioner is equally emphatic, as he attempts to remain solvent under trying conditions, that he is also concerned with protecting national park values. To many people, conducting a business for profit in a national park somehow doesn't seem right. To the concessioner, who is guided both by the rules of free enterprise and government regulation, a profit of less than 4 per cent doesn't seem quite right, either.

Paying what seems to be a rather high price for a hotel room, which may turn out to be something less than lavish, and then standing in a long breakfast line while a college boy with more weighty matters on his mind boils the eggs beyond the requested three minutes, many a visitor echoes Mather's declaration that this kind of treatment doesn't add much to a vacation trip. Letters to senators or congressmen or the Secretary of the Interior will compare service and prices in the parks unfavorably with those outside the park. The injured party generally threatens to take his business elsewhere, and the concessioner often wishes that he could do the same.

Restaurants elsewhere may have a 365-day season, but in the large Western parks where snows come early and stay late, the concessioner's season lasts about seventy-five days, from mid-June until the end of August. Fresh supplies are handy to the city restaurant; the park concessioner is at the end of the line. Business enterprises in the city draw from a ready work force; labor is the concessioner's biggest problem.

For the opening of the season he must recruit dozens, hundreds, or even thousands of employees, a great many from the college campus. He must bring them to the park, provide them with dormitory quarters, give the new ones some training, and start right off providing high-quality service. With the close of the season, his seasonal employees depart; he may be able to keep on only a handful of permanent employees. Throughout the winter his capital investment is buried under deep snow.

His construction costs are generally higher than those of outside competition. Carpenters and masons and road crews cannot commute from homes to the job; the contractor either supplies accommodations or pays a premium for the employee to supply his own. The construction season is also short, and construction of major facilities may involve closing down the job for one or several winter seasons.

The operating restrictions are equally severe. Plans and designs and materials for new facilities must be approved by the Park Service, which regulates all rates and prices and approves all items of sale. The concessioner may be required to open early in the season and close late, periods in which he has little if any chance for making a profit, all to ensure that the public gets its money's worth.

On the credit side, while he is not permitted to advertise within the park, the concessioner is protected from competition and is guaranteed a steady flow of potential customers, although vacation travel can fluctuate with the economy. He has captive customers with no other place to go within the park. (An alternative does exist, for the traveler can go outside the park in search of a better deal.)

It is, however, the considered opinion of the banking community that a national park concession is not a blue-chip operation. The land upon which a building is constructed by the concessioner remains the property of the government, which also retains title to the building itself. If the Park Service and the concessioner make a wrong guess as to what the public might want in future years, requiring the concessioner to make a heavy investment, there is nothing the Park Service can do to keep him from going under.

SOUVENIRS

A good many people who have nothing but praise for the quality of the food and accommodations, and who have been grateful for the chance to explore the parks with a decent respect for the comforts of life, do find considerable fault with the souvenir business. "Why do you allow junk to be sold in the parks?" they ask Park Service friends. Privately, park administrators have been heard to ask themselves the same question.

One blunt answer, which sums up the concessioner's side of the argument rather well, comes from Hil Oehlmann, an elder statesman of the concessioners, who is as knowledgeable and as sensitive to park matters as any Park Service veteran. "I do not consider it a responsibility of the National Park Service and its supporting organizations to improve the public taste," he has declared on more than one occasion, "and certainly no such duty devolves upon the concessioners in the parks."

Probably the only explanation of the souvenir situation is that credit for the quality of souvenirs sold in the parks can be shared equally by the concessioner, the park superintendent who approves all items sold, and parents, who make the whole thing possible. Children in particular have a desire to take home a remembrance of their visit, and concessioners feel they are meeting this need.

One reason for souvenir sales is evident from the balance sheet. The two leading services, food and rooms, require substantial outlays of capital and large staffs of trained employees. Faced with the enormously complicated and often disastrous job of trying to operate a restaurant (one of the highest risk enterprises imaginable) at a profit, the concessioner understandably regards his line of souvenirs as a life preserver, a good markup, easily sold, and a healthy profit. Souvenir sales undoubtedly are critical to the solvency of some concession operations.

Yet, deciding which are the good and which are the bad souvenirs involves a value judgment with which park superintendents have about as much difficulty as do parents. A few years ago a citizens' committee appointed by the Secretary of the Interior to study once again the souvenir problem found the concessioners, who have their own committee for monitoring souvenir sales, irritated by the continual criticism. Although unanimously of the opinion that there was extensive room for improvement, and that at one end of the scale there existed a collection of items that should not be allowed in a national park, the committee itself divided on items in the gray area. Writer Michael Frome, long an implacable critic of junk souvenirs, put sweatshirts high on his list of inappropriate items, but gifted designer Charles Eames, who had nothing but scorn for the "home furnishings" sections of many stores, retorted, "I will defend with my life the right of the American child to buy a national park sweatshirt."

In fairness to the concessioners, "good" souvenirs are hard to come by. Handcrafted articles are preferred, but no source of such articles exists on the scale required by park concessioners. Crafts tend to be the products of low-income cultures, like those of Appalachia or the Indian reservations.

(Probably 90 per cent of the articles sold in the Smithsonian Institution's fine-craft shops are from foreign countries.) Eames and committee member Lloyd New, director of the Institute of American Indian Arts in Santa Fe, proposed that a line of meaningful park souvenirs be developed: old-fashioned flip books showing the movement of animals; place mats, calendars, and playing cards using good art work and photographs; silkscreened cloth items with designs taken from the patterns observable in the park landscape.

Ultimately, souvenir inventories reflect public preference, and the quality of souvenirs sold in the parks will probably continue to respond to the buying habits of the traveling public. (Readers will please excuse this disgression: In this writer's opinion the Park Service, the concessioners, and the public can and should do better, but the outlook is not hopeful. Someone must be buying all those chenille bedspreads lining the highways of America.)

The Concessioner Problem

The nature of the concession operation makes it a continual source of dissatisfaction in Congress. Few activities in government have been examined and re-examined as many times. Secretaries of the Interior, the General Accounting Office, three committees of the House of Representatives, and the Office of Management and Budget have conducted separate studies. There has always been a lingering suspicion that somehow it isn't right to grant a preferential contract with an exclusive right to do business and to make money in a government preserve. Finally, in 1965, the Concession Policy Act wrote into law the established policies of the Park Service.

Congressional anxiety, in the past, has been stimulated by Park Service policies toward concessions that seem to run counter to normal procedures for handling government business. Concession contracts, for example, are not awarded on the basis of competitive bidding, with the contract, as is the case in most operations, going to the low bidder. The prospective concessioner's proven ability is a primary factor in the selection, along with evidence that indicates what his attitudes are likely to be toward public service and the need to conserve park resources.

The concessioner does not face competition, another source of criticism. He operates much like a public utility, which also has been found to work best with regulation replacing competition. If two or more concessioners were to be established in a park, they would have to be allowed freedom to become truly competitive in the areas of advertising, prices, and services offered. Since the decision as to how many hotel accommodations or service stations must be a Park Service (rather than a concessioner) decision, competition isn't in order in the parks.

Although, as a general rule, one concessioner controls all or almost all of the business in a park, there are many exceptions to the rule—depending, among other things, upon the amount of business. The Park Service may also decide that the public interest will be best served if one or more additional concessioners provide specific services. By law, every concession contract must be submitted to Congress for review before it can be executed by the Director.

Another source of continued criticism is that segment of the public that believes it inappropriate to provide civilized comforts in an area supposedly established primarily to preserve the opportunity for a wilderness experience. In its 1962 report on concessions in the federal government, the Outdoor Recreation Resources Review Commission concluded that providing concession facilities in the national parks represents a continuation of the preservation and use dialogue and that "there has been a dichotomy within the agency between the purist, wanting the least possible amount of park development, and the recreationist, dedicated to development and expanded use within the limits of the Park Service's conservation and preservation concept." Under pressure from the general public on both sides, the Outdoor Recreation Resources Review Commission observed that the Park Service has steered something of a middle course.

There are some half-dozen federal agencies that utilize private concessioners in supporting their recreation programs (the Bureau of Reclamation, the Forest Service, the Army Corps of Engineers, the Tennessee Valley Authority), but the Park Service has the largest operation. Park concessions require a substantially larger investment, do a greater business, and have a greater variety of business activities represented.

Other park agencies have taken different approaches to concessions. The state of California, which operates one of the most extensive of the state park systems, chose to build the facilities with state funds and to lease them to private enterprise for operation. During the golden era when income from state oil leases was made available for state park operation, funds were available for development, and the system worked well. Now those funds are not sufficient to meet operating expenses, and a recent study recommended that private enterprise be invited to develop needed facilities.

Canada chose an entirely different system, establishing enclaves within the national parks as town sites where, with little restriction, competition among private businessmen was allowed to determine the range and quality of services available to the public. This method has not been without its severe headaches, and regardless of which approach has been taken to concessions in parks, most administrators would admit to an occasional thought that there must be a better way.

GOVERNMENT ACQUISITION

Although concessioners respond with reasonably good humor to most suggestions for improving their operations, one subject is taboo in polite conversation: the recurring proposal that the government should assume actual ownership of concession facilities.

In good times, when vacation travel is up and concessions tend to do as well as possible, the proposal of government ownership is seldom encountered. During the Great Depression of the 1930's, park concessioners were in extreme difficulties. With the Depression, followed by a veritable embargo on travel during World War II as a result of gasoline rationing, concessioners were forced to close down some or all of their facilities. It was during this period that Secretary of the Interior Harold Ickes began to advance the idea of the government's acquiring the concession facilities. After the war, Ickes's successor, Julius Krug, announced that it would be official policy to work for government acquisition of facilities, with operation by either nonprofit distributing companies or by private enterprise under lease from the government.

In some parks, where concession facilities were needed, no private business could hope to operate at a profit, and none could be found willing to make the necessary investment. The establishment of Mammoth Cave National Park in 1941 gave Ickes the opportunity to establish a new kind of concession organization, National Park Concession, Inc., a nonprofit distributing corporation operating in parks where private enterprise would not risk operations. National Park Concessions has made it possible to provide needed services at Isle Royale, at Big Bend National Park, and also on the Blue Ridge Parkway.

The Concession Policy Act, passed by Congress in 1965, seemed to terminate the government ownership discussion, but the sale of the Yellowstone Park Company the following year set in motion a sequence of events that once more reopened the question. One of the oldest family-operated concessions, still under the direction of the third generation of a family that had come to Yellowstone in 1891, the Yellowstone Park Company had been in serious financial difficulty for some years. Public complaints against the level of service were increasing, as were the operating deficits. The company was purchased in 1966 by General Host, one of the modern conglomerates, whose diversified holdings included bakeries, food-processing companies, and mining interests. Announcing that great things were in store for Yellowstone and the Park Service now that commercial matters were in the hands of professional managers of large enterprises, General Host proceeded to post a disappointing record. The promised revolution was hardly apparent, and General Host found that national park concessions are not necessarily business bonanzas.

In Yellowstone, and in a number of parks, it is evident that improved management techniques, no matter how dazzling, cannot overcome the built-in handicaps. Required by its contract to modernize its facilities, General Host found that the combination of high construction, operation, and maintenance costs, coupled with excessive interest rates required to obtain capital, plus the short season, made the chance of recovering its investment an extremely remote one.

With the acquisition of concession companies by several conglomerates, certain patterns seem likely to develop. The family-operated concession, in most instances, accepted the fact that service to visitors in accordance with national park requirements was a condition of doing business. In a period of tight money and vanishing profits, the financial managers heading the conglomerate empires may have a different motivation when it comes to determining whether the level of services and the maintenance of facilities in the parks can be sustained.

Testifying before the House Appropriations Committee in April, 1971, the Park Service Director announced that almost one-third of all park concessioners lost money in 1970 and that an equal number, from a financial point of view, could be considered only marginal operations. He informed the committee that he intended to request appropriations to purchase the holdings of General Host and concluded, "I am confident that that is just a prelude to buying out the possessory interests of a number of other concessioners."

A formidable obstacle to government acquisition has always been the cost of purchasing concession interests, and the Office of Management and Budget turned down the Director's 1971 request to include funds in the Park Service budget for purchase of the General Host contract.

THE PARK SERVICE–CONCESSION PARTNERSHIP

Since it is the expressed policy of Congress "to encourage and enable private persons and corporations to provide and operate facilities and services . . . deemed . . . desirable for the accommodation of visitors," the concessioner and the Park Service association is generally referred to as a partnership, although that term is not wholly accurate. Both combine to provide the necessary visitor services, commercial and educational, but in carrying out their assigned roles, the two do not exhibit all of the behavioral patterns of traditional partners.

The Park Service has the regulatory responsibility, yet this authority is not quite as rigid as it sounds. True, the Park Service approves the price of a hamburger sandwich and its size, but there are a lot of intangible factors in a sandwich. Unlike other businesses, if the concessioner wants to raise his prices, he must receive permission to do so. Occasionally an impasse is reached, and the concessioner may feel the need to seek an audience at a higher level, although this is a tactic that has unpredictable results. Still, it is an always unnerving experience for the Director to schedule a meeting with the Secretary on a concession problem only to find that the concessioner has been there before him.

The term "partnership" is perhaps more applicable to the working relationship between concessioner and the Park Service employees in the parks. Many of the concessioners now operating started out as quite small family enterprises and grew with the park. The fact that many have spent a good portion of their lives living in a park has had no less an impact upon them than upon Park Service employees. It often happens that the Park Service people, who transfer frequently, are the transients, while the concessioners provide the real continuity. The reason they chose to stay in business, often under less than ideal economic conditions, is probably little different from the reason that people working for the Park Service stay. Both happen to enjoy the life.

For reasons, therefore, that are not much different from those that have drawn some unusual characters to the ranks of the Park Service, some uniquely talented people have chosen the life of a concessioner and through their efforts have conferred broad benefits upon the national parks. Some have operated relatively small concessions. The general area of photography has understandably drawn more than its share of gifted people.

Now eighty-one, Emory Kolb led one of the first parties after Major Powell to run the Colorado, making his first trip through the Grand Canyon in 1911. He was in business before Grand Canyon National Park was established in 1919. Kolb still operates his photographic studio, perched on the rim of the Grand Canyon at the entrance to the Bright Angel Trail.

The master photographer Ansel Adams and his wife Virginia have operated a book and photography studio in Yosemite Valley for more than twenty-five years. A Sierra

Club member since 1919, and on the club's board of directors since 1934, Adams is almost as well known for his conservation activities as for his incomparable photographic records of national park scenes.

One could not develop a list of the people who have made significant contributions to the parks without including a substantial number of concessioners. The story of the Yosemite Park and Curry Company, until recently a family-operated business, suggests the richness of concession traditions, for the company dates back nearly twenty years before the establishment of the Park Service to David and "Mother" Curry.

Curry and his wife began their national park careers in 1894 by leading summer tours to Yellowstone in prairie schooners but in 1898 moved their operation to Yosemite. Camp Curry, which originally consisted of seven tents, a cook, and a few college student helpers, in 1971 celebrated its seventy-fourth year. As a result of Stephen Mather's efforts, the Curry Company was consolidated with its competitors in 1925 to form the Yosemite Park and Curry Company.

The Curry family continued to control the company and in 1948, after the death of Mr. Curry, who had also served as president of Stanford University, management of the company passed to David Curry's daughter, Mary Curry Tressidor. Mrs. Tressidor had an abiding concern for the park, which manifested itself in countless ways, some of which brought little or no profit to the company. She donated money for needed research programs and for publications. A lover of the back country, she personally supported the Yosemite High Camps, tent camps that ring the valley at high altitudes, providing, for those willing to hike the High Country, one of the most memorable experiences available in any national park. It is doubtful whether the camps have ever operated at a profit, for all supplies—including clean sheets—have to be brought in by pack mule, but, when the Park Service was forced by budget restrictions to eliminate a ranger naturalist who conducted nature tours out of the camps, the company provided his salary in order to retain the quality of its service.

While the nature of business operations in the parks makes problems inevitable, Stephen Mather's salty-tongued biographer, Robert Shankland, concluded that concessioners deserve considerably more praise than criticism, for without them the parks could not have existed, and few have found the exercise profitable. "Others have plugged along with the parks for many years and, though understandably hopeful of showing a profit, have worked freely for the principle of national-park inviolability and have conducted themselves far more like conservationists than anyone has demanded or expected of them."

VIII
How to Establish a National Park

In July of 1924, on the train platform at Gardiner, Montana, the northern entrance to Yellowstone, the story of the establishment of Grand Teton National Park began. Dragging on for more than a quarter of a century, it suggests the intensity of emotions that are aroused and the powerful influences brought to bear when lands public or private are proposed for national park status.

On this momentous July day Horace Albright, then superintendent of Yellowstone, arrived at the station to greet the distinguished philanthropist John D. Rockefeller, Jr., who with his sons John, Nelson, and Laurance was making a get-acquainted visit to Yellowstone. Albright had been warned by a cautious Washington office functionary not to present any park problems to his celebrated guest, a technique often followed by park superintendents who become disheartened following established procedures for problem-solving.

Albright obeyed this time, but two years later Rockefeller returned with his family for a more extended visit and Albright was unable to resist the rare opportunity. Both he and Stephen T. Mather had been pushing the idea of national park status for the Grand Tetons, and after guiding the

Rockefeller party through Yellowstone, he took them down to the Jackson Hole country, which lies just a short distance south of Yellowstone. A strategic stop was made on a hilltop overlooking the Snake River and Jackson Hole with the Teton Range in the background, one of the superlative landscapes in America.

Here Albright described the worthiness of preserving "this sublime valley" as a national park, and pointed to the filling stations and billboards beginning to invade the valley. Unless someone could acquire these lands, the character of the entire valley would be despoiled. A particularly ugly complex of telephone poles, which obscured the view of the mountains from the stopping place Albright had carefully selected, buttressed his contention. No further argument was required; Rockefeller asked only that a plan be prepared by the Park Service for a Grand Teton National Park.

The broad, flat valley of Jackson Hole, lying at the base of the rampart range of the Tetons, was the key, and the following year Rockefeller organized the Snake River Land Company to begin buying out the privately owned lands in Jackson Hole. Using the cover of a land purchasing company was an obvious necessity to avoid the speculation and inflated prices certain to result if Rockefeller were known to be involved. Although the subterfuge was later a cause of bitter controversy, Rockefeller would seem to have paid fair prices. Wyoming required land to be assessed at true value; by 1933 Rockefeller had acquired 35,000 acres, assessed at $520,000, for which he paid $1.4 million.

One stratagem for preserving Jackson Hole, which had been previously advanced, was to expand Yellowstone's southern boundary, and during this period the proposal was revived. It quickly brought the Park Service and Forest Service into combat, since the proposal would transfer 800,000 acres from Forest Service to Park Service jurisdiction. The resulting feud, which aroused passions nationally as well as locally, required the appointment in 1925 of a Presidential committee to arbitrate the dispute between the two stalwart, and unbending, conservation organizations. In the resulting compromise, all of the Jackson Hole valley area was excluded, probably because the Forest Service had considerably more local support, and in 1929 a small Grand Teton National Park was established, consisting only of the eastern side of the Teton mountains, whose granite peaks were relatively unforested.

Residents of Jackson Hole were not especially concerned by the inclusion of the mountains within a national park, but they were highly suspicious about the possible utilization of the valley lands being acquired by the Snake River Land Company. By 1930 Rockefeller's involvement was confirmed, and a Jackson newspaper charged that the people had been "betrayed," for the obvious intent of Rockefeller and the Park Service was to expand the park to include the valley. Bitter opposition developed—from livestock interests with powerful friends in Congress, from the dude ranchers and outfitters, from state officials fearing loss of tax revenues, from boosters who wanted no government intervention in their determination to "see Wyoming grow."

Much of the land in the Western states is still in one form of federal ownership or another, upward of 50 per cent in many states. There is an ambivalent feeling toward this land, locally, but there is also deep resentment against nonresidents when plans are drawn up "back East" to tell local people how neighboring public lands should be managed. In his *Conservation: Now or Never*, Nicholas Roosevelt comments upon this phenomenon:

> It is difficult for Easterners to realize the depth of the antagonism of politicians, businessmen, ranchers, chambers of commerce and almost everyone living within an easy reach of National Forests or Parks against the initial setting aside of these re-

serves and against all efforts to enlarge them or to tighten the regulations governing their use.

Actually, the private lands purchased by Rockefeller, while critical, represented only a small part of the lands needed for the expanded park. The remainder were public domain and forest lands, which local residents much preferred to be continued under administrative regulations that would permit logging, mining, grazing, hunting, and development of recreational enterprises.

By 1933 the land acquisition program was virtually complete, but the opposition was so bitter there was no hope of congressional action to accept the Rockefeller lands and enlarge the park, and the controversy continued throughout the 1930's. Several congressional committees held hearings in Jackson, with local sentiment hewing to the theme that they were "being beaten out of their heritage." The Senate passed a park bill in 1934, but the House killed the measure because of Wyoming opposition. During the 1930's and 1940's, the Jackson Hole controversy was a factor in every level of Wyoming politics. The governor and congressman who favored the park plan were soundly defeated in the 1938 elections.

Rockefeller was a target of scathing abuse throughout the controversy, and, still waiting for the government to accept the donation of the lands he had purchased, Rockefeller wrote to Secretary of the Interior Harold Ickes in 1942 indicating that if the national park proposal was infeasible or if the President did not establish the area as a national monument he must reluctantly dispose of his Jackson Hole lands. This was more of a strategic move on the part of conservationists to break the log jam than a sign of Rockefeller impatience, and the effort was successful.

Ickes, a longtime enthusiast for the park plan, won over President Franklin Roosevelt, and in March, 1943, the President established by proclamation a Jackson Hole National Monument, extending the boundaries of Grand Teton National Park into Jackson Hole—as Congress had refused to do. Although ostensibly based upon the Antiquities Act, which gave the President authority to protect "scientific" features as national monuments, Roosevelt's bold stroke hit an exposed nerve on Capitol Hill, and outraged congressmen declared it "a subterfuge to thwart the will of Congress by Executive action." Ranchers staged cattle drives across the valley to show defiance, bills were introduced in Congress to abolish the national monument and amend the Antiquities Act, and a rider was attached to every Interior appropriation bill from 1944 to 1948 prohibiting the Park Service from spending a penny on the Jackson Hole National Monument.

When, after World War II, another drive was launched in Congress to abolish Jackson Hole National Monument, the climate had changed. Perhaps it was the ever increasing number of tourists arriving in Jackson Hole, which suggested the benefits of national park status might be considerable. Certainly the growing strength of the conservation organizations was a factor. Finally a compromise was hammered out and in 1950, twenty-six years after Rockefeller's visit to Yellowstone, President Harry S Truman signed the bill establishing the Grand Teton National Park.

KEEPING OUT THE DEAD CATS

Each session of Congress produces a vast number of proposals for additions to the national park system. In the Ninety-first Congress (1969–70), the House considered 108 bills proposing new parks; the Senate had 51. During the two-year period 13 of the proposals were authorized by Congress.

Some of the bills that failed to pass have appeared and

will reappear as regularly as the cherry blossoms around Washington's Tidal Basin, but until the right senator arrives in Congress, or departs, no action will take place. The proposed Prairielands National Park, in Kansas, was first proposed some forty years ago. The park would preserve one of the few remaining stretches of grassland prairie; it might also provide delayed balm to former Director Conrad L. Wirth and former Secretary of the Interior Stewart L. Udall for the widely publicized photograph of them being ordered back to their helicopter by an irate landowner during a survey trip.

Often, however, bills to establish new parks deserve a merciful death. The problem of maintaining the standards of the national park system is ever present, and while all sites that qualify should be brought in, those that don't should be left out. Yet there is an equal need to preserve historic sites and recreation areas of less than national significance on a scale far beyond the capacity of the national park system. The national parks would have been swamped long ago were it not for the parks and other preserves administered by federal and state agencies.

Partly as a means of providing relief and support for the national parks, Director Stephen Mather set out to strengthen the state park movement by organizing a state park conference in 1921. At the time only twenty states had parks of any kind, most of which were inadequately financed and undeveloped. Looking down the road a long way, Mather told the assembled representatives from state, county, and municipal organizations, "I believe we should have comfortable camps all over the country, so that the motorist could camp each night in a good scenic spot." The National Conference on State Parks, formed by the delegates, effectively promoted the state parks, which tend to be closer to population centers and more easily accessible. Although occupying only one-fourth of the acreage of the national parks, the nearly 3,400 state parks in 1970 served three times as many visitors, 474 million.

The matter of standards is inevitably personal, and at times geographical. An area that seems superbly qualified for national park status east of the Mississippi, in a region heavily populated, might seem less significant in one of the Western states. Congressmen have been known to recommend areas containing scenery that at best could be described as anemic, and local boosters constantly push for legislation to establish some minor curiosities as national parks purely for the financial bonanza of having the National Park Service designation on the Esso road map.

In 1916 alone, there were bills introduced for sixteen new national parks, which would have doubled the number existing. Fortunately, and perhaps proving the system, Congress passed only two, Hawaii Volcanoes in Hawaii and Lassen Volcanic in California; the rest of the proposed parks were fairly dreadful. In one three-week period of the 1920's, bills were introduced to establish High Knob National Park in Virginia, Nicolet National Park in Wisconsin, Yakima National Park in Washington, Killdeer National Park in North Dakota, Wonderland National Park in South Dakota, and eight more pieces of less-than-spectacular wonders scattered around the country. Claims are often made for historic sites, ranging from the purely insignificant to the hilarious, most of which are clearly worthy of oblivion.

One of the most scandalous, or perhaps only whimsical, monstrosities of this sort ever proposed was the "All-Year National Park," sprung on the Park Service in 1922 by none other than the Secretary of the Interior, Albert B. Fall (later the villain in the Teapot Dome scandal) and bearing the unmistakable touch of that ill-fated cowboy personality. Consisting of a dozen or so assorted tracts of undistinguished real estate, miles from each other, the proposal was enriched by the contribution of numerous chambers of commerce, and few likely sources of tourist-fleecing had been overlooked. Still, the Park Service should have been forewarned, for Fall was once quoted as saying, "Whenever in the public lands I can find a pleasant place for local people to go up and camp, there I shall have a national park."

The role of the National Park Service in the establishment of new parks is, in part, to serve as a professional consultant to the Congress, identifying areas worthy of consideration, preparing extensive study plans, evaluating the proposal in relationship to the other areas of the system, and making final recommendations. As in the case of all consultants, the Park Service's advice may be disregarded.

For it is Congress, and not the National Park Service, which is the ultimate architect of the national park system. The Director of the Park Service proposes; the House and Senate Interior and Insular Affairs committees dispose. But saying that Congress has shaped the national park system is a way of saying that the people have made the determinations. Would that all such examples of the democratic process turned out so well.

While it is axiomatic that all bureaucracies tend to proliferate, the Park Service not excluded, in the sensitive area of selecting parks to be added to the system, the Park Service has taken a generally conservative position. Of fifty-one proposals made to authorize historical parks in one year, the Park Service endorsed only two—with the stipulation for one site that historical research must first prove the authenticity of the structural remains. In the earthy terminology of one colleague: "You've got to keep the dead cats out!"

To some, the Park Service position probably seems more liberal. When a Director of the Park Service, under questioning, announced that he would favor establishing a national monument as magnificent as Glacier Bay, even though it meant accepting mining, a prominent conservation magazine headlined the statement "Park Service Leader Abandons National Park Standards." Park standards are indeed personal; faced with difficult choices the directors of the Park Service have thought it wiser to take a practical view rather than a rigidly doctrinaire position.

Probably the greatest danger to the integrity of the national park system is not, however, the occasional substandard area that somehow slips through. Those that aren't quite good enough present the gravest problem. If the park system began to include these areas, which are pleasant and moderately attractive, the distinction between truly national significance on the one hand and local pride on the other would be increasingly blurred, and the original idea of national parks would steadily erode toward mediocrity.

Getting Park Bills Through Congress

The Grand Teton example illustrates some of the extremes involved in establishing new parks, but not all. Many require even more time. A proposal to set aside the Indiana Dunes area, on the south shore of Lake Michigan, was first reviewed by Mather in 1916; it happened also to be one of the first bills upon which George B. Hartzog, Jr., testified when he became Director in 1964, but it did not pass until 1966, just fifty years after it had been proposed. It was, by then, only a remnant of the original proposal and badly fragmented, all that could be salvaged from industrialization of the lakeshore.

The first effort to preserve the coastal redwood forests of California came in 1852, when a joint resolution introduced in the State Assembly cited the loss of the redwoods and urged passage of a law to make these forests common property of the citizens of the state, and not subject to trade and traffic. The times were hardly ripe for this level of statesmanship, and the resolution did not pass. Congress authorized the first study of a Redwood National Park in 1919, and the climate had improved but little. A redwood park bill did finally pass in 1968. By this time, of the nearly 2 million acres of redwoods that had once existed, 50,000 acres had been set aside in state preserves, and 200,000 acres were owned by lumber companies. It was estimated that, at the existing level of cutting, the lumber companies would finish off the virgin redwoods in twenty years.

All new parks must be established by an Act of Congress. (The reluctance of Presidents to establish national monuments by proclamation is discussed in Chapter X.) This requirement ensures that the interval between introduction of legislation and its passage will be several years. The delay is not, however, without value, for it is in accordance with the tradition in this country that no one should be deprived of his private property without due process.

A bill to establish a new park may originate in the Department of the Interior and be introduced as an administration bill. It may also be prompted by local people through their representative or senator or may result from the personal interest of a member of Congress. Regardless, the bill, which must pass both Houses, is referred to the Interior and Insular Affairs committees of the House and Senate. The Department of Interior is requested by the committee to comment, either favorably or in opposition to passage of the bill, and the Park Service prepares this report, although the Secretary of the Interior may not always accept the conclusions.

Hearings on the bill are held in Washington, but the committees also schedule public headings locally, to allow individuals most directly affected to be heard from and to get a sense of the general attitude toward the park bill. Understandably, those whose property lies within the proposed boundaries of the park are seldom in favor. A proposed new park is about like a proposed new highway—most everyone is for it so long as the right of way doesn't go through his front lawn.

Highway projects are, however, executed with considerably less indulgence in the democratic process than parks. A new highway does not require an Act of Congress. Despite fears or claims to the contrary, the National Park Service has no power to take land from anyone. It can receive this authority only from Congress by specific legislation. The individual whose land may be involved in a park proposal at least has the satisfaction of knowing that it takes a majority vote in the House of Representatives, a majority vote in the Senate, and the signature of the President of the United States before his land can be acquired by the Park Service. And he may well be able to live out his years before this can happen.

"Senatorial courtesy" is always a determining factor in the attitude of Congress toward a park bill. If the affected congressman does not support the park proposal, his colleagues on Capital Hill will seldom ignore his position. It is therefore easier for local residents to block establishment of a park than for supporters elsewhere in the country to bring about passage. Faced with this dilemma, Congress has in recent years written legislation granting flexible arrangements for property owners, which might allow them to retain their residency for a specified number of years, including life tenure.

When a bill is passed and signed by the President, the area is "authorized" and becomes a part of the national park system. No magical change takes place on the ground, however. A cadre of experienced Park Service employees must be selected and transferred to the new assignment. Priorities of needs for the park must be established, and funds included in the annual budgets to provide for planning, design, and construction requirements. Specific research studies may be necessary before any development can take place, requiring the specialized talents of an aquatic biologist, an architectural historian, or a wildlife management specialist. Development of a new park is not unlike the development of a modern "new town," which is created from scratch. With a number of new parks to activate every year, the Park Service transfer and promotion policy gets a workout.

This lapse between authorization of the park and the actual appropriation of funds for land acquisition unfortunately can be accompanied by an enormous increase in land values. When Point Reyes National Seashore, just north of San Francisco, was authorized in 1962, the estimated cost of land acquisition was $14 million. But appropriation of the land acquisition money took a number of years. Speculators subdivided properties, hoping that when homes were built property values would be so high that the government could never afford to acquire the lands; by the time the $14 million had been expended, the cost had gone almost out of sight. Although nearly $58 million has been spent for acquisition, all of the land has not been acquired.

Land acquisition costs constitute a substanital portion of the Park Service budget, $70 million for fiscal 1972. Yet it was not until 1961, with the authorization of Cape Cod National Seashore, that Congress for the first time established a precedent by appropriating the funds needed to acquire the lands. Before 1961, all major parks were set aside from the public domain, were donated by the states, or were the result of private philanthropy. Cape Cod was the first instance of the federal government's purchasing an entire park.

Despite the formidable logistics involved, a substantial number of park bills are passed, and the national park system continues to grow. In one of the most productive intervals in Park Service history, during a short period of only a few weeks in late 1970, five major park bills were signed into law: Apostle Islands National Lakeshore in Wisconsin, Sleeping Bear Dunes National Lakeshore in Michigan, Gulf Islands National Seashore along the Florida and Mississippi coastline, Voyageurs National Park in Minnesota, and the

Chesapeake and Ohio National Historical Park in the Potomac River Valley.

The Art of the Possible

It would be nice to report here that new park areas are always selected and their boundaries drawn on the basis only of ecology, historical integrity, and the public weal, and this phenomenon does occur. But land is highly coveted, and the public lands are as vigorously defended by the administering agency as are the private lands. Only Alaska has vast reaches of wilderness remaining, and despite the immensity of their realm, Alaskans traditionally have regarded national parks as one more evidence of federal interference, which might better be restricted to the lower Forty-eight.

Attractive possibilities do remain for developing national parks out of the territories of other federal agencies, usually those of the Forest Service and occasionally those of the Department of Defense; but when this kind of campaign is launched, powerful political and economic legions appear, strongly entrenched and armed to the teeth. One is reminded of Confederate General James Longstreet's observation that combat troops, like young ladies, are suspicious of movements about their flanks.

In the case of proposed seashore areas there are, for example, few extensive stretches of attractive beach that do not already have private development. During the recreation survey of the Atlantic coast, carried out by the Park Service in 1955, Assateague Island, in Maryland and Virginia, was a likely proposal, having only a few dozen cottages, and located within a half-day's drive of Washington and Baltimore. However, the island had already attracted the attention of a real estate promoter; it had been subdivided, and much of it had been sold. The extent of development plans and the projected cost of buying out the properties were such that no feasible proposal could be made.

Then, in 1962, a violent tropical storm struck Assateague. Only a few of the completed homes escaped destruction from the storm, which changed the configuration of the shoreline and left many lots under water. Shortly afterward property owners were notified by local authorities that the projected method of sewage disposal was a health hazard and would not be permitted. With the support of many residents of the area who believed the undeveloped thirty-three miles of coastline would be of greater value as a public recreation area, Assateague was established as a national seashore in 1965.

Some recent proposals for new parks, particularly those in urban areas, have posed almost insurmountable problems in terms of cost. The proposed Gateway National Recreation Area, now before the Congress, comprising a complex of lands around the harbor of New York City, includes 23,000 acres. This desperately needed recreation area would be easily accessible to a metropolitan population of more than 10 million persons. The federal government would donate lands valued at $161 million; New York City and New Jersey would contribute lands valued at $100 million; additional private property required for the project would cost an estimated $40 million—by far the most expensive single project in the history of the National Park Service.

Citizen Contributions

Particularly in the period before 1961, the generosity of private citizens enriched the national park system, and the Park Service has been able to turn to private philanthropy as have few other government agencies. Acadia, the first national park in the East, resulted from the efforts of a group of Bar Harbor summer residents headed by George B. Dorr of Boston, including the Rockefellers, who wanted to preserve the beauty of the neighboring islands and coastal lands against commercial intrusions.

States have also contributed to the establishment of many parks. Accepting the offer of the state of Texas to contribute the land for Big Bend National Park, Congress authorized the park in 1935. Money was scarce in the Depression years, but in 1944 Texas presented deeds for nearly 700,000 acres, and Big Bend was established. In order to establish Cape Hatteras, the state of North Carolina and Mellon Foundations each contributed half, while Harpers Ferry was a gift of the state of West Virginia.

Often, however, the efforts of individual citizens have been decisive, not through donation of funds, but in generating the necessary public support. Mount McKinley and Sequoia National Parks can largely be attributed to the work of a handful of people, led by Charles Sheldon in Mount McKinley and Col. George Stewart in Sequoia.

The giant sequoias were barely discovered before speculators and lumbermen were busily at work. Logging that began in the 1860's had wiped out the accessible groves a half-century later. Much of the devastation, in the words of the Secretary of the Interior, was "useless, wasteful, lamentable." The wood of the great trees is so extremely brittle (as opposed to the wood of the coastal redwood) as to be of little commercial use. Saws could not bring them down, and when they were finally hacked and blasted with gunpowder into manageable size, most of the potential lumber had been lost, and the splintered remains were burned. The Converse Basin, once as splendid as the Giant Forest in Sequoia National Park, was gutted completely, and apparently the crew foreman had a final twinge of conscience— or longing for immortality. He left one single tree standing in the 6,000-acre grove, named the Boole Tree after himself, which measures 112 feet in circumference at the base and is larger than the General Sherman Tree in Sequoia National Park.

Observing the vicious practices of the lumber goons Col. George Stewart, a California publisher, and a few friends determined to preserve some of the remaining groves in a national park. As receiver of the land office at Visalia he was able to have the surveyor general in San Francisco suspend private entries in the sequoia groves. Fake claims and dodges of all kinds were utilized, and even the Giant Forest was saved only at the eleventh hour. Stewart fought back, a local resolution appealing for national park protection of the big trees was adopted, and in 1890 the park was established.

The love of the North Country drew Charles Sheldon, a self-trained naturalist who had retired from profitable business interests to devote his life to wilderness research. Few other men have possessed his scientific curiosity, his dedication to the wilderness, and his physical stamina. Beginning with a study of the desert bighorn sheep, he continued his observations northward along the backbone of North America, through the Canadian Rockies into Yukon Territory, and finally into Alaska. Moved by his first sight of Mount McKinley, Sheldon built a small cabin on the Toklat River and spent a year exploring and recording the region. Enduring the Alaskan winter under such primitive conditions would have been an ordeal for most men. Leaving his cabin in June, 1908, Sheldon noted in his journal, "No words can describe my sorrow and regret as I led the horse out of the woods from the cabin to the bar and started down the river."

A member of the Boone and Crockett Club, which was influential in the establishment of several national parks, Sheldon devoted himself to establishing a Mount McKinley National Park. Nine years later, he personally carried the bill passed by Congress to the White House, and stood by President Woodrow Wilson to receive the pen used in signing the legislation.

IN-HOLDINGS

The casual park visitor presumes that once a park is established, everything within the park boundaries is parkland, and the Park Service has absolute jurisdiction. Unfortunately, this is seldom true. Particularly in the case of the large parks, pockets of lands that were in private ownership before the park was established have never been acquired, and most parks still contain "in-holdings," varying from small plots to subdivided residential communities. Only seven of the thirty-six national parks are completely in public ownership.

Lake MacDonald in Glacier National Park in Montana is a glaring example of private ownership and development, and park visitors driving along the shore of this superb mountain lake are generally puzzled by the string of houses and cabins bordering the western end of the lake and irritated by cyclone fences which enclose privately owned stretches of beach. There were 16,000 acres of privately held lands when the park was established in 1910, including timber lands owned by lumber companies and private homes on Lake MacDonald. Since the latter included summer cottages of both the senators from Montana, a considerable factor of "externality" was added to the acquisition of private lands in Glacier.

The Park Service has no control over private lands within the parks. The owner of an ocean front property in Virgin Islands National Park brought in a bulldozer to strip sand from the beach for commercial sale. In the Taylor Slough area of the Everglades, quick-buck operators slashed roads through the unspoiled saw grass country to peddle "waterfront" lots. As a result, park visitors may see sawmills and lumber yards, trailer courts and souvenir stands, garbage dumps and mining operations.

The only recourse against the commercialization of private

lands within the parks is to purchase the properties. It is Park Service policy not to acquire against the owner's will any land unless it is required for essential visitor facilities, or if its use is a detriment to the park. Costs of such lands are astronomical; acquisition costs of the in-holdings in the national park system are estimated at nearly $200 million.

TAXES—AND OTHER ECONOMIC CONSIDERATIONS

The economic factor should be acknowledged as a powerful stimulant to establishment of national parks. It may well be, in some cases, the most influential factor either for or against, because parks affect the local economy, and local support or opposition is often the deciding factor.

If the proposed park will take more than half the land in the county off the tax rolls, it is understandable that local businessmen are interested in learning what alternative sources of revenue may appear.

If the economy of a region depends upon the lumber industry, the prospect of changing the administration of an area from the Forest Service to the Park Service has little appeal for those likely to lose their jobs at the sawmill. But for many in the local communities, the prospects may look considerably better: service station owners, merchants, hotel, motel, and restaurant owners and their employees.

Economic projections of the expected results from establishing a park are often made as a part of the study plan, and the effects of previously established parks on the regional economy is often introduced as evidence. Wholly innocently, Park Service estimates of the number of visitors the proposed park will attract may sometimes be on the liberal side. A few years after the establishment of Canyonlands National Park, by which time several hundred thousand visitors had been predicted, there were only fifty thousand, a number that delighted those concerned for the protection of the park features but disappointed those hoping for a tourist windfall.

In all probability there are few cases in which parks have not significantly advanced the local economy. Having Grand Canyon, Wupatki, Sunset Crater, and Walnut Canyon in Coconino County, Arizona, and having Mesa Verde and Aztec in and about Montezuma County, Colorado, accounts for more than 50 per cent of the income of these two counties. Nationally, the economic impact of the national park system is an important element of the travel industry economy. It accounts for $6.4 billion in expenditures in the travel, recreation, and supporting industries, and $4.8 billion in personal income for businessmen adjacent to, or along, the routes leading to the parks.

It has been said that if the state of Virginia had set out to restore Colonial Williamsburg purely for travel promotion purposes, it would have recaptured its entire investment just from the state gasoline tax paid by those traveling to Williamsburg. All the rest of the money spent within the state for goods and services would represent a monumental return on the investment. A hasty calculation, even with scant data, suggests this may be somewhat overstated, but the basic premise is sound—as Disneyland has proved.

Always the Dam Builders

It is almost always true that establishment of a park ensures permanent protection of the natural features. Yet only recently the projected dams on the Colorado River would have flooded a portion of Grand Canyon National Park. Modern civilization is consuming its natural resources —minerals, forests, hydroelectric sites—in ever larger gulps. So long as the amount of available land was sufficient to supply the required raw materials, commercial threats to the parks were less of a danger. As the population increases and as technology multiplies the consumption per person of natural resource products, exploitation of park resources becomes a more distinct threat.

An internationally known mineral engineer, Charles Park, and Dave Brower, one of the most effective conservationists in modern times, were subjects of a 1971 *New Yorker* magazine profile in which each expressed the opposing views of park use.

"Minerals are where you find them," said Park. "The quantities are finite. It's criminal to waste minerals when the standard of living of your people depends upon them. A mine cannot move. It is fixed by nature. So it has to take precedence over any other use." Declaring that minerals should be extracted wherever found, for the good of the people, he concluded, "If there were a copper deposit in Yellowstone Park, I'd recommend mining it."

To which Brower replied with a question: "Should America have to go without much to leave its finest wilderness unspoiled?"

The dam builders have long found the parks irresistible, and following patterns almost as predictable as that of migrating birds, and equally unfathomable, they grind out new justifications on their mimeograph machines. On the subject of dams, however, park people are inflexible, for they have heard all the arguments (civilization as we know it will disappear without the salutary influence of this particular technological miracle; damming the river will vastly increase recreational values because people can "use" lakes better than rivers). The dam builders were nearly successful in Dinosaur National Monument.

Dinosaur was set aside in 1915 to protect an eighty-acre dinosaur graveyard in Utah. The chance result of stream action depositing the remains of countless dinosaurs in a single bed, the profusion of fossilized skeletons made it a paleontologist's laboratory, and a great many skeletons were excavated by museum and university expeditions. Because the monument is located within the superlative canyon region cut by the Green and Yampa rivers, the monument was enlarged in 1938 to include 210,000 acres of canyon country.

Then one day in the mid-1940's Director Newton Drury noticed in the Federal Register that the Bureau of Reclamation, a sister agency within the Department of the Interior, had staked a claim for two reservoir sites in Dinosaur that would flood the monument area from one end to another. No one had felt the need to inform the Park Service of this project, and with commendable restraint the Park Service suggested to the Secretary of the Interior that a misunderstanding must be involved, perhaps the Reclamation Bureau did not realize those sites were already spoken for as a part of the national park system.

There was, it turned out, no misunderstanding. Reclamation was in the business of producing hydroelectric power to help pay for irrigation projects. If a couple of the twenty-seven dams proposed for complete development of the Upper Colorado happened to fall within national park areas, it was regrettable, but power came before scenery. The ensuing fracas turned into the fiercest of all battles over the waters of the Colorado River.

If constructed, the dams would be the first such invasion of a national park since Hetch Hetchy was authorized in 1913, and there were known to be nearly thirty other potential dam sites within national parks on the dockets of the Bureau of Reclamation and the Army Corps of Engineers. The fight was drawn between those favoring the complete harnessing of the river by power dams in all major canyons and those who would leave the most scenic of the canyons unspoiled. The Park Service urged the Secretary to deny the application for the Dinosaur dams, but in 1950 Secretary Oscar Chapman approved the project, although offering the opinion that this action should not be regarded as a precedent for other parks.

Bills were introduced in succeeding sessions of Congress

to authorize construction, and the controversy became a national issue. Conservation forces placed their hope for defeat of the dam bill on a campaign of arousing public opinion, and they proceeded to generate the strongest defense of national park integrity in history. Chapman told his successor it was "the hottest controversy" of his administration.

Public reaction, and questionable engineering factors, forced the Bureau of Reclamation to drop the Split Mountain dam early in the struggle, but it put together a fascinating set of arguments for the Echo Park site where the Green and Yampa Rivers meet: the lake would vastly increase the recreational value of the monument; increased costs to the rest of the Upper Colorado project from the loss of this site might adversely affect the welfare of the region; and finally, only the Echo Park site would prevent a horrendous evaporation loss. General confidence in the infallibility of engineers was badly shaken when astute investigation of the figures forced the Reclamation Bureau to revise downwards, twice, its estimate of the actual evaporation loss from alternative sites.

Victory seemed to go to the dam faction when, in 1955, a bill with eleven sponsors from the affected Western states received almost impregnable support from President Dwight D. Eisenhower, Secretary of the Interior Douglas McKay, the Corps of Engineers, and the Federal Power Commission. But public protest against construction of the Dinosaur dam had mounted to such a level that it posed a threat to the entire Upper Colorado project, and the solid ranks of the dam builders began to crumble. To save the larger project, the bill was rewritten, excluding the Echo Park dam, the conservationists withdrew their opposition, and the Upper Colorado storage enterprise was passed.

That the Dinosaur National Monument stakes were extremely high was confirmed when the Director of the National Park Service resigned in the midst of the conflict. Something more of a conservationist-philosopher than his activist predecessors, Newton Drury was disillusioned by interbureau bickering and took no pleasure in political horse trading. He was intensely devoted to the parks and stubborn in defending them in principle and in fact.

Although Oscar Chapman favored the dams, Drury had spoken out strongly against them. The Secretary countered with an invitation that Drury consider new employment: for face-saving purposes a position as special assistant to the Secretary, newly created, at a lower salary; or as a real growth opportunity, the job of governor of Samoa. Unwilling to engage in this kind of political hanky-panky, and concerned that the office of the Director not become involved in public quarrels, the uncompromising Drury resigned in April, 1951, and was promptly selected by Governor Earl Warren to head California's state park system.

A few years earlier Drury had stated the case against attempts to justify use of park resources for commercial purposes:

> If we are going to succeed in preserving the greatness of the national parks, they must be held inviolate. They represent the last stand of primitive America. If we are going to whittle away at them we should recognize, at the very beginning, that all such whittlings are cumulative and that the end result will be mediocrity. Greatness will be gone.

IX
Life in a National Park

A national park may well be the destination for a million vacationing travelers, but for quite a number of Park Service and concessioner employees and their families, it is both a place to work and a home. Working and living in a park community, under the special conditions existing there, are probably the most distinctive features of a career in the Park Service.

As a general rule, when the park is located in or near a town or city where housing is available, government quarters are not provided—except that one or more employees may be housed within the park to provide an extra measure of protection in case of emergencies. In many historical parks employees are assigned quarters in restored period houses, a rare and memorable experience, although climbing the stairway to the second floor can resemble the final assault on Everest. Conceivably, there could be some unpleasantness with the superintendent about window air-conditioners, television aerials, and kiddies' tricycles on the lawn.

But in the national parks, and in most of the national monuments, seashores, lakeshores, parkways, and recreation areas, government housing is provided. In the manner of the

Volkswagen beetle, and for much the same reasons (although with a touch more of style), Park Service housing is built according to standard plans, two- and three-bedroom, single-floor homes, with materials appropriate to local conditions. Placed, when possible, out of sight of the visitors, the houses are clustered together somewhat in the spirit of a small suburban development, but with a remarkably enriched landscape design. To protect taxpayers from frills and give Park Service architects a challenge, Congress has placed a ceiling on the amount that can be spent for each park residence.

Some parks have quarters that predate the era of the standard plan, a few of which encourage wifely witticisms of the "But why didn't you tell me you joined the Peace Corps?" variety. The Southwestern monuments have a few buildings that reflect a time when craftsmen, utilizing native materials and an appreciation of the beauty around them, created superb living environments. Standard-plan housing does ensure equal treatment for all employees and often eliminates the problem of trying to fit old furniture and drapes into a new house after a transfer.

If the park is far removed from civilization there is some compensation, however. Rental rates for government quarters are established on the basis of rents charged for comparable housing in the neighboring towns, which in more remote locations may be modest. Percentage reductions are made based on the distance to the nearest shopping and medical centers and other necessary locales.

Minor Inconveniences

Family life in a park community to some degree reverses accustomed life styles. Most citizens have all the necessities of life at hand. Their problem is to get away. For park families, even the normal conveniences of civilization can be a problem. Shopping, which may involve a 200-mile round trip or more, may be made the occasion of a social spree much as earlier pioneers used their infrequent opportunities to get into town.

Keeping medical and dental appointments also can become substantial projects, particularly during the winter snowstorms. It has happened so often that stories of racing for the hospital with an overpregnant wife hardly merit much conversation (although losing the race still does). One enterprising ranger who didn't quite make the hospital in time is said to have collected the standard pediatrician's fee from Blue Cross for services rendered, although next time around the patient elected to forego the financial advantages and take a more conventional approach to childbirth.

Some park families rely on the latest edition of "Merck's Manual" (*The Merck Manual of Diagnosis and Therapy*, first published in 1899). It is apparently the all-age predecessor to Dr. Spock (although one ranger reported, "I found it never worked too well on my own complaints—everything I tried to diagnose came out either acute alcoholism or conversion hysteria"). Since the manual is dedicated to "the Doctor of Medicine and to his colleagues and aides in the allied professions," a park naturalist feels medically qualified as a "colleague" and keeps his copy on the shelf right beside the Peterson *Field Guides*.

Schools can be a real problem. Although a county's economy is not always a measure of the quality of its school system, good schools and good teachers cost money, and in thinly populated regions school funds are often meager. Only a few of the parks have their own schools, and long bus rides are sometimes involved.

In some of the most isolated areas Park Service families may resort to mail-order education. The Calvert System, a correspondence course in the form of home-study kits from first grade through high school, is available from the Calvert

School of Maryland. For the children, having a teacher who is also your parent and a classroom that is also your dining room presents diverse opportunities. An alternative, used by employees in remote locations such as Big Bend National Park in western Texas, is to board children during the week at the nearest community, 125 miles away.

An important bit of data on personnel forms is the age of the employee's children, and "require adequate schools" is a frequent comment in the section in which the employee is asked to indicate what health, schooling, or other restrictions should be taken into account in selecting him for a new assignment. As a general practice, younger employees with children who have not yet reached school age are sent to the most distant outposts, a period of their lives they later seem to cherish the most and about which they will reminisce with little urging.

Sometimes living with the people you work with can create trying circumstances, for it becomes difficult to sort out official and personal attitudes. If the ranger's small boy clouts the superintendent's small girl over the head with his pogo stick, the ranger and the superintendent may have to work a little harder to maintain the warmth of their interpersonal relationship. "In a way, these things are sort of entertaining," said one who survived such difficulties, "which might say something about the quality of the entertainment available."

Primitive conditions can, however, inspire park people to improvise, and observing some of the more inventive methods of combating tedium, one suspects the spirit of the World War II Seabees has survived. In Death Valley, where there is little summer action except heat prostration, employees grappled for some time with the problem of how to prevent undue loss of government property from fire, although admittedly the fire danger in Death Valley is not particularly high. The result was a masterful justification for construction of a reservoir. Should fire ever come, the reservoir stands ready, although lowering the water level might interfere with the evening swim before dinner.

Some of the parks that are most attractive to visitors may be somewhat less than ideal places in which to live. The Glacier National Park fog has been blamed for occasional personality clashes among employees—it would be indelicate to include wives—and the claim that Mount Rainier has matched the Biblical forty days and forty nights of precipitation has the ring of truth. During the winter of 1970–71, at the Paradise Visitor Center in Mt. Rainier National Park, a new world record was recorded of 1,018 inches (more than 84 feet) of snow, with the final snowfall recorded on May 30. Under these conditions, cabin fever is not unknown, and the long winter may resemble an extended sensitivity training course.

WITHOUT SOCIAL DISTINCTIONS

Because of occasional hardships and inconveniences, hospitality is one of the most common characteristics of the park community. It is a trait that has happily permeated the entire Park Service organization, prevailing even over the rampant apathy one senses in the Washington corridors of some agencies. Employees who have been in the Park Service a few years have friends, or friends of friends, in almost every park, and with this additional lure, families on vacation tend to visit other parks. No employee on travel orders fails to adjust his official itinerary to include any park within even remote striking distance, a practice encouraged by an enlightened management, although not expressed in writing.

A ranger whose father was a career army officer once remarked that he joined the Park Service because it reminded him of military life in which the family moved to a new post every few years, invariably met friends from previous assignments, made new friends, and absorbed the culture of a new locale. The park community, like a military post, is a transient one, but the rigid caste system between officer and enlisted man on an army post is not present in a park, where there could be a tendency to establish social distinctions between the uniformed and professional people and the blue-collar employees. Some distinction, based upon education, experience, or natural interest does exist; transfers and promotions are considerably less available to maintenance workers; but snobbery is refreshingly absent, and the Park Service makes a continued effort to eliminate any preferential treatment, real or fancied, which may develop. Acceptance in the park community depends as much upon possession of relevant talents as it does upon official position. The ability to produce an impeccable dry martini is highly prized, naturally, but top marks are also given to a good wildlife photographer, a good dry fly fisherman, or a good camp cook, attributes only rarely found in administrators. The prudent ecologist, fresh from academe, elects a couple of additional semesters of practical application under the trail crew foreman. If a person has been educated beyond his intelligence, it begins to show when he can never seem to get the hang of a four-wheel-drive Jeep.

Remarkable careers have been fashioned in the Park Service by people who entered as untrained technicians but who possessed quick intelligence and a ready capacity for growth. Al Lancaster is a good example. As a young bean farmer in southeastern Colorado, he was fascinated by the Indian relics that his plow turned up. The arrival of a Chicago Field Museum party in the 1920's gave him the chance to work in the excavations; he absorbed technique observing the archeologists and was an avid reader. Al entered the Park Service as a laborer but brought with him an instinctive knack of knowing how to build things. Steadily he developed the science of preserving ancient Indian ruins, and ultimately became the outstanding authority on ruins stabilization in the Southwest. Although he had never finished high school, he was teacher to a generation of professional archeologists both within and outside the Park Service and received the Department of the Interior's Distinguished Service Award.

There is admittedly one enigma surrounding life in the parks: what, for example, does a ranger really do during those long winters? It seems likely, however, that if one could somehow explore the situation he would find the answer is about the same as to the equally puzzling problem of what a Scot wears under his kilt—although it may be ill-advised to pursue the subject in either case.

But there is no riddle as to what Park Service people talk about when they get together: shop, shop, shop. Not, for many, because they are unaware of what is happening in the world outside, but because they regard their occupation not as a job but as a way of life. Assigned to a regional office and living in a city suburb after a good many years in the parks, an associate observed that for the first time in his career he was living among people who didn't talk about Park Service business all the time. It was, he conceded, a welcome change that he intended to enjoy thoroughly—until he wangled a transfer back to the field.

THE SEASONALS

The park year has two seasons rather than four—the "travel season" and the "off season." With the exception of a few parks, the travel season coincides with the public school vacation months of June, July, and August. Efforts to spread the impact have been only partially successful in encouraging people to try the spring and fall months, but if the logistics are possible, there is no better time to experience the parks. Particularly with the advent of the snowmobile, winter use in some parks is on the increase, with Yellowstone now counting twenty thousand machines during a winter.

Because of the wide fluctuation in visitor use, it is not economical for the Park Service, or the concessioners, to retain large permanent staffs throughout the year. Instead, during the summer the small number of permanent interpretive and maintenance employees become the supervisors who direct the work of the "seasonals," temporary employees hired for the duration of the summer rush. The total employment of the Park Service almost doubles during this period, adding nearly two thousand additional uniformed rangers, naturalists, historians, archeologists, and information receptionists, and about the same number of maintenance workers.

For the concessioners, of course, the use of seasonal help is even more substantial. Providing reasonably appropriate housing for seasonal employees is a problem for both concessioner and Park Service, but those who elect a seasonal job are less concerned with housing standards than with something to do in their off-duty hours; fortunately they have each other.

The contribution of the seasonals can be simply stated: they operate the parks in the travel season. To the visitor they are the Park Service, for almost all uniformed employees encountered are seasonals. Many of the seasonal interpreters are university or high school teachers, who return year after year because they like the work. It couldn't be the pay. In most cases the seasonals man the visitor centers, conduct the guided walks, give the evening campfire programs. The parks could not be operated without them. Some move on to another park after a few years; others never get over their first love and remain in one park for an entire career.

Dean of the seasonals is Wayne Replogle. "Rep" began his career as a Yellowstone seasonal naturalist in the summer of 1930 and possesses an encyclopedic knowledge of the park. Still a member of the University of Kansas faculty where he once coached the football team, "Rep" has accumulated only one black mark on his record: he received an official reprimand in 1936 for making a solo assault on the East Face of the Grand Teton.

A considerable number of Park Service employees began as seasonals. Some take the job during college or graduate study, with no thought originally of making the Park Service a career, but somehow they get hooked. Others who have difficulty getting a permanent appointment work a number of years seasonally prior to achieving career status.

ON THE MOVE

People who enter the Park Service can expect to live in a large city, a small village, or a remote outpost located either near the Arctic Circle or in the subtropics. Employees living on Liberty Island in Upper New York Bay have one of the best of all views of New York City with its teeming population; those living in the crumbling citadel of Fort Jefferson in the Dry Tortugas Islands off Key West have plenty of free time to watch one of the greatest of all wildlife spectacles when incredible numbers of sooty terns gather on Bush Key for the nesting season.

Moving to a new park area may require a substantial adjustment for the whole family. Obviously for those exchanging the cool green forests of Shenandoah National Park in Virginia for the sandstone formations of Canyonlands National Park in Utah, a new life style is in order. As it most often happens, the desert seems at first particularly forbidding to those unfamiliar with its singular attractions, but continued association seems to create an inevitable fascination, and when the time comes, most families feel a distinct reluctance to leave.

A ranger is expected, first of all, to know his park thoroughly, and when he transfers he begins a learning process that never stops until he moves on to another park and starts again. Like the fabled mountain man, he needs to be able to find his way to the most remote points about as easily as most people proceed to the corner drugstore. And beyond the physical features of the park, a substantial knowledge of its natural and human history is also required.

For the historian transferring from the Cumberland Gap country of Daniel Boone on the Kentucky-Tennessee border to the Carl Sandburg home in North Carolina, the geographic distance is not far, but he too must go back to school and absorb an entirely new chapter of American history.

Differences of opinion among biologists over the ultimate impact of horses on forest ecology is matched by disagreements among park historians over the true interpretation of historical events. Custer Battlefield National Monument, in Montana, has produced continuous controversy and has recently, in fact, entered upon an even more intense era of contention, but the perennial contenders for leadership in this area have been the group of Civil War battlefields south of the Mason and Dixon Line—the so-called Cannon and Chigger circuit. One could hardly imagine a position more fraught with temptation than that of a Southern-born Park Service historian, whose duties require him to interpret the Civil War. Such historians manage to suppress sectional allegiances—with rare lapses. Several years ago members of a Department of Interior management survey team, while making a swing through the Virginia military parks, detected what they considered to be a restrained, yet noticeable, partiality in the battlefield markers toward the exploits of Southern arms. Even at Appomatox the theme seemed to be that of a noble but misunderstood people upon whom a kindly Providence had bestowed all of the manly virtues but by some oversight had neglected to supply sufficient guns and butter. When the leader of the survey team called the matter to the attention of the regional historian in Richmond, that courtly scholar replied angrily: "Suh, I am unbiased!"

SUPERINTENDENTS, RANGERS—AND WOMEN

"When the Morfield Canyon campground is full," the superintendent of Mesa Verde once observed, "I'm the mayor of the second largest city in this section of the State." The 450-site campground alone holds nearly two thousand people; adding the other visitors in the overnight accommodations along with permanent and seasonal employees and their families enhances the superintendent's claim. Running a national park, in addition to all the other problems involved, is a lot like running a small city.

Illustrating this point to a congressional appropriations committee, for the purpose of obtaining sufficient funds to do the job properly, Director George B. Hartzog used the following statistics from one national park: a permanent population of more than 1,000 concessioner and Park Service employees and their families; 500 miles of roads and trails; an elementary school, a high school, and a hospital; fourteen sewage disposal systems; more than three hundred Park Service buildings and employee residences; eight campgrounds which accommodate more than five thousand campers.

To this must be added the additional complexities created by a daily influx of twenty thousand visitors, for which hotels, cabins, restaurants, stores, and service stations are supplied, staffed, and operated by the concessioner, along with his own extensive complex of residences, offices, and warehouses. The fleet of vehicles that the Park Service requires to patrol, maintain, and repair the road system would match the motor pool of most comparable cities.

In the lifetime of most career Park Service people, the job of operating a national park, large or small, has grown increasingly complex, the tempo has quickened, and superintendents are not always certain whether their role is that of mayor or steward of precious natural and historical resources. The respectful behavior of people in the national parks has been, until recent years, one of the traditions. Now crime is a rising problem. The "flower children" migrate to the parks and the life styles of some produce a distinct cultural shock among other visitors. Rangers at entrance stations who check in the motorcycle caravans do so under a strict policy that every visitor must be treated equally and the enforcement of regulations cannot be selective.

Yet, if the freaked-out few were excluded, those compelled to rattle the more sedate clientele with bizarre public acts, the majority of young people who hitchhike or arrive on foot are probably seeking, and finding, the kind of experience for which the parks were originally set aside. With their bedrolls they head for the back country, perhaps no less mindful of John Muir's creed than those who enter the park in air-conditioned comfort.

Parks are operated under policy regulations established to maintain consistent management practices in the three categories: natural, historical, and recreational. To these might be added: urban and cultural. Urban parks have their own special problems, and cultural parks constitute a new concept, now being presented to Congress. However, even within a single category, there are wide variations. In the recreational category come parks in locales as various as the civilized and inhabited landscape of Cape Cod and the stark desert of Glen Canyon, and policy guidelines must allow for individual variations.

As a result, the way a park is operated reflects to some degree the personality of those in charge. The likelihood of individual difference is enhanced by the practice of delegating major responsibilities to the superintendent, rather than to Washington. Considering the wide variety of parks, the differences in attitudes of employees, and the reasonable latitude given the superintendent to make local decisions, it is understandable that a new superintendent, sizing up the situation, may feel impelled to spend the first year getting the place shaped up—his way. The system has a lot in its favor; administrative arteriosclerosis is avoided, master plan teams are kept busy, and employees start meeting report deadlines, until they get the new man broken in.

The conflicting viewpoints of Park Service people toward preservation and use policies, opinions strongly held and strongly expressed, probably constitute one of the strongest ingredients of the organization's character. Before decisions are made, arguments are advanced from all sides and from all levels. Those who end up in the minority may or may not be charitable in defeat. Although conformance with approved policy is required publicly, no Park Service Director has ever ordered internal adherence, although it might well shorten coffee breaks. Apparently not satisfied with conventional avenues of communication open to the discontented, whose use is encouraged, a Park Service underground newspaper has made an appearance.

A perpetual gripe of field people is conveyed by that tiresome old phrase "We're out here on the firing line," which would seem to suggest all other offices are burdensome administrative and supply detachments far removed from the scene of battle. Like most such analogies, this one is wildly inaccurate. While the regional and Washington offices are staffed almost entirely by people who have spent a good part of their careers in the parks, no one in Washington, in the eyes of field personnel, can really understand the problem. All of which would suggest that in this respect, at least, the Park Service differs little from other organizations administered from a central headquarters.

Yet one must reluctantly admit that the constant and driving pressures exerted upon the executive leadership of the Park Service can, on the rarest occasions, divert emphasis from park operations to throwing up barricades against the latest assault on the budget or a threat to reduce personnel ceilings. Spared this grueling existence, Park Service people in the field are less likely to forget that maintaining the parks unimpaired has primacy over all other endeavors.

Being responsible for some of the most priceless remnants of the national heritage, trying to be responsive to often inscrutable instructions arriving from higher authority, facing an insurrection from seasonal rangers who think shoulder-length hair looks fine under the wide-brimmed Stetson, the park superintendent wears his several hats and somehow holds everything together. A perceptive architectural consultant came back from one park with the conclusion that the superintendent reminded him of a rancher, and this analogy is not far off. Let the master planners develop their schemes, let the regional director send his management appraisal team, let reorganizations make it impossible to determine who is running the store. The superintendent goes right along running his ranch.

The title "ranger" is one of considerable respect, the most respected in the organization, with a long tradition going back before 1900. Not particularly awed by Prince or President, whom they have frequently served, rangers can point to the legendary Billy Nelson, who once guided King Albert of Belgium on a back-country trip. "Hey, King," he shouted over the campfire, "shoot me that side of bacon, will you?" And recognizing an authentic free spirit of the New World, the King of the Belgians smilingly tossed Billy the bacon.

With a history of such heroic feats, it is only natural that the ranger-types at times have tolerantly regarded their interpretive brethren as well-intentioned—and on the whole competent—specialists (or "nature fakers," as they call them), perhaps inclined a bit to bookishness, and never developing much appetite for law enforcement work. To their credit the interpreters invariably speak well of the rangers ("tree fuzz" to the interpreters), admire their ability to build a career on robust vitality, and accept them as equals, in most things. To the visitor, all uniformed employees are rangers, the person to whom one goes for information or for assistance, and inspired by this simplistic line of reasoning the Park Service has placed all interpretive positions in the ranger category. Something ineffably fine may be lost in the translation.

Lest this account be unduly criticized for using the generic "he" when referring to rangers, it should be noted that a substantial number of female historians, naturalists, and archeologists wear a handsomely styled uniform, compete for promotions, draw quarters, and share equal assignments, particularly in the administrative and interpretive field, although a couple of women have also achieved superintendent status. Catching the spirit of the times, some of the ladies are demanding full equality with rangers, including fire fighting and back-country patrols. Although in the Park Service organization that kind of progress may take a little longer, during the summer of 1971, Yellowstone was employing female naturalists, biologists, truck drivers, corral helpers, and flag women on road construction.

In the only fairly distant past, park rangers, like cowboys, were somewhat discouraged from matrimony by the conditions of their work. When the oldline superintendent ordered a winter tour of the back country, he wanted the ranger to have his gear packed, horse saddled, and be on his way within the hour. The advent of the married ranger changed the climate, for his eagerness to meet the standard of 300 miles of ski or snowshoe patrol each month waned steadily. "It's nice to have a hot stove to come home to," as one wife observed. But it may not be fair to blame the arrival of the ranger's wife, for, about the same time, the ranger's paper workload increased so drastically, or so he laments, that he began to have about as much trouble getting away from the office as his Washington counterpart.

The girl who becomes a "rangerwife," as the unpaid but absolutely essential position is generally referred to, often must exchange familiar surroundings and civilized amenities for the likes of berry-picking and moose-watching. If the district ranger station is also the ranger's residence, she must respond to all emergencies in his absence. Knowing how to raise the radio dispatcher on the communication system and to sign off with "Ten Four" comes in as handy as remembering, when the Director visits the park, that he likes his Scotch with no ice, and water on the side.

Quite a lot of socializing is done in the parks, particularly when other diversions are lacking, and official visits from regional and Washington dignitaries generally spark social gatherings of greater or lesser size, as is befitting to the rank, and influence, of the guests. During the travel season an almost endless procession of VIP's arrive in the parks: distinguished or famous public figures, motion-picture companies, writers, congressmen singly and in committees, and the ubiquitous National Geographic photographer. Many become dinner guests, and although they are something of a drain on the larder, many are delightful people.

During his tenure on the Secretary of the Interior's Advisory Board, publisher Alfred A. Knopf traveled widely in the parks and became an effective and tenacious fighter in their behalf. Finding a special refreshment in his visits to the parks, the urbane Mr. Knopf, always recognizable by his electric blue shirts, prudently avoided cultural shock by including among other necessities packed away in the trunk of his car a case of his favorite wine.

Park Service people found Alfred Knopf a charming and unpretentious companion. Apparently the affection was returned. Writing in *This Is Dinosaur*, he said:

> It is hard to imagine more dedicated people than those who run the Parks. I have never met a single one whom I would not be glad to meet again, and I have invariably regretted the time to say goodby. The range of their interests, their high intelligence, their devotion, make them a separate and wonderful breed.

X

Relationships with Congress

The Park Service Director serves a number of masters. None is more demanding than the Congress of the United States. Conservationists protesting against suspected departures from traditional park practices can hope for a sympathetic reception from the Director, perhaps even for a modification in policy. But requests from Congress get immediate response, particularly from members of the Interior committees. Additional supervision is received, in the case of individual parks, from the two senators and the congressman from the district in which the park is located, who constitute the "congressional delegation" for matters involving that park.

In accordance with established practice for all federal agencies, there are two committees each in the House and Senate which dispense advice and consent—and funds—for the operation of the National Park Service, although the actual work is done by subcommittees of the four parent committees. The Interior and Insular Affairs Committee in each House handles the substantive matters involving the Department of the Interior; in the case of the Park Service, all legislation that would establish new national parks and all bills involving park policy. Subcommittees of the Appropriations committee in each house pass upon the Park Service request

172

for appropriations. When a new park bill is written by the Interior and Insular Affairs Committee, the amount of money that can be appropriated for land acquisition and development is usually specified. The actual appropriation of those funds is a function of the Appropriations Committee.

The Director makes a considerable number of official appearances before these committees each year. He and his staff must be prepared to explain to the appropriation subcommittees, intelligently, every item of an exceedingly long and complicated budget, and it is not uncommon for the Director to be asked such questions as why he needs an additional ranger and a maintenance man at Fort Laramie. Interior and Insular Affairs subcommittees hold a number of hearings on new park bills in Washington and in the field, and all of the committees make a practice of personally reviewing park operations.

While it would be an obvious exaggeration to describe the attitude of agency heads before congressional committees as reverent, that term might come closer to the mark than the suggestion of any hint of the defiant or truculent. There is actually supposed to be a historical marker somewhere in a committee room on Capitol Hill commemorating the site where an agency head once spoke disparagingly to a committee member, but the likelihood seems most improbable. Probably the low tolerance of the committee members for anything resembling delaying tactics from agency witnesses stems from the knowledge that this is their best chance. During the rest of the year their experience is often similar to that of President Harry Truman, who once remarked rather glumly that it was easy enough to give orders to the departments—the problem was that nothing seemed to happen.

A delicate balance exists in the relationships involving the Congress, the President, and an executive agency. One of the best examples of the kinds of stresses that threaten the balance took place at the close of the Johnson Administration.

THE MILLS OF THE GODS GRIND SLOWLY

In almost the last hour of his Presidency, Lyndon B. Johnson concluded one of the more ambitious efforts of the executive branch of the federal government to engineer an expansion of the national park system. It involved a behind-the-scenes exercise in power politics, a seeming effort to bypass the authority of the Congress, and provoked an offer to resign from Secretary of the Interior Udall just forty-eight hours away from the close of his eight-year term. In his *Christian Science Monitor* comment on the events, reporter Robert Cahn declared, "A synopsis of the political maneuvering would make a classic case study for students of political science and executive legislative relations."

It began in mid-summer of 1968, as President Johnson approached the final six months of his term in the White House, when he asked his Cabinet officers to recommend things that might be accomplished by executive action during this period, particularly those which could not possibly get through Congress in the short time remaining. For Secretary of the Interior Stewart Udall, the invitation presented a long-sought opportunity to set aside parklands, which the President is authorized to do under the Antiquities Act of 1906 but which has been done only rarely in more recent times because of congressional opposition.

One small phrase from the Act, "and other objects of historic or scientific interest," had offered Presidents an opportunity which they had used with a most liberal interpretation, particularly in terms of what constituted an object of "scientific interest." To Congress the practice of establishing national monuments caused increasing irritation. It came to be regarded as a route taken by the executive branch to bypass the authority of the legislative branch. After the President proclaimed a national monument, however, it was necessary to come to Congress for funds to operate the area, and here Congress could exercise its veto power.

The last previous effort to thwart Congress took place during the Eisenhower years. A bill to establish a Chesapeake and Ohio Canal park had long been stalled in Congress, and two days before the end of his term the President used the Antiquities Act to set it aside as a national monument. Congress was incensed, and to make sure that the lesson would not soon be forgotten, it turned down the Park Service's request for funds to activate the C&O Canal every year afterward. To avoid such unpleasantness, letters were exchanged between the Secretary of the Interior and the Interior committees agreeing that the Antiquities Act would not be used without prior clearance through the committees, except in emergencies, and President Johnson had used the authority only once—to add Ellis Island to the Statue of Liberty National Monument.

Although well aware of the ultimate confrontation with Congress that would result should the Antiquities Act authority be invoked to establish new parks, Udall decided to take advantage of the President's offer by arranging to bring into the national park system those areas that were eminently qualified but for which legislation might be difficult or long drawn out. The Park Service was asked to prepare a list of possible additions. Udall had been under pressure from conservationists to pursue this cause for some time, and he now invited several groups to make their recommendations.

A provisional list of seventeen areas was selected, from which Udall made the final selection of seven, discarding several that were certain to create interdepartmental warfare, particularly with the Department of Agriculture's Forest Service, and therefore might jeopardize the entire project. A considerable portion of the selected lands were under the jurisdiction of the Bureau of Land Management, which gave wholehearted cooperation to the undertaking. Putting the package together was a formidable job, for it involved authenticating the status of the lands, documenting the legal requirements, and providing the maps, charts, photographs, and other papers required to prepare the official proclamations and necessary to put together a presentation for President Johnson's review. The known preference of the President for bar graphs and large color photographs was not overlooked.

On December 11, 1968, the presentation was made to President Johnson in the White House. The reception was warm, enhanced by the enthusiasm of Lady Bird Johnson, who had taken great interest in the parks and made a distinguished contribution to the entire conservation field. But the project was recognized by Johnson and his staff as having significant political implications. In addition to several legal matters requiring extensive study by the Department of Justice, the President raised the obviously most difficult problem—congressional clearance. This task was given to Udall, with instructions from the President to "touch all bases on the Hill."

In the first of a series of excruciating coincidences, President-elect Nixon had announced only a few hours before the White House meeting that the new Secretary of the Interior was to be Walter Hickel, governor of Alaska. A number of the proclamations dealt with lands in Alaska, which in fact constituted the largest part of the total acreage involved. What kind of endorsement and support would these parklands receive from the new Administration, the President asked?

Fate intervened for the second time within a week. It was understood that the President would sign the proclamations on December 19, as a "conservation Christmas gift" to the nation. The preceding day he came down with the flu, was taken to Walter Reed Hospital, and spent the holidays recuperating in Texas. However, in his final State of the Union Message delivered on January 14, the President made oblique reference to the park plan, announcing that while much land had been set aside for conservation during his Presidency, "There is more going to be set aside before this administration ends."

Apparently, all bases on Capitol Hill had not been touched. Udall had briefed the congressional delegations from the states involved and had gained the support of Senator Henry Jackson, chairman of the Interior and Insular Affairs Committee in the Senate. But Jackson's opposite number in the House, Wayne Aspinall, the key to congressional approval, had not been briefed, in all probability because of his known dislike for Presidential use of the Antiquities Act. When he learned of the proposed action in the last week of the Johnson Administration, the battle was joined.

Congress, in the person of Representative Aspinall, was adamant and made its views known to the White House. Establishment of new national park areas, the Antiquities Act notwithstanding, was the function of the Congress. There was no immediate threat, since the lands included were already federal property. "I saw no emergency," Aspinall told Robert Cahn. "There was no need to by-pass Congress. And if the President wanted to go ahead, we just wouldn't activate the areas."

To most observers, Aspinall's position was dictated not by his attitude toward preserving national parks but by his regard for the authority of the Congress. A few years before, when Udall and the Park Service had been willing to compromise and to permit mining in order to pass the Canyonlands National Park bill, it was Aspinall who held for the "pure" park and who was instrumental in its passage.

Acutely sensitive to this rare chance to preserve a significant portion of the remaining wild country, and knowing from his own experience in the House how long the legislative route might take, Udall urged the President to take direct action. Keenly sensitive to the legitimate prerogatives of the

Congress after his years as Majority Leader in the Senate, and yet not unmindful of the significance of his opportunity, Johnson waited.

In the final days of the Administration, Udall and Johnson, who had achieved a distinguished record as partners in furthering the cause of conservation, became bitter adversaries. On the Saturday before the inauguration of the new Administration on Monday, on the basis of information or of reasons which he did not divulge, Udall anticipated Presidential approval by authorizing the release to the press of an announcement that the proclamations had been signed; perhaps the release was made on the basis of misinformation, or perhaps Udall was willing to risk everything in the hope of forcing Johnson's hand.

Seeing the news coming in over the wire service ticker in his office, Johnson phoned Udall and ordered immediate retraction of the story. During what was apparently a difficult conversation the President refused to accept Udall's resignation or to indicate what his final action would be. On Monday morning, in probably the last official act before welcoming the new President to the White House and accompanying him to the ceremonies, Johnson signed the orders establishing one small new national monument of 26,000 acres and adding some 350,000 acres to three existing areas.

The result was certainly worth the long effort, for parklands are hard to come by and longer campaigns have been considerably less fruitful for the Park Service. But for those who labored in the vineyards and who joined the long vigil in Director Hartzog's office over the final weekend, awaiting the call that never came, the crushing disappointment will not soon be forgotten. In announcing the signing of the proclamations, President Johnson enunciated the facts of political life, particularly with respect to the relationships among the White House, the Department of the Interior, and the Congress. Of the proclamations he had decided not to sign, he said, "The taking of this land without opportunity for Congressional study would strain the Antiquities Act far beyond its intent. . . . Such action, I am informed, would be opposed by leading members of Congress having authority in this field."

Knowing from experience the pitfalls ahead, the Park Service staff had at the beginning of the exercise judged that the odds were decidedly against success. But understandably, as the climate seemed to improve, the unprecedented scope of the enterprise had infected all concerned. Under the circumstances, the uncharacteristic optimism was excusable, for the stakes were indeed high.

Had the President signed all of the proclamations, nearly 8 million acres would have been involved, and by this one stroke of the pen the national park system, which had been laboriously enlarged over a period of ninety-seven years, would have been increased by more than one-fourth.

XI

Relationships with Other Federal Agencies

After the ceremony of officially swearing in Stephen Mather as first Director, Secretary of the Interior Franklin K. Lane casually remarked, "By the way, Steve, I forgot to ask you—what are your politics?" It was a reassuring way of telling the new Director that the job of running the national parks was not considered to be within the realm of partisan politics, and that Mather, a well-known Republican, was welcome in President Woodrow Wilson's Democratic Administration. The first Director served under three Presidents and five secretaries, surviving the change of administrations when Warren G. Harding was elected in 1920, and this tenacity established a typical pattern for his successors.

There have been seven directors in the fifty-six-year history of the Park Service; excluding one Director who served less than a year as an interim appointment, the average tenure has been a little over nine years. None has ever been removed as a political measure, and with the possible exception of the directorship of the FBI, this must be regarded as one of the unusual records in government. Admittedly, however, there have been one or two uneasy incumbents during certain changeovers who thought a precedent might be in the making. Of Interior's dozen major bureau chiefs who welcomed Secretary of the Interior Walter Hickel aboard in January, 1969, only George B. Hartzog of the National Park Service and the able William Pecora of the Geological Survey were still around to bid Hickel farewell when he departed, rather abruptly, less than two years later.

The Secretary may have a shorter tenure, but he both appoints the Director of the Park Service and reserves to his office the major policy decisions affecting the national parks that are not matters of legislative mandate. A Director would be considered imprudent not to consult the Secretariat on matters of moment, and it is considered bad form to catch the Secretary or the assistant secretary by surprise, particularly in a matter likely to stimulate public attention. This, however, suggests a more precise operating procedure than in fact exists; a bureau chief seldom lacks influential friends in various places, including Capitol Hill, any of whom may feel impelled, when prompted, to intercede in his behalf. It is a venture not without risk, however.

There have always been, and there always will be, two contrary forces at work within every department of the federal government. This little-known phenomenon provides bureaucratic confirmation of Newton's Third Law of Motion, that for every action there is an equal and opposite reaction, with a resulting tendency to solidify the status quo. On the Departmental level at the beginning of an administration, a new team is put together, which shortly begins to sense that each bureau seems to be marching to its own drummer. One of the first objectives, inevitably, is to break down bureau intransigence and to weld the separate agencies into a single unified Department. This is the centripetal force.

Calling upon experience gained in countless previous engagements, the crafty bureau chieftains battle to preserve their treasured prerogatives, some few of which might rise above the mundane; and this is the centrifugal force. After a well-fought campaign, the Department emerges the winner, forcing from the bureaus agreement that without exception the name of the Department will always appear above the name of the bureau, or in larger type.

THE PARK SERVICE AND THE FOREST SERVICE

Considering that, in the opinion of veteran government watchers, the most celebrated interbureau rivalry in all government involves the Forest Service* and the Park Service, it is always startling to learn that relatively few Americans are actually aware of the feud. Even worse, they are as likely as not to refer to park rangers as forest rangers, an inexcusable slip. On the other hand, that minute section of the citizenry that is well informed on the antic behavior of the federal bureaucracy apparently expects to witness a fist fight every time park and forest rangers meet.

In fact, Forest Service and Park Service people get along famously and cooperate in many ways, particularly in the field where they have close operating relationships. But on the bureau and departmental level, where policies are made, tradition is strong, and neither side is permitted to forget the firmly entrenched attitudes of its constituency. The long history of conflicting and competing objectives has developed in each agency a keen but wary respect for the ability of the other to stir up mischief.

The Forestry Reserve Act of 1891, although it consisted of only a few lines added to an omnibus public land bill, turned out to be one of the most important measures enacted by Congress in the history of conservation in the United States. It gave the President authority to set aside as forest reserves, later called national forests, timberlands from the then vast public domain. No congressional action was required, a sig-

* A separate volume in this series is devoted to this agency: Michael Frome, *The Forest Service* (New York: Praeger, 1971).

nificant difference from the requirement that each national park must be established by Congress. Before a group of Western senators attached another rider that took the power away in 1907, four Presidents had set aside more than 175 million acres. Theodore Roosevelt alone was responsible for 150 million acres, more than five times the amount of land presently included in the national park system. A person could today begin at the Canadian border and hike through the states of Washington, Oregon, and California, remaining within national forests almost entirely on his 2,000 mile journey to the Mexican border.

The Act ensured the future protection of much of the nation's timber and watershed resources. But since the forest preserves covered a good portion of the undeveloped lands of the West, they included areas of superlative natural and scenic value that would become increasingly attractive as recreation lands. Thus was triggered an inevitable conflict between, on the one hand, lumbering, mining, and grazing interests, which were dependent upon the "sustained-yield" policies of Forest Service administration, and, on the other, the conservationists, who came to believe many of the scenic forests would be of infinitely more value to the nation as national parks.

Many national parks in the West are partially or entirely surrounded by national forests. When the Park Service sought to alter original boundaries, in order to effect more natural borders along mountain ranges or to include migration routes of wildlife overlooked in the enabling legislation, such expansion could only be accomplished at the expense of adjoining national forests. Almost without fail when new parks were proposed they lay within the domain of the Forest Service, and as new national parks were carved out the Park Service cost the national forests more trees than Paul Bunyan.

Political leaders, whether elected or appointed, dislike exceedingly to preside over the dissolution of their dominions.

There is simply no known way to convince any agency head that removal of even a portion of his sovereign territory will be to his advantage. Anticipating trouble to come, when legislation was proposed to establish a National Park Service, the Forest Service was totally opposed, believing that, with minor adjustments to its operating procedures, it could handle the recreational and inspirational needs of the American public, fitting them in with the somewhat more specialized requirements of the mining, grazing, lumbering, irrigation, hunting, and other interests comprising the multiple-use fraternity.

By establishing the new bureau of national parks, Congress settled the argument of whether one or two agencies would have responsibility for administering the parks and the forests. The decision, in retrospect, seems particularly inspired, for it placed the two agencies in direct competition, rather an intelligent way to handle such matters. The Park Service was quickly on the move and proceeded aggressively to establish its position as the agency to which the federal recreation lands should be entrusted.

Over the years the two agencies developed totally different constituencies, which in modern times have exerted powerful influence on policy decisions. It could hardly be expected that the purposes of, say, the Weyerhaeuser timber combine and those of, say, the National Audubon Society would be in harmony, or that either one would be shy about making its opinions known in the proper places. The economy of many regions depends upon the following process: a forest ranger cruises his district and marks the mature trees for cutting; a lumber company is awarded a contract for felling and processing the trees; the local county gets 25 per cent of the revenue from the sale. The prospect of changing an area from a national forest to national park status has little appeal for those likely to lose their jobs at the sawmill. With conservation and travel interests supporting a national park proposal, and with commercial interests grimly fighting any exclusion of public lands from development, the position taken by rival candidates has been known to influence the outcome of elections.

Perhaps more basic to the relationship between the Forest Service and the Park Service are philosophies upon which agency loyalty and tradition are also based. The professional forester, trained in silviculture, endeavors to develop a healthy stand of timber and sees the value of converting mature trees into lumber, useful for people's daily needs and providing economic benefits for those who harvest and process the wood. Opposed to this utilitarian approach is the Park Service philosophy, which allows the overmature tree to live out its span and, dying, to rot on the ground, perhaps even becoming a "bug tree" and providing a breeding place for insects which in turn can attack healthy trees. To the forester, thinking of wasted two-by-fours, such practices go against the grain. He thinks of forests in terms of productivity; for him lumbering is a more logical approach to forest management than preserving the trees for their scenic value.

This is not to say the Forest Service professionals do not respect and defend national parks; they do. But locking away *additional* productive forests, for unproductive uses, strikes them on the whole as a piece of irrational behavior. The opposing philosophies were plainly defined by a Forest Service statement that describes the motivation of those who grow trees for the board feet therein, and those who do not:

> Many people like big timber and do not understand or appreciate vigor or thrift in a tree. To them, a large overmature, spiketopped, catfaced, conky old veteran is magnificent, has character and is much to be preferred to a thrifty intermediate tree.

And may God have mercy on the redwoods.

INTERIOR VS. AGRICULTURE

In his State of the Union Address of January, 1971, President Richard M. Nixon proposed one of the most sweeping reorganizations of the executive establishment ever advanced. From six existing departments and a number of independent agencies four new departments would be established: Human Resources, Community Development, Economic Affairs, and Natural Resources. The proposed Department of Natural Resources would consist primarily of bureaus from the Department of the Interior, but there would be a number of other agencies transferred to the new Department.

The fundamental purpose of the new Department of National Resources would be to deal with the problem of overlapping and at times conflicting management policies affecting the nation's natural resources and to develop a more effective mechanism for coordinating and integrating all related land, resource, and environmental programs of the federal domain. A major component of the new Department, Land and Recreation, would bring together all federal land-managing agencies, including the National Park Service and the Forest Service, which would be transferred from the Department of Agriculture.

With the exception of lands set aside for special uses by agencies such as the Atomic Energy Commission and the Bureau of Reclamation and those reserved for Department of Defense installations, the remaining public lands of the United States are managed by four bureaus, all of which would be placed in the Land and Recreation component of the new Department: the Bureau of Land Management, the National Park Service, the Bureau of Sport Fisheries and Wildlife, all from Interior, and the Forest Service from Agriculture. A fifth agency, the Bureau of Outdoor Recreation, has no land-managing responsibility but plays a strategic role in coordinating all federal recreation programs; it also administers the Land and Water Conservation Fund, from which Congress appropriates funds for land acquisition to the Forest Service, the Bureau of Sport Fisheries and Wildlife, and the Park Service.

The Bureau of Land Management administers nearly 500 million acres of public lands, almost two-thirds of the total land in federal ownership, with 60 per cent located in Alaska. Bureau lands consist largely of the remnants of the original public domain, those not suitable for selection by homesteaders, or land not included in national parks and forests. The Forest Service administers nearly 200 million acres, most of which are in the West. Together, the Forest Service and the Bureau of Land Management manage almost 90 per cent of all federal lands. The Bureau of Sport Fisheries and Wildlife (in its wildlife refuges) and the National Park Service each manage about 30 million acres.

In the over-all administration of these federal lands there are fundamental choices that must be made, choices which continually pit the interests of one segment of the public against the interests of another. Such decisions are becoming increasingly difficult to make. Determining whether the need for oil from the Santa Barbara channel or from the North Slope of Alaska outweighs the environmental disasters that might result from extraction exemplifies the sort of dilemma surrounding the use of the public domain.

Almost any segment of public land could be utilized for lumbering, grazing, mining, or for water for irrigation or for developing hydroelectric power. It could also be given over to mass recreation and used for camping, picnicking, fishing, or winter sports. Or it might be reserved for more intangible products, spiritual values, and utilized as a wilderness retreat, a sanctuary. Originally, there was enough land, and as the land-managing agencies were established, the distinctions between them were clear, so that each could carry out its own specialized mission. There was more land then and fewer people, allowing a higher tolerance for slippages between agencies.

President Nixon's massive reorganization plan, particularly as it affects relationships between the departments of Agriculture and Interior, was only the most recent effort toward coordinating the programs of the two federal departments most concerned with conservation matters. Nor was it the first major effort to create a single Department of Conservation that would consolidate all resource-managing agencies under one authority.

The national forests, when first established, were administered by the Department of the Interior, but in 1905 Theodore Roosevelt moved the Forest Service to Agriculture, under Gifford Pinchot. The reason given for this action was that forests were set aside primarily to supply a continuing yield of timber, in the manner of a farmer producing a crop. With the Department of the Interior assigned the task of disposing of the public domain, the Agriculture Department assumed an early leadership in the field of conservation.

A tradition of competition—if that is an accurate term to use in connection with government departments that do not always agree—had developed between the Interior and Agriculture departments by the time Harold Ickes took over the Department of the Interior in 1933. Ickes seemed to have two burning ambitions: (1) to revitalize the reputation of the Department of the Interior and (2) to transform it into a Department of Conservation, largely by taking the Forest Service away from Agriculture. Thriving on rancorous argument and knowingly insulting every one of his top Interior Department staff, Ickes labeled himself "America's No. 1 Curmudgeon, or Sour Puss." Confident that wrongdoers abound in government, he terrorized the Department of the Interior employees by personally roaming the halls seeking out counterspies—or even worse, loafers.

Ickes battled for years in vain, trying to get Congress to

change the name of the Interior Department to the Department of Conservation, jousting publicly with Agriculture's Secretary Henry Wallace over transfer of the Forest Service, the keystone of his plan, and all the while extracted vague promises from President Franklin Roosevelt, who apparently considered it all good fun. While he didn't get the Forest Service, Ickes did get the Biological Survey and the Bureau of Fisheries (later consolidated into the Fish and Wildlife Service), and the Bureau of Mines. He also exacerbated relationships between the Interior and Agriculture departments.

In January, 1963, Secretary of Agriculture Orville Freeman and Secretary of the Interior Stewart Udall signed a joint letter to President Kennedy, which press cynics promptly tabbed "the Treaty of the Potomac." The pact confirmed there had been a history of "public controversy" between the two departments, but the two chieftains proclaimed: "We have closed the books on these disputes and are now ready to harmoniously implement the agreed upon solutions." Considering the amicable spirit that marked the peace pact announcement, the prediction of the end of hostilities between Agriculture and Interior was understandable, although, as it proved, somewhat premature.

The controversies in question revolved almost entirely around issues of dispute between the Park Service and Forest Service. In an era of rapidly expanding demand for outdoor recreation, the relationships between the two agencies had become even more abrasive. Writing in *American Forests*, a former assistant chief of the Forest Service, Edward C. Crafts, noted that its "Operation Outdoors," designed to upgrade the entire recreation potential of the forests, "was a defensive counterprogram to the National Park Service's Mission 66." The Multiple Use Act of 1960, a piece of landmark legislation for the Forest Service, which included recreation as a primary forest use, was aimed in part to block increasing public pressure to create new national parks out of the national forests. Crafts noted: "We so badly wanted recreation included in the listing for strategic reasons in order to help us in our recreation activities and incidentally in our competition with the Park Service."

Seeking comparability with the Park Service in the field of outdoor recreation, and adopting the slogan "They Shall Not Pass" with respect to establishing new national parks out of national forest lands, the Forest Service had flatly denied the Park Service permission to study the North Cascades park potential. Although the Potomac pact cleared the way for a joint study of the North Cascades region by the two agencies, with the Bureau of Outdoor Recreation serving as referee, five years of exceedingly arduous negotiations followed. The constituencies, local and national, of both agencies were active combatants, and by the time a North Cascades National Park bill passed Congress in 1968, the so-called Peace of the Potomac was a little tarnished.

In its study of the proper use of the public lands and the most effective method of achieving their intelligent management, published in 1970, the Public Land Law Review Commission noted that because the Forest Service was not under the same policy direction as the other public land agencies, there were "unnecessary differences in policies between the Forest Service and bureaus within Interior," that these differences had led "to conflicts between them, particularly over the use of national forest lands for national parks, that have been a source of embarassment to national administrations; to confusion on the part of the using public; and to expensive duplication of staff, offices, programs, and facilities."

A particularly thorny example of the "unnecessary differences" between the Park Service and Forest Service, which at times have frustrated Presidential administrations, arose out of the Forest Service decision to create an all-year recreation resort in the Mineral King basin adjacent to Sequoia

National Park. Although the Disney company was selected to develop the $50 million project, it was promptly stymied by the refusal of the Park Service to grant a permit for construction of a high-standard road across parkland, the only access to Mineral King. The interagency dispute quickly escalated into an interdepartmental battle, and was finally settled by the White House in favor of the Forest Service, curiously just about the time that the Redwood National Park controversy, which involved Forest Service interests, was settled in favor of the Park Service.

It was observed by the commission that both the Forest Service and the Bureau of Land Management were moving "almost irresistibly" toward similar objectives in their programs involving consumptive use of natural resources, with the lands of both agencies "managed for the same products and under similar multiple-use authorities." The commission concluded that the Forest Service should be merged with the Department of the Interior into a new Department of Natural Resources. It was also noted by the commission that the Forest Service had a long record of significant research accomplishments and of immensely successful cooperative relationships with the states and with private landowners—a record that was unmatched by the Interior agencies and that would greatly improve their capabilities.

It seems possible that the prolonged contest begun forty years ago by Harold Ickes may finally achieve its goal, but it must be accomplished over the strong objections of a powerful element of the body politic.

The present writer would add only a couple of wholly personal notions of some of the resulting effects, should the grand design be realized with respect to the Forest Service and Park Service. The first is that the National Park Service would be placed in direct association with one of the truly elite agencies of the federal government. In the dedication, pride, and discipline of its highly professional personnel, the

United States Forest Service has few equals. The Park Service would have to be on its mettle, and the close association just might be beneficial.

The other thought is occasioned by an apocryphal dialogue between two Greek philosophers, who were not quite contemporaries. Said Archimedes: "Give me a fulcrum and I will move the world." To which Diogenes countered: "Will it be better off in some other place?"

XII

Relationships with Conservation Organizations

The management of the national parks is a matter of concern, not only to the Department of the Interior and the Congress, but to an ever expanding concert of conservation organizations, which keep a close and frequently critical eye on park matters and forcefully challenge policy decisions with which they disagree. As a special interest group, these organizations are capable of large-scale lobbying efforts, although technically they do not constitute a lobby. Most generally, their counsel to the Director exhorts him to return to "true national park standards," from which, one would gather, the Park Service always seems about to be departing.

"Conservationists and the lovers of our national parks in general are becoming increasingly apprehensive about the trend toward some national parks becoming recreational resorts." Thus spoke the National Parks Association back in 1958, and on this theme it has spoken for much of its history. Founded in 1919, "To defend the National Parks and Monuments fearlessly against assaults of private interests and aggressive commercialism," the National Parks Association is the only conservation organization formed primarily to protect, or guide, the national parks. To show its broader concern, it recently adopted a new title, National Parks and Conservation Association.

The National Aububon Society, whose beginnings go back to the saving of Everglades rookeries from plume hunters shortly after 1900, has worked for the establishment of wildlife refuges and the adoption of migratory-bird treaties with Mexico and Canada. It is also one of the few conservation agencies that manage lands, maintaining more than 1 million acres for rare bird species. The Izaak Walton League works for a variety of wildlife and natural resource projects, as well as piscatorial matters. Both organizations have strong interests in national park management.

The plea of Aldo Leopold that remote wild areas throughout the country be preserved was the rallying cry of those who founded the Wilderness Society in 1934. In keeping with its founding philosophy, the society holds to the belief that as much of the national parks as possible should be kept in absolutely primeval condition, and that management of park wilderness so that it is used and experienced on its own terms constitutes the true purpose of a national park.

Each of the considerable number of organizations involved has a somewhat different purpose and attracts membership with different interests. The National Resources Council of America is an affiliation of some sixty individual organizations, which helps consolidate member influence and conducts studies in the public interest on such projects as the proposed Rampart Dam in Alaska and the recommendations of the Public Land Law Review Commission. The Nature Conservancy is almost exclusively involved in locating and acquiring small tracts, primarily in emergency cases where the land can later be turned over to land-managing agencies, such as the Park Service. The Wildlife Management Institute, which is concerned with research and the training of wildlife managers, and the National Wildlife Federation, which coordinates the work of local sportsmen's groups, represent specialized interests.

The Conservation Foundation serves the cause, in part, by raising funds to conduct studies of various conservation matters, including projects in other countries. It sponsored the recent survey "Man and Nature in the National Parks," which suggested there is too much of the former at the expense of the latter. When the National Parks Centennial Commission decided to conduct a public dialogue as a part of its program of preparing a long-range plan for the national parks, the Conservation Foundation was chosen to direct the symposium.

These organizations are headed by some of the truly great figures of the conservation movement. To them the Secretary of the Interior and the Director of the Park Service frequently turn for advice and assistance, and from their ranks have selected members of special committees and task forces to examine troublesome areas of policy. Congress looks to these leaders for advice when considering important new legislation, and many have made distinguished contributions. The late Howard Zahniser was more than any other person responsible for passage of the Wilderness Act. That eloquent poet and guide from the North Country, Sigurd Olson, has served as a personal adviser to the directors of the Park Service on matters of wilderness preservation for many years. No other man understands better the wilderness of North America, and no other writer has described its beauty in finer prose.

If the voices of the more impassioned conservationists were less strident and they were less positive of their own infallibility, their pronouncements might receive even greater heed. The difference between the Park Service and the conservationists is, according to the scholarly study of the parks by John Ise, "the difference between men who have a practical job to do, in getting new parks, in making the parks accessible to the public, in making friends for them, and in protecting them from the invasion of commercial interests, on the one hand, and on the other hand men of fine idealism who do not have these responsibilities."

All conservation organizations, some to a greater degree than others, support or seek to defeat park and environmental legislation pending before the Congress. Legally they can do so only as an "educational" activity, a nice distinction, which in some fashion is different from lobbying. If guilty of lobbying to influence legislation, a conservation organization could lose its tax-exempt status, a generally mortal blow. By placing full-page advertisements in major newspapers that condemned a bill to dam the Colorado River at Grand Canyon and urging readers to make similar expressions known to their congressmen, the Sierra Club lost its tax-exempt status—but has since prospered from a substantial increase in membership.

The Sierra Club, founded by John Muir in 1892 to promote the welfare of Yosemite National Park, is probably the best known of all the conservation groups, and an enormous debt is owed the Sierra Club by the Park Service. In the words of one assistant secretary of the Interior, the Park Service has "no stauncher friend, no more useful critic." When, during World War I, the Secretary of the Interior was seized by a patriotic spasm and ordered 50,000 sheep to be grazed in Yosemite, he cut off the Director's protests by declaring: "This is war!" Reflecting a moment upon the awesome decision, he added, "But don't let the Sierra Club find out."

"Finding out" is what the conservationists do best, as was the case in the Chesapeake and Ohio (C&O) canal episode.

In January, 1954, the *Washington Post* commented editorially on a bill before Congress that would authorize the National Park Service to acquire land along the C&O canal for construction of a scenic parkway. Operations had been suspended in the 1920's on the historic canal, founded by George Washington in 1784, which provided a water route for commerce between Washington and Cumberland, Maryland, a distance of 185 miles. The Park Service, in cooperation with the Bureau of Public Roads, had prepared the parkway plan, which would utilize the towpath and at times the bed of the canal itself for the right of way.

With the best of intentions and for purposes wholly laudable, the Park Service occasionally courts difficulties when it seeks to make available to many an experience being restricted to only a few. This is the over-all philosophy of national parks; it also generates a majority of the conflicts between the Park Service and the conservation community. A parkway, predicted the *Post*, would "stir the enthusiasm" of most intelligent citizens, for "the lovely Potomac Valley could thus be made available." Rather than destroying natural and scenic values, a reservation being expressed here and there, the roadway "would enable more people to enjoy beauties now seen by very few."

Justice of the Supreme Court William O. Douglas, never noticeably restrained by judicial decorum when expressing himself on conservation matters, quickly placed himself in the camp of those who regarded the parkway as a disaster. A lifelong wilderness enthusiast and conservationist, Douglas replied to the *Post* editors, challenging them to get up out of their swivel chairs and join him on a hike along the length of the canal, predicting the trek might help them appreciate the true value of the canal: "It is a refuge," he wrote, "a place of retreat, a long stretch of quiet and peace at the Capitol's back door."

A few months later Douglas, the two *Post* editors, and some forty other citizens set out bravely from Cumberland for the eight-day ordeal. The duel between the Supreme Court and the Fourth Estate captivated the nation's capital, where newspaper editors customarily regard themselves less accountable than members of the High Court. The hike along the towpath generated nationwide interest and the predominant sympathy was for Douglas, one man trying to buck the system.

Only nine of the originals were around at the finish, but

nearly fifty thousand well-wishers were on hand for what turned into a victory celebration. After tending to their blisters, the game *Post* editors concluded that the Park Service plan should be substantially modified, and it was. Justice Douglas and those interested in preserving the splendor of the Potomac Valley formed the C&O Canal Association, and the organization, led by Justice Douglas, had to make a ceremonial march along the towpath every year from 1954 to 1970 before the passage of a park bill, for which they could take considerable personal satisfaction. By then the original idea of building a parkway had long since been abandoned.

XIII
Yellowstone's Children

The distinguished American student of conservation history Roderick Nash, dissatisfied with an effort to list American contributions to world civilization (the spirit of philanthropy and the public school, among others), spoke out in a recent essay on behalf of one distinctive American contribution omitted from the list—the national park. Establishment of Yellowstone National Park was the first instance in world history of preserving a great tract of unspoiled landscape for public use.

Nash comments in "The American Invention of National Parks" that, since Yellowstone, "we have exported the national park idea around the world. We are known and admired for it, fittingly, because the concept of a national park reflects some of the central values and experiences in American culture." In the century since Yellowstone was created, more than 1,200 national parks or equivalent preserves in almost one hundred countries have been set aside, and they have been fittingly called "Yellowstone's children."

The United States pioneered the national park movement for a number of reasons, the first of which was largely an accident of history. Because the country was settled from east to west, it happened that a modern culture existed along the eastern seaboard while vast tracts of unexplored wilderness existed in the West, even throughout most of the nineteenth century. Among the city dwellers who occasionally sampled the wild country, there began to develop a strong sentiment for preserving nature, and this group began to voice its regret over the passing of wilderness from the American scene.

Another reason for the park movement developing in the United States was the wealth and extent of the country's natural resources. Few nations could have afforded either the costs of taking so much land out of production or the expense of providing facilities and services. Nations struggling at subsistence levels had other priorities to meet.

The final important factor was the presence in the United States of a democratic political tradition. In many cultures, the practice of protecting tracts of land in their natural state could be traced back for thousands of years, and preserving game in the royal preserve was an English tradition. But the great estates were maintained to protect the land from, not for, the people.

Well before Yellowstone was established, Henry David Thoreau observed that the kings of England had even destroyed entire villages to protect the king's game, a practice fine for the wildlife but tough on the people. In the United States, Thoreau concluded, "we who have renounced the king's authority" should have our national preserves where wildlife is protected, yet "not to hold the king's game merely, but to hold and preserve the king himself." In a democracy, the king was, of course, the people, and the national preserves contemplated by Thoreau became the national parks.

It would be a disservice to the world park movement, however, and to the contributions that many nations made to the development of the national park idea to suggest that other countries simply copied the American experiment. Yellowstone did provide a stimulus; "the seedling sown in Wyoming was transported to flourish in both islands of New Zealand," reported a park service administrator from down under. But it was primarily an idea that made a timely appearance, as nations began to concern themselves with the need to preserve a part of their natural and cultural heritage.

The emerging concept of conservation in the United States during the latter part of the nineteenth century owed much to European influences. Carl Schurz, who, as Secretary of the Interior in 1877, first proposed a system of national forests, was born in Germany and knew from his observations in Europe the value of professional forestry methods in checking erosion and maintaining watersheds. Because professional training in forestry was unavailable in the United States, Gifford Pinchot enrolled at the French Forestry School in Nancy, where he studied under an Englishman responsible for forestry developments in British India.

AMERICAN AID

It is, however, to the United States that many nations turn for advice and assistance on park matters, particularly developing nations that are only beginning to establish national parks. An almost constant flow of park administrators come to observe park operations and to discuss mutual problems. Some attend sessions at the training centers in Grand Canyon and Harpers Ferry. Others are detailed as observers to a national park or to the regional or Washington office staffs. Most travel widely throughout the park offices, and one tends to encounter park visitors from far-off lands almost as a part of the daily office routine.

Park Service people have found, to their advantage, that while supposedly giving advice, they have the opportunity to learn quite as much as the trainees. Generally unable to approach funding levels available to manage the American parks, park people from other countries are no less committed to national park ideas. Nor do they fail to point out, politely, gaps that seem to exist in American parks between the philosophy preached and the actual practice.

An effective means of exchanging ideas among park people is the International Seminar on the Administration of National Parks and Equivalent Reserves, better known as the "Short Course." Held each summer since 1965, it brings to the United States about thirty representatives (a busload) for a course of study at a selected university and an extensive tour of American and Canadian national parks. Jointly sponsored by the University of Michigan, the National Parks Service of Canada, and the U.S. National Park Service, and supported by the Conservation Foundation, the seminar has been attended by more than 200 participants from seventy countries.

It is physically impossible for the Park Service to keep pace with the demand from overseas for American expertise in the field of park planning and development. Every year teams and individuals are sent to various countries on assignments that may vary from technical assistance on a specific problem, to the development of a master plan for a national park, to the planning of an entire national park system. A good many career Park Service people have the opportunity for travel assignments of one kind or another, and in the last decade the Park Service has sent off close to fifty delegations to some twenty-five countries.

The following account of the intercontinental wanderings of one Park Service planning team, although certainly not typical, does suggest the flavor of those assignments. As it journeyed from country to country, it not only threatened to match the legendary odyssey of Ulysses returning from the Trojan War but, with an admirable flair for drama, ended up planning a national park for the site of Troy.

The adventure began in 1966 when the Park Service sent an adviser and a team of twelve professional employees—engineer, architect, landscape architect, archeologist, museum curator, and seven other specialists—to the Royal Hashemite Kingdom of Jordan. Supported by funds from the Agency for International Development, their assignment was to prepare master plans for several proposed national parks, to train counterparts who would participate in the planning and eventually administer the parks, and to advise the government of Jordan on park matters. At the same time, the head of the proposed Jordanian park system came to the United States for one year of training with the National Park Service at all levels of the organization.

When the Arab-Israeli War broke out in June, 1967, members of the team were in the war zone, and some were reluctant observers of the hostilities. Suspecting that peace in the region would be a long time coming, the Park Service evacuated families to Greece. Providentially a request came from the government of Iran, and the team did a short stint of park work there before moving on to Athens, laying groundwork that resulted in a later request for park planning aid from the Greek government.

Accepting an invitation from Turkey to develop a master plan for Goreme National Park, the team (which understandably was growing smaller with each migration) moved to Ankara, but with the cooling of the scene in the Middle East and the adjournment of hostilities, the team returned to Jordan and completed its assigned project by the end of 1968.

In early 1969, now reduced to four members, the team set up headquarters in Turkey, to plan and design eleven new national park areas and to train counterparts for eventual administration of the parks. Enriched by the experience of working in four countries on two continents, the team finally returned to the United States in late 1971.

WORLD RECOGNITION

Inevitably, as the national park movement began to take root in many countries, the need for international action was recognized, and support was generated toward developing a world organization that could promote nature conservation and serve both as a clearinghouse for information and a source of aid to countries wishing to establish national parks. Largely through the efforts of Dr. Paul Sarasin, founder of the Swiss National Park, an International Conference for the Protection of Nature was held in Basel in 1913, and agreement was reached among participating nations from Europe, Asia, and North America to establish an international commission.

World War I intervened, and in its shattering aftermath efforts to activate the commission failed. Finally, through the initiative of the Netherlands, an International Office for the Protection of Nature was established at Brussels in 1928. Its activities were severely limited and ended with the outbreak of World War II. Switzerland again took the initiative after the war, and with the support of France and the newly created Economic and Social Council of the United Nations (UNESCO), a conference was held at Fontainebleau in 1948. There the International Union for Conservation of Nature and Natural Resources (IUCN) was founded.

The IUCN has become the voice, and often the instrument, for worldwide action on environmental matters. One of its major objectives is to encourage establishment of national parks, preserves, and wildlife sanctuaries. More than seventy countries are represented in its membership, comprised of sovereign states, governmental and private organizations, and international groups.

At the 1958 IUCN General Assembly held in Athens, the International Commission on National Parks was constituted to promote the worldwide park movement. There were no established criteria to identify, among the many kinds and types of reservations throughout the world, those which qualified as national parks. What was needed was a recognized standard toward which all nations could work. In 1959, endorsing the national park concept as a contribution "to the inspiration, culture and welfare of mankind," the United Nations requested IUCN to develop a World List of national parks and equivalent reserves.

The World List, entitled *United Nations List of National Parks and Equivalent Reserves* and now in its second edition (1967), accepts 1,204 national parks and equivalent reserves from ninety-three countries; these selected areas encompass more than 230 million acres and approach an impressive 1 per cent of the land surface of the earth. Africa leads all continents, with 41 per cent of the total acreage, North America (north of the Rio Grande) has 38 per cent, Asia contains 8 per cent (of which Russia accounts for 3 per cent), Central and South America have 5 per cent, Oceania has 4 per cent (with 2 per cent in New Zealand), and Europe 3 per cent. The United States has 25 per cent of the total acreage, followed by Canada with 10 per cent.

Two types of areas are included on the World List, "National Parks" and "Equivalent Reserves." To qualify as a National Park, the area must have been established by the central government, which in turn guarantees three basic considerations are fulfilled: (1) that legal protection is provided against all exploitation of the resources, including hunting, agriculture, stock grazing, lumbering, or mining; (2) that, if the population of the country is less than fifty people to the square kilometer, the minimum size must be 5,000 acres, and, if more than fifty people, the selected area must contain 1,250 acres; and (3) that the area is adequately staffed and funded to maintain and protect the resources. Additionally, the governing authority must permit or provide facilities for visitor use and enjoyment, declared to be one of the major reasons for the existence of national parks.

To qualify for inclusion on the World List as an Equivalent Reserve, the area must also meet the above three considerations. It is classified as a Strict Natural Reserve if visitor use is not permitted; it is classified as a State Park or a Provincial, Cantonal, or other Local Authority Reserve if the area is not under the jurisdiction of the central government authority; it is classified as a Private Reserve if the area is administered by a nongovernmental organization.

In the following section there is a brief description of the status of national parks in countries around the world. The World List has served as the official reference for this. Understandably, the difficult task of assembling the World List was complicated by lack of data and incomplete information submitted. Areas that some nations have designated as "National Parks" are omitted from the World List, because they do not meet the criteria. A future edition will bring the World List up to date and include the many areas newly established.

Hopefully it is not too chauvinistic to observe, as an introduction to reviewing the world park movement, that the remarkable record of the United States in the field of conservation is often overlooked these days. As the face of a once beautiful land is ravaged by that depressing cluster of roadside culture best described as "neon guano," there is a tendency to emphasize what has been destroyed. One can also take considerable pride in what has been saved.

In his recent book, *The Environmental Revolution*, the British writer and conservationist Max Nicholson suggests that if one is looking for the origin of the world conservation movement, he should look to the United States before 1900, when an able group of scientific and professional leaders were urging the federal government to assume responsibility for solving resource problems in the national interest. From this agitation emerged a number of strong federal conservation agencies, including the present Forest Service, the Bureau of Sport Fisheries and Wildlife, and the National Park Service. Nicholson concludes, "All these developments in the United States during the three closing decades of the nineteenth century may be said, for the first time in any country, to have put conservation on the map as a serious public issue."

A glance at the United States entries on the World List reveals the extent of nature preservation in this country by many different federal, state, and private organizations, on a scale unmatched elsewhere. So many American national parks and equivalent reserves are included (284) that the customary descriptive data could not be included. To a person reasonably well acquainted with preserves in the United States, it would seem that in order not to engulf the world inventory, selection was made on a somewhat representational basis.

It is also significant that only about one-third of the U.S. entries on the World List are areas administered by the National Park Service. Something over one-third are made up of "wilderness," "wild," and "primitive" areas from the Forest Service, these being generally free from roads or commercial intrusions, in which hunting and grazing is regulated and whose natural values are of the highest quality.

Twenty wildlife refuges, administered by Interior's Bureau of Sport Fisheries and Wildlife, are recognized on the World List. Many of these preserves, while not selected for their scenery, have national park qualities. At more than 8 million acres, roughly the size of Massachusetts, the Arctic National Wildlife Refuge in Alaska is the largest single preserve in the world.

The World List also includes eighty-nine state parks, and again one is impelled to suggest this is a representational selection. Some state park systems are administered with exemplary professionalism and fiscal support (although some are not) and would rival the national park systems of some countries. Also included on the World List are a few areas administered by the National Audubon Society, the Nature Conservancy, and the Smithsonian Institution.

It would be unrealistic, however, to attempt to compare the national parks of other countries with those of the United States, for each country has of necessity responded according to its own opportunities and its own capacities. Densely populated nations do not have large unpopulated tracts of land available, and land is often the most precious of all commodities. Only in an affluent but sparsely settled country such as Canada is the American-type park possible. The great wildlife parks of Africa, on the other hand, are far larger than any of the American parks.

Many countries believe that the most important natural areas should be reserved for scientific study, and that their resources would be damaged by the freedom that visitors are allowed in national parks. They have developed a system of Strict Nature Reserves, in which total protection is enforced and the public is excluded. "The ban on visitors to Strict Natural Reserves is in effect waived for naturalists engaged in research," is a typical observation of the World List. A small country such as Belgium, which has no national parks, has National Nature Reserves in which grazing, hunting, or fishing is not permitted and original conditions are being restored. England in its nature reserves, Poland and Argentina in their national parks, and Germany in its *Naturschutz* parks probably carry out more scientific research than is done in the American parks.

Canada and Latin America

Among all countries Canada, whose geography and frontier history parallel those of her neighbor to the south, comes closest to the United States in the development and operation of its national park system. It was the first to follow the American example, with almost an identical beginning. Construction workers pushing the Canadian Pacific Railroad through the Canadian Rockies in 1885 came upon a cluster of hot mineral springs much as had the 1870 Yellowstone Expedition. Although some of the men filed claims, in the hope of future profits from the tourist trade, the Canadian Government followed the American example and reserved the springs from sale or settlement.

In 1887, the Rocky Mountain Parks Act enlarged the Banff reservation to include mountain scenery, with wording almost identical to that of the Yellowstone Act of fifteen years earlier. Canada established "a public park and pleasure ground for the benefit, advantage and enjoyment of the people." The American version set aside "a public park or pleasuring ground for the benefit and enjoyment of the people."

In 1911, Canada's Dominion Forest Reserves and Parks Act was passed by Parliament, which authorized establishment of a Park Service organization even before its U.S. equivalent was created in 1916 and was, in fact, an argument used in the congressional debates on the American bill.

Canada has kept pace comfortably with the United States in park matters, establishing its first historical park in 1917, well before the first U.S. historical one was authorized in 1930. At latest count, there were twenty national parks totaling nearly 19 million acres, some of which are far larger than the biggest U.S. parks. Many Canadian parks are as heavily used by Americans as by Canadians, with such spectacular destinations as Banff National Park particularly popular. In 1932, the Waterton-Glacier International Peace Park was created, authorized by the Canadian Parliament and the United States Congress. A truly international park was established in 1964 at Campobello Island, New Brunswick, the summer home of Franklin D. Roosevelt and the place where he contracted polio. The Canadian and American park systems equally share operating costs and management direction.

Canada has organizationally separated its national parks and historical sites, with both administered by the National and Historic Parks Branch of the Department of Indian Affairs and Northern Development. Canada's provinces also administer extensive park systems, with some of the extremely large provincial parks well worthy of national park status. British Columbia and Ontario, for example, have established some 400 provincial parks.

With the exception of but a few countries, such as Argentina, the Latin American nations have not yet built extensive national park systems, and many countries have no national parks. The obstacles are formidable: promising areas are often inaccessible and rarely visited; economic difficulties have placed developments required for national parks in low priority; a particularly complex land ownership pattern offers additional difficulties in acquiring parklands, with private property, licensed and unlicensed villages, farmlands and other forms of ownership offering extreme legal complications.

Typical of many countries, the generosity and vision of one man, Dr. Francis P. Moreno, helped stimulate the park movement in Argentina. He was bequeathed eighteen thousand acres from the government as a reward for his contribution to the exploration of the Patagonia Cordillera. Dr. Moreno gave the land back to the government for a national park in 1903, declaring that protection of such lands was an excellent tool of human progress, "for the greater benefit of present and future generations, thus following the example of the U.S.A. and of other nations who own superb national parks." Later enlarged and established as a national park in 1922, it is one of a dozen national parks in Argentina, many of which are extremely large and well protected.

Europe

The comparatively tiny but heavily populated continent of Europe, with its incomparable cultural heritage, has had a long and sophisticated tradition of living with the land. For a great many centuries, a skilled and hard-working peasantry has converted natural ecosystems into parklike settings, and the national park concept has been shaped by this tradition.

Almost all European parks and reserves were established long after original vegetation and wildlife had been considerably altered or even destroyed by many centuries of cultivation, and they represent only a fraction of the original habitats of the continent. But while some lack spectacular scenery and wildlife populations, their unique value is the display of living landscapes characteristic of large areas of Europe.

Although one could scarcely overlook the Commons Open Spaces and Footpaths Preservation Society, founded in 1865, the beginnings of a program to acquire parklands and historic sites in Britain came with the creation in 1895 of the National Trust for Places of Historic Interest or Natural Beauty, suggested by a slightly earlier Massachusetts organization with a similar title.

Great Britain has one of the most pleasant, if artificial, countrysides in the world, and one of its leading conservationists remarked how extraordinary it seemed "that with so many parson naturalists in England the national park idea did not originate there." But proceeding with that deliberate caution that has so often saved the British Empire from temerity, a National Parks Act was not passed until 1949. Picking up speed, Britain has since established ten national parks, none of which is less than 100,000 acres in size, the ten totaling 3.25 million acres, a remarkably extensive system, except that most of the land within the limits of the designated park is privately owned.

Although it contains many towns and even industrial sites, Britain's park system strikes a compromise. The national parks are so designated because of their outstanding natural beauty and are protected by the designation against further destruction by industrialization or haphazard urbanization. None of England's parks meet the criteria of the World List, which notes that these parks "from a social point of view have a considerable importance"—a monumental under-statement. In a country inhabited for more than four thou-sand years, with little publicly owned land and with trespass forbidden in most privately owned areas, the British national park constitutes a magnificent contribution to the conserva-tion of the English countryside. Widely used and enjoyed by the British people, its unique flavor has been perfectly described as "a thinly inhabited region where the natural scenery is safeguarded for amenity and recreation."

Of the many species of native mammals inhabiting Europe's Alps, the elk, deer, wild horse, beaver, wolf, and bear had all been exterminated during the seventeenth and eighteenth centuries. Among the few that barely escaped extinction but were severely threatened are the ibex and the chamois. The movement to preserve these species helped create national parks in several countries.

Long a Royal Hunting Reserve of the Kings of Italy, Gran Paradiso in the Italian Alps was established as a national park in 1922 by King Victor Emmanuel to save the few remaining ibex. One of the three French national parks ad-joins Gran Paradiso and was also established to protect the ibex. France has twenty-seven additional Reserves included on the World List, quite a few of which contain dubious encroachments, but as the World List delicately explains, "it has been necessary to waive in some degree the criterion requirements laid down by the International Commission on National Parks, in order to fit in with the peculiar circum-stances obtaining in France, a country in which the distribu-tion of habitats and of private ownership of land is of ancient origin and highly diverse."

The whole of Switzerland, that dazzling gift of the Alps, might almost be classified as a national park. Its high Alpine valleys, cool climate, and poor soil have preserved the natural setting from agriculture and compelled a commitment to livestock grazing. The Swiss ecology, happily, has produced an unspoiled landscape, *Heidi,* and Swiss cheese. Swiss National Park, the country's only such preserve, is well known for strictly regulating visitor-use patterns. One of the two Reserves included on the World List is the Forest of Derborence, only 120 acres, but the last virgin forest remaining in Switzerland.

The small countries of Austria, Denmark, Belgium, and the Netherlands, with relatively large populations for their size, have no national parks, but each has made great effort to preserve remaining natural areas. With much of its land reclaimed from the sea, Holland demonstrates an utterly flat landscape that could not exist without man, yet it has eighteen Reserves on the World List.

As a United Nations document, the World List does not include nonmember nations such as East Germany, which contains numerous and well-managed reserves. Within West Germany's federally owned lands, agriculture, forest production, hunting, and fishing are all practiced according to scientifically established principles, and none qualifies for inclusion in the World List.

Poland has a long tradition of conserving natural resources, and has eleven national parks, one of which contains the largest virgin forest in Central Europe as well as the only remaining herd of European bison. The Tatra National Park in the Carpathians is one of the best examples of an international national park, with both Poland and Czechoslovakia protecting their respective parts of the Tatra Mountains by adjoining national parks. Joint scientific efforts have been carried out since 1924; the Czech park, High Tatra, has well-developed accommodations, campgrounds, and trails;

the Polish park, Tatras, serves 1.5 million visitors a year.

Since 1909, Sweden has maintained the largest natural preserves on the European continent, and in 1962, when it established its sixteenth national park, of nearly 500,000 acres, it was the largest in the Swedish national park system. Contiguous with two other national parks, a bird sanctuary and a forest preserve, the complex covers more than 2 million acres and forms a conservation area larger than any on the continent—a land of forbidding mountains, glaciers, and moraines, with Alpine vegetation above the tree line among the most beautiful in the world.

ASIA

Many Asian countries have enormous populations and a long history of settlement and cultivation, with the result that there are no wildlife concentrations of the kinds found in Africa and few inhabitable places where natural scenery exists in its original condition, excluding such remote regions as the mighty Himalayas. The density of population and economic scarcity are serious obstacles to the development of national parks. India's situation is typical, for the primary need to improve the nation's standard of living has made it extremely difficult for India to provide the high degree of protection required for national park status, although five national parks are included on the World List.

As a result of American occupation of the Philippines, a law was enacted in 1932 providing for the establishment of national parks, since extended by the Republic Act of 1953. Twenty-three national parks have been established, and several preserve sites of Philippine history, including Bataan National Park, scene of the surrender of American-Philippine troops to Japan in 1942.

Reserves had been initiated in Russia shortly before the Revolution, but the present legal basis for Nature Reserves was laid down in 1924 by the Presidium of the Central Executive Committee of the U.S.S.R., which defined protected areas as "those portions of the national soil which are forever made subject to total protection and removal from all economic exploitation." Russia has fifty-one Reserves on the World List, in both Europe and Asia, the largest approaching 2 million acres, and there is a current proposal to establish Russia's first national park in the vicinity of Lake Baikal, which will cover 3 million acres.

The most extensive and highly developed national park system in Asia is that of Japan. Compared to her Asiatic neighbors, Japan is a tiny country, with a population exceeding 250 people per square kilometer. As a result, one of the characteristics of the Japanese national park is that it generally includes cities, towns, or villages, as well as agricultural or forestry lands.

The Japanese parks are an integral part of the native's social life and are much more extensively used than the American parks. Mt. Fuji alone receives some 25 million visitors a year, almost half the number of visitors to all of the national parks in the United States. Because of the exceptional way in which Japan has sought to achieve protection of its limited natural resources while providing for maximum public enjoyment, the twenty-three national parks were judged accordingly and included on the World List, although not meeting the "total protection" standard. Had the criteria been strictly enforced, it "would have had the effect of giving a quite false idea of the vast, coherent and praiseworthy efforts of the Japanese authorities towards 'the protection of places of scenic beauty and also, through the promoted utilization thereof, a contribution to the health, recreation, and culture of the people.' "

AFRICA

On the endless plains of Africa are found the significant remnants of that community of plains animals and peoples which, during the Pleistocene era, existed in one version or another throughout the grasslands of the world. In North America, the wolf, the bison, and the grizzly bear have almost vanished, and the native Indian has been driven from his ancestral lands. In East Africa, great bands of wildlife coexist with native populations and their domestic herds, living out their lives in a manner little changed over the centuries.

Africa's Sahara is a more effective barrier to the spread of plants and animals—and man—than the oceans. East and south of the great desert region more than sixty national parks and preserves provide a permanent sanctuary for the vast herds of African wildlife, easily the most spectacular and diverse animal populations left on earth.

A typical description from the World List of one such preserve (Dinder National Park in Sudan) suggests the diversity: "Giraffe, hartebeest, reedbuck, roan antelope, bushbuck, oribi, waterbuck, greater kudu, several species of gazelle, dik-dik, buffalo, lion, ostrich. Black rhinoceros, leopard, cheetah, elephant (during rains), hyaenas [sic] and jackal also recorded." The Director of the National Parks of Kenya has observed, "A journey across the Serengeti measures up to the historical descriptions of Africa in the last century."

In 1919, King Albert of Belgium visited a number of national parks in the United States, and in the course of his journey met in Yellowstone with two noted American zoologists, Fairfield Osborne, who had been on Stephen Mather's first mountain trip in 1915, and John C. Merriam, along with Victor van Straelen, who was to become one of the leading figures of the world park movement. Out of the discussions came an active plan to protect the vast herds of wildlife in Africa and to use such reserves for scientific studies.

Hunters were already threatening to exterminate the gorilla, and in 1925 Albert National Park, in the then Belgian Congo, was established as the first national park in Africa and the first park anywhere devoted to systematic scientific research. Now containing almost 6 million acres, it is three times the size of Yellowstone.

An even earlier effort to preserve African wildlife came from the legendary Boer leader, and later President of the Transvaal Republic, Oom Paul Kruger, who set aside the Sabie Game Reserve in 1892. With the help of Europeans who foresaw the extermination of South African wildlife, Kruger National Park was established in 1926, now the third largest national park in the world.

Growing concern over the plight of African wildlife culminated in the London Conference for the Protection of African Fauna and Flora held in 1933. Out of the conference came some of the great national parks of eastern and central Africa, but the conference also helped stimulate creation of national parks elsewhere in the world, and many countries establishing national parks after 1933 followed the criteria laid down by the London Conference.

A factor in the development of the African parks was the inconceivable numbers of animals killed by hunters and poachers, who killed for food, for hides and skin, and to supply the Far East with rhinoceros horn, a popular and presumably well-tested aphrodisiac. Using poisoned arrows, snares, and pits, native poachers took a terrible toll. One park administrator estimated that before strict measures effectively reduced poaching some 150,000 large animals were being killed each year in Kenya.

A director of one of the East African national park systems has pointed out that parks in his country had begun as nature sanctuaries, where people were allowed only "on sufferance." Now, however, the objective is to encourage as many people as possible to visit the parks. The result, he noted, would not be the flood of visitors which many countries have: "Our problem is the converse—and will remain so for generations: how to get sufficient visitors into the parks to make them a viable part of the country's economy."

Recognition that the game populations of Africa constitute a world resource helped create the early movement for national parks during the colonial era of African history. But the legendary Great White Hunters, whom Hemingway reported—or created—have almost disappeared. On the modern safari the rifle has been largely replaced by the long-lens camera and the spotting scope. Travel agencies in many countries book African wildlife tours, and national parks have become a major factor in providing much-needed foreign exchange.

The scenic beauty of Africa is less well known outside the continent, although those familiar with its snow-capped mountains, mighty river systems, and breathtaking waterfalls believe African landscapes the equal of any continent. A number of significant geologic features are preserved by national parks. Victoria Falls, one of nine national parks in Rhodesia, contains the mile-wide cataract on the Zambesi River that plunges nearly 350 feet. Mt. Kilimanjaro, highest mountain in Africa (19,340 feet), is now a game reserve, which Tanzania is planning to establish as a national park.

Agonizing decisions will soon have to be made, however, to determine whether the need for economic growth outweighs the values of protecting Africa's natural heritage. With most of the African nations seeking to improve the standard of living of their people, Africa possesses more than a third of all the potential water power in the world, only a tiny portion of which has been used to generate electricity. A current proposal to dam the great cataract in Uganda where the Victoria Nile roars through a narrow rock gap over a 140 foot precipice has created world attention. Whether Murchison Falls National Park will be destroyed by the dam project in part rests with the World Bank, target of strong pressure from world conservation organizations.

Despite the obvious differences between the social and economic patterns of Africa and of the United States, the problems facing their national park administrations are remarkably similar. During a recent visit of an official of the South African park system, who was in the United States to observe the American parks, he put the following questions: "The young people seem to show little interest in our traditional interpretive programs; how can you reach them? Is it best to build visitor facilities within the park or keep them outside? When should the number of visitors to a park be restricted, and how?" The discussion could well have been about Yellowstone instead of Kruger National Park.

AUSTRALIA AND NEW ZEALAND

As befitting a sparsely populated land with endless space, Australia has an impressive number of parks and preserves. Each of its six mainland states and the island of Tasmania has established its own national park system, with seventy-two areas accepted on the U.N. World List. Administration of the parks is provided by a special National Park Board made up of local officials and residents, assisted by conservation organizations, an intriguing departure from the usual reliance on central control.

There are a great many lesser parks and preserves administered by the states. Western Australia has more than 450 nature reserves and Queensland, with twenty-five national parks on the World List, has also designated some seventy-five "National Parks" of over 1,000 acres (presumably the equivalent of American state parks) and several hundred "scenic areas" of less than 1,000 acres.

Australia needs its preserves, for perhaps no other country in the world has suffered such devastation from the introduction of exotic animals. Rabbit, domestic cat, European fox, rat, mouse, and wild dog (dingo)—their populations have exploded until they have threatened the national economy and rendered marsupial species almost extinct.

New Zealand calls to mind splendid mountain landscapes of glaciers, lakes, and waterfalls, heavy forests, and Alpine meadows. In the opinion of some, its park system rivals the American system. It began in 1887 when a Maori chief, concerned that his tribe's holy places in the mountains be protected, gave them to Queen Victoria as "a sacred place of the crown and a gift forever from me and my people." The Maori lands were included when Tongariro National Park, the first in New Zealand, was established in 1894. All are effectively managed and protected, although both sport fishing and hunting have become traditional activities, and some exotic species have been introduced, including wallabies from Australia. Not included on the World List are more than 1,000 scenic reserves and historic sites, which are managed by the National Parks Authority.

1972: THE CENTENNIAL YEAR

At the conclusion of the First World Conference on National Parks held in Seattle in 1962, the delegates noted that the centennial of Yellowstone would occur in 1972. A resolution was adopted, recommending that, because Yellowstone "created widespread response throughout the world," the centennial should be properly celebrated by "a conference to be held in Yellowstone Park and attended by representatives of all countries."

Two other major international conferences, with purposes closely related to the Yellowstone conference, were scheduled for 1972. In June, the United National Conference on the Human Environment in Stockholm was to bring together delegates from 130 member nations. The Canadian, Maurice Strong, as Secretary General, has declared the environment "the most international of all the great issues facing the world today." One of the proposals on the agenda is a World Heritage Trust, which would obligate nations to protect environmentally critical areas of the world such as Angkor Wat, Murchison Falls, and the Florida Everglades, along with endangered wildlife.

The International Union for Conservation of Nature and Natural Resources was scheduled to hold its triennial General Assembly at Banff National Park, in Canada, the week prior to the Yellowstone Conference. The second World Conference on National Parks was to be held in Grand Teton and Yellowstone National Parks in September, where more than five hundred delegates were to exchange ideas and to discuss the ultimate problems of park conservation to be faced during the second century of the park movement. A National Parks Centennial Commission, authorized by Congress and headed by California publisher and conservationist William L. Lane, was to coordinate the commemorative activities scheduled throughout the centennial year.

XIV

A Look at the Future

The greatest challenge facing the nation as it prepares to celebrate its two-hundredth anniversay in 1976 is the creation of a truly livable society, one that reveres all life, respects natural processes, strives to improve the quality of life for each citizen, and places human values above all others. Looking to the second century of national parks, which begins in 1972, the challenge to the leadership of the National Park Service is to consider its task not only one of park tending and of serving as stewards of land, scenery, wilderness, and history, but also of managing parks in a way that expresses a compassion for human values.

The decade of the 1960's has been termed a conservation decade. During those years the annual reports of the Department of the Interior, bearing such titles as *Quest for Quality, Population Challenge, Man: An Endangered Species,* expressed the growing suspicion that something had gone wrong with traditional patterns involving man and his natural world. A special report to the Senate Interior and Insular Affairs Committee, entitled "A National Policy for the Environment," suggested that achieving environmental sanity would involve moral standards:

If it is ethical for man to value his chances for survival, to hope
for a decent life for his descendants, to respect the value that
other men place upon their lives, and to want to obtain the best
that life has to offer without prejudicing equal opportunities
for others, then the cornerstone of environmental policy is
ethical.

Young people particularly are sensitive to the basic issues
of materialism vs. nonmaterialism and the protection of
natural values from economic exploitation. They are also
unwilling to accept established social patterns as predestined,
and on college campuses—and in national parks—have given
notice that the decade of the 1970's may be remembered as
one of conservation confrontations.

A number of subcultures have made up the customary
pattern of park visitors: families, always the largest single
unit, along with campers, tour groups, backpackers, retired
couples. To these have been added in recent years a new
subgroup, variously identified as "flower children," "long
hairs," or "earth people," "bikers" of the motorcycle brotherhood, and the political "revolutionaries." On the first travel
holiday weekend of the first year of the new decade, representatives of these countercultures triggered the first civil riot
within a national park.

AN INCIDENT IN YOSEMITE

On July 3, 1970, several hundred young people who had
been gathering in Yosemite for some weeks congregated in
Stoneman's Meadow, a flat, grassy stretch in the center of
Yosemite Valley surrounded by campgrounds. Their behavior had become an increasing irritation to the ranger staff
and to many visitors, particularly in the campgrounds, and
there were numerous complaints of the noise of tape recorders

and radios played far into the night, along with complaints about dope, profanity, nudity, and sex. A 7:00 P.M. curfew in the meadow was ignored, after which mounted rangers drove the people from the meadow.

But the next day youth groups were back, and there was an angry undercurrent. Rangers posted signs announcing that the curfew would again be enforced; the young people continued to play guitars, smoke marijuana, and throw Frisbees. As hundreds of spectators lined the meadow that evening, the rangers again sought to clear the meadow by force. Retreating before the charge of the horsemen, the young people picked up rocks and bottles, which they hurled at the horses, driving the heavily outnumbered ranger force from the meadow in confusion.

No one could take pride in the episode of Stoneman's Meadow, and the aftermath was equally unfortunate. Unable to restore order, the Park Service called upon the police jurisdictions of the nearby cities of Fresno and Merced and Madera and Mariposa counties. By midnight nearly one hundred policemen had arrived in the park. Divided into squads led by rangers, they made a sweep of the campgrounds. More than one hundred arrests were made between midnight and morning, there were a series of ugly encounters, police and ranger vehicles were damaged, and there were injuries on both sides. The accusations and counteraccusations that followed were highlighted by a widely publicized letter to President Richard M. Nixon from a Florida physician, a witness to the events, who condemned the Park Service for unwarranted brutality against a peaceful gathering.

The unhappy affair was considerably more complicated than this brief account indicates. The doctor's letter provoked immediate responses from other witnesses who denied that excessive force had been used and praised the rangers for their efforts. But the July Fourth weekend in Yosemite has had a far-reaching effect upon the entire Park Service organization. It will be some time before the Park Service sorts out its own attitudes. There is agreement that until a way is found for mutual understanding and respect to exist between the Park Service and the youth culture groups, there will be difficult times ahead.

The traditional role of the park ranger, that of protector of park resources and host to park visitors, was not equal to the requirements of the incident at Stoneman's Meadow. The rangers, including a number of seasonal employees, were desperately trying to handle a situation for which they were ill equipped by reason of training, equipment, and ideology. Should another disturbance occur, however, it will be treated differently.

Rangers are now undergoing a 500-hour retraining program. Sensitivity to the problems and cultures of minority groups and of young people is emphasized. Included are sessions in criminal law, firearms, narcotics, and crowd and mob control. Also stressed is the policy that park visitors, of whatever appearance, are not to be manhandled by hard-nosed police types.

"We were the friendly rangers," said one chief ranger, "who, when we saw an infraction, pointed out the error and talked with the violator." Now as he dons a riot helmet and practices with pistols, clubs, and chemical Mace, the ranger, who has always been the Park Service's protective force, finds his duties ever more demanding and complex. Recognizing the many urban problems making their appearance in the parks, the Park Service seeks a way to respond appropriately to antisocial behavior and the politics of confrontation without destroying the quality of the park environment experience for the great majority of visitors. Yet, as in the case of the universities, the Park Service has found that persistent demands from the young have forced a timely re-examination of attitudes and policies, which may yet transform the Yosemite incident into a healthy step forward for the organization.

Overuse in the Parks

Although the presence of the hippie types is disturbing to some, a considerably greater problem for others is the threat of overuse of the parks. Articles in magazines and newspapers have chronicled a level of use considered to be unwarranted. Observing congestion in the most heavily used parks, instead of the traditional peace and quiet the parks are supposed to offer, the writers believe the time has come to restrict visitor use. That the Park Service has not begun to impose stiff regulations on visitors is also a source of bitter criticism. "Our National Parks are headed hellbent for a crisis," in the opinion of one *Field and Stream* writer. "Not even the President of the United States appears able to persuade the entrenched leadership of the National Park Service to face up to it," he declares, adding that the Park Service "is afflicted with a syndrome that 'Parks are for People.'"

President Nixon mentioned the problem when he visited Grand Teton in the summer of 1971:

> The growing popularity of our parks has created a number of serious new problems as millions of Americans have sought the recreation and respite they provide. Traffic congestion and crowded campsites are becoming more common. In many places, natural systems have been over-burdened and damaged by the presence of too many people. Wild animals and unique plants have often been crowded out of their traditional habitat. In short, we are beginning to understand that there are limits to the amount of use our parklands can withstand, and that as more and more people seek the great rewards of outdoor life, the experience can be somewhat diminished for each of them.

The President and the Park Service are no less eager than concerned journalists and conservationists to remedy the situation, but the only available solutions involve painful choices.

Generally the Park Service goal has been to provide an

opportunity for all visitors wishing to visit parks to do so, without giving preference to any group and under conditions that have the widest public acceptance. In the past, both ends of the visitor spectrum have supported this policy, those preferring wilderness solitude and those enjoying the sociability of the campgrounds. The twain did not often meet or interfere with one another's pleasure, but now the sheer numbers of people have begun to impinge upon everyone's enjoyment.

An inhibiting factor that has prolonged more positive action has been that, so long as use of the parks by the two groups was compatible, the Park Service could avoid the uncomfortable role of discriminating against either the "mass recreationists" or the "purists." For a democratic society, the choice that seems more and more inevitable has strong implications of cultural elitism. In future years, restrictions on the number of people who will be able to enter the parks is inevitable, and the determination of how this can be done equitably presents one of the most crucial decisions that the Park Service has faced in its history.

It will require an approach rather more complicated than, as some critics have suggested, simply locking the gates and hanging up a FULL sign. Although all campsites in the parks have historically been awarded on a "first come, first served" basis, an experiment was scheduled for 1972 whereby campgrounds in several national parks were reserved through the nationwide "Ticketron" apparatus, with potential park visitors throughout the country able to obtain confirmed reservations for campsites in advance of their trip to the park. If this system operates successfully on a small scale, the feasibility of expanding the system to include other facilities will be considered. The possibility of developing some kind of system applicable to the total park, which would require advanced reservations for all visitors, is an ultimate consideration. When and how the reservations of the "no shows" will be disposed of, a continuing problem for most vacation travel enterprises, is only one of the perplexing elements that must be solved.

The benefits of a reservation system might be considerable, but the total problem is infinitely more complex. Effective solutions will depend upon a comprehensive planning approach on the scale now being applied to the Yellowstone and Grand Teton master plans.

A NEW KIND OF MASTER PLAN

These plans, now under consideration, will likely serve as models for all future master planning. They are based, first of all, upon the evident fact that a park cannot stand by itself but must be considered as a part of the region in which it exists. The regional highway systems, the multiplicity of available recreational opportunities, and the location of tourist accommodations and services, along with the recreational developments on adjoining federal or state lands, require that a park master plan must be conceived as a part of a regional plan.

It is significant, but for the Park Service rather disheartening, that at present the average stay in Yellowstone is only thirty-one hours. Considering the size of the park and the variety of experiences available, and the distance most people have traveled in order to see the park, the amount of time allotted to Yellowstone seems terribly meager. People spend considerably more time going to the seashore or the mountains for a weekend. Obviously, half the people spend less than thirty-one hours and a substantial portion of all Yellowstone visitors enter and leave the park the same day.

These statistics can be variously interpreted: people simply aren't that interested in parks; or they may be unaware of just how to go about taking advantage of park programs; or people may be disappointed that what they experienced failed to meet their expectations. There are doubtless an unknown number of park visitors in each of these sample groupings. It seems likely all would profit from an opportunity to find out, before making the decision to enter the park, just what parks are like and what activities and experiences might be expected. And if there are to be restrictions in the future, both on entering a park and on the means of travel within the park, it will be necessary to inform people as early as possible.

For Yellowstone, Grand Teton, and all national parks, a steadily diminishing role for the private automobile is foreseen, along with a corresponding increase in the use of alternative means of transportation.

The development of a transportation system that enhances, rather than diminishes, visitor enjoyment of the park involves formidable problems. The point at which the visitor is successfully separated from his automobile involves sizable logistical problems, for it will require the development of parking lots, either within or outside the parks, capable of handling thousands of vehicles. Emptying automobiles of all personal gear, suitcases, loose ends, and particularly camping equipment and smoothly transferring the load to a transportation system will pose a not insignificant obstacle.

For several years a free shuttle bus system has been provided in Yosemite Valley, subsidized by the Park Service. Operation of a fleet of buses in this relatively small area of less than eight square miles costs $300,000 a year. With people leaving their cars behind, the valley has been much less congested, but if fares were charged, considerably fewer people would elect to use the buses.

Since Yellowstone and Grand Teton cover an area greater than the states of Rhode Island and Delaware combined, the logistical and financial problems involved in excluding automobiles and providing some other form of transportation become apparent. Colonial Williamsburg, which provides a free shuttle bus service for its restored area, requires twenty-five buses for a round trip of four miles—but the round trip distance from Jackson, Wyoming, at the southern entrance to Grand Teton, to Gardiner, Montana, at the north entrance to Yellowstone, is more than three hundred miles!

The new master plan concept of Yellowstone–Grand Teton begins with the development of information centers in the gateway towns surrounding the two parks. All traffic will be directed to these points, where the visitor can receive a thorough briefing; he can determine, among available options, including transportation systems, what activities he wants to engage in, and if necessary obtain reservations. The primary emphasis will be to give the visitor a sense of what the park is like, and to break it down into understandable units. Initially, he will proceed from the gateway towns to the parks in his own automobile; eventually, he will undoubtedly be taking a park transportation system.

If the Park Service, and the many gateway towns that adjoin almost all parks, can cooperate in the development of these gateway centers, many of the facilities needed by visitors could be provided within the center complex. It would be a giant step forward if private enterprises were to develop facilities aesthetically attractive, which might also be within the reach of families of limited means. It might require a technical-assistance program to support private development of park-related facilities. Government support might also take the form of a federal recreation development authority, which would build such facilities and lease them to private operators.

Entering the park, the visitor will proceed to one of several threshold communities, developed areas from which the actual exploration of the park can begin. The goal, initially, will be to separate the visitor from his car at this point, and three separate transportation systems will be required, in the large parks, to meet the needs and the interests of the several major components of the total park visitor pattern.

For those who want to see as much as possible or who want to get acquainted generally before making specific forays, one system will make a continuous loop tour. For those who want to go directly to points of interest, to trail heads to begin a hiking or backpacking trip, a second transportation system will be available. A third system will provide individual shuttle transportation within the larger threshold areas, such as the geyser basins, or between major points of interest.

These systems, and they may turn out to be buses, funiculars, tramways, or combinations of all these, will accommodate the "through traveler" who is satisfied with the general tour; the recreational user who wants more than passive sight-seeing and who wants to do some hiking and camping to get away from the developed area; and the true wilderness traveler who wants to pass as quickly as possible through the outposts of civilization into the wild country.

With this kind of approach, the Park Service can limit the number of people entering the park, or using a part of the park, or engaging in particular kinds of activities. Visitor use will be dependent upon the capacity of the transportation system, which in turn will be geared to the capacity of the park to absorb use. The tendency on the part of many has been to hope that a magical figure can be discovered that will determine just how many people a park can safely accommodate.

A more reasonable approach seems to be one of working out levels of use that can be tolerated, both by the visitor and by the resource, for the given number of activities and geographic areas that make up the total park and to tie each of these elements into the transportation system. The levels of tolerance will require the considered experience of park administrators, as well as sociologists and ecologists, working toward levels of use that will not impair the experience of visitors or do damage to the park resources.

With this approach, the past tradition of counting visitors will have to be refined considerably before a ceiling number for visitors can be developed. Each visitor is presently counted as one, which results in a deceptive set of statistics. One person driving out of Denver goes through Rocky Mountain National Park along Trail Ridge Road, stops at a few overlooks, and continues westward, having spent only a few hours in the park. Another enters Rocky Mountain to camp and spends a week, hiking in the back country and fishing the mountain streams, attending the evening campfire programs, and spending hours in the museums.

The person who stays the longest has the most meaningful experience; he also contributes considerably more toward the development of the park—his requirements are far more exacting than those of the quickie visitor in terms of water and sewage facilities, campgrounds and concessioner accommodations, parking lots and museums.

An overnight stay has been a traditional part of the national park experience and has always been considered a most desirable one. In certain parks it is doubtful whether overnight use could, or should, be eliminated. But available overnight use among the many who desire it may be a part of the reservation system, with the length of stay drastically curtailed. Conversion to day use in itself could create as well as solve problems. Roads could well be jammed by "commuting" traffic as all visitors try to enter in the morning and leave in the evening.

Responsibility to Meet Social Needs

The conservation world has been generally united in its attitude toward most environmental matters. There may be variations in intensity of interest, depending upon whether the subject involves endangered species, preservation of historic buildings, or the establishment of a new national park. But with only infrequent disagreements among the many organizations in the field, conservationists have shared similar objectives. And those who defend the cause of the environment have been relatively free from criticism.

Some people are beginning to express different views about the direction and the goals of conservation. Rather than the national parks being damaged by swarms of people who overrun the facilities, they believe too large a segment of the population has been denied use of the parks. These critics hold that poverty, race, and the disintegration of life in the inner cities have never been concerns of the conservation movement, yet they are the crucial social problems most deserving of national attention. What happens to the recreational experience of people in the great natural preserves should not be treated separately from what is happening to the people living in the most blighted urban areas.

Writing in *Parks and Recreation* magazine, July, 1971, Peter Marcuse, in an article entitled "Is the National Parks Movement Anti-urban?," suggests that it is an exaggeration to say the conservation movement is antipoor, antiminority, antiurban. He concludes, however, that considerable doubt exists "whether the values and needs of all men in our society are being fairly and equally met in the approach to natural areas that the conservation movement has thus far adopted."

In June, 1971, early in his administration, Secretary of the Interior Rogers C. B. Morton issued a policy directive to the Park Service, outlining the areas he wished to receive special attention. He noted that many parks are little used by financially underprivileged citizens and asked that a special study be made of techniques for making the parks more accessible. "Perhaps we need to find ways of developing lower cost accommodations for families and organized groups," Morton said, "so that we can truly broaden the use of the National Park System to include all social and economic groups."

Either the goals and the strategies of the conservation movement and particularly that part of it concerned with the
strengthening of the National Parks can be restructured, re-
defined, broadened, or perhaps only re-interpreted to have
something to offer to the large numbers of the excluded in the
ghettos and slums of our cities, or conservationists will join
the other legitimate targets of those pressing for greater dignity
and freedom and the opportunity to enjoy the good things life
has to offer, regardless of consequences.

No one would seriously contest that visiting parks and
historic sites is an activity directly proportional to income.
National Parks are essentially a middle-class experience.
They are hardly within the scope of families hard pressed for
bus fare to travel to the local zoo. The culturally disadvantaged are not a significant part of the statistics of national
park travel, and black families are seldom encountered in the
campgrounds.

The question being raised is wholly relevant and one which
conservationists and the National Park Service must ponder,
for it requires a re-examination of conservation's obligation
to the individual human being. If the purpose of conservation
is a healthful and attractive environment, it should be an
environment healthful for people and enjoyed by people, not
nature for nature's sake but nature for people's sake. Otherwise, from the vantage point of the poor and the jobless,
wilderness preservation might well be included with exploration of the moon as programs too remote to be relevant,
which compete for funds needed to solve excruciating social
problems.

EVERGLADES—AN EARLY WARNING

A crucial problem of the future is whether the national
parks can actually survive. Considering the disastrous sequence of events which have devastated Everglades National

Park in the last decade, survival is not assured. The most spectacular example yet of conservation brinkmanship, Everglades is one of the first national parks to face extinction. Because it adjoins a large metropolitan complex in the heavily populated East, it was the first to undergo such an ordeal. One suspects it will not be the last.

The Everglades story epitomizes the modern dilemma: how to balance the intangible benefits to the whole society that result from national parks against the significant economic benefits which can be realized by local communities— but only at the expense of the integrity of the park. The Everglades experience is hardly comforting to those who expect the decision would obviously be in favor of the park.

Dedicating Everglades National Park in 1947, President Harry S Truman announced, "We have permanently safeguarded an irreplaceable primitive area." The culmination of a half-century struggle to preserve a portion of the unique subtropical region of southern Florida, establishment of the park seemed, as the President promised, to ensure it permanent protection. But the Everglades is a region wholly dependent upon its water supply, and few people realized at the time how delicately the ecosystem is balanced.

Historically, the unfailing rain clouds rolling in from the ocean had fed the long curving river of saw grass, the true Everglades, which extends from Lake Okeechobee southward to the tip of the Florida peninsula. For more than one hundred miles the land loses less than two inches of elevation to the mile, and the pure, sweet water had moved almost imperceptibly southward, over rich peats and limestone aquifers, turning brackish as it reached the mangrove swamps along Florida bay. The timeless flow of the 50-mile-wide river supported an abundance of life unsurpassed on the North American continent.

In the mangroves, white pelicans and roseate spoonbills and herons ceaselessly foraged the shallow water for fish and in the deeper sloughs alligator and anhinga gathered to feed upon gar and bream. Where a slight elevation created hummocks and pinelands, bobcats and panthers slipped through the shadows. Flocks of egret and ibis, numbering in the hundreds of thousands, floated like huge clouds across the landscape. "When we try to pick out anything by itself," John Muir once observed, "we find it hitched to everything else in the universe," and his classic definition of ecology aptly described the interdependence of life in the saw grass community, which he viewed in 1867 during his 1,000-mile saunter from Kentucky south through Florida to Cuba.

During the 1960's it became increasingly evident that the ecosystem of the Everglades region was being irrevocably altered. Believing the rich muck was going to waste under water, agricultural interests were draining off the water, only to discover that, when exposed to air and the heat of the sun, the dried material oxidizes. In some districts 40 per cent of the organic material vanished into the air.

The citrus, melon, and vegetable growers of south Florida have been heavy users of DDT and other pesticides and fertilizers. Sediments sampled from within the park show concentrations of chlorinated hydrocarbons of an order of magnitude one thousand times greater than in the water passing overhead, the result of biological magnification through the food chain in which each successive predator accumulates all the pesticide residues from the fats of his prey. The long and complex food chain pattern of the Everglades makes it terribly vulnerable to the poisoning effect of pesticides.

The same year that the park was established, hurricanes smashed across Florida. The bill of $60 million for damages, coupled with loss of more than two thousand lives from similar storms in the previous decade, provoked demands for preventive measures. Over the next twenty years the Army Corps of Engineers carried out the Central and Southern Florida Control Project, and the river of grass south of

Okeechobee was systematically drained, diked, and culti-vated. Everglades National Park no longer received its ancient flow of water from the impartial bounty of nature but from a formula devised by the state of Florida and the Corps of Engineers.

In 1962, Levee 29 was completed along the park's northern boundary, and the floodgates along the Tamiami Trail, which allowed the south-flowing waters to enter the park, were closed. Henceforth, the flow of water would be artificially controlled, and "The River of Grass," in the words of one scientist, "after 5,000 years had ceased to flow." In combina-tion with the drought years that followed, the results were catastrophic to Everglades National Park. Water levels fell to a low beyond anything previously known, and species of aquatic life managed to survive only because of pockets of water remaining in the deepest holes. The park estimated that 90 per cent of the original alligator population had been lost, and of 1.5 million wading birds when the park was established, probably fewer than 50,000 survived.

The decision in the mid-1960's of the Dade County Port Authority to build an international jetport along the north boundary of the park, big enough to swallow up the four largest airports in the United States, seemed to be the final death blow. Yet the controversy that it provoked finally aroused national concern. Particularly helpful to the conser-vation cause were such Neanderthal utterances as the reply of Florida's transportation secretary to criticisms of the destructive impact of the jetport on the wildlife of the Everglades: "Alligators make nice shoes and pocketbooks."

Such contemptuous disregard helped supply needed sup-port to conservation efforts led by the National Audubon Society, which once again entered into combat to save the Everglades. Interior's report on the effects of the airport, compiled by a team under the direction of Dr. Luna B. Leo-pold of the Geological Survey, provided tough conclusions;

the jetport would "inexorably destroy the South Florida ecosystem and thus the Everglades National Park." Magazines
and newspapers trained their guns on the jetport issue, and
in January, 1970, President Nixon announced an agreement
reached by the Department of the Interior, the Department
of Transportation, the Dade County Port Authority, and
Collier County that no further airport construction or development would be permitted beyond the single training strip
already in operation.

So far as the precious places of this country are concerned,
there is a critical difference, perhaps one of environmental
maturity, between the two possible approaches to a project
on the scale of the Everglades: either the decision is made
to carry out such projects because the precise consequences
are not known; or decision-makers take a stand on the position that no action will be taken that will alter the earth
until the ultimate impact has been studied.

In a perceptive account of "The Bitter Struggle for a
National Park" in the April, 1970, *American Heritage*, John
Mitchell of the Sierra Club reasoned that at stake is the
future integrity not of one park but of all national parks, that
Everglades is a test case, reflecting "the challenge that all
citizens face wherever the landscape is being poisoned and
the forces of nature abused. Indeed, if Everglades National
Park is to be saved, it will be done because discrete segments
of our society will have found a way to work together. If that
can be accomplished," Mitchell concludes, "then perhaps
what the park has taught us can begin to save America."

Give Us the Tools

The end of the Mission 66 program, in 1966, coincided
with the escalation of the Vietnam war, and since that time
nondefense agencies have taken budget cuts. In a period of
expanding responsibilities, and with new parks to activate

each year, the Park Service has struggled to keep pace. "If sharp cuts are forced on the national parks budget and we don't have enough rangers to protect the national parks and maintain their quality," said Representative Julia Butler Hansen, chairman of the House Appropriations Subcommittee that handles the Park Service budget, who frequently finds ways to express her own high regard for the national parks, "I would recommend that we close those parks with lowest priority of use."

In August, 1971, Director George B. Hartzog set forth the plight of the parks in a report to the Secretary of the Interior. Between 1960 and 1971 there were eighty-one new parks added to the national park system. Yet, since 1966, funds appropriated for visitor-use facilities had actually declined by $30 million annually. Of new parks established since 1960, there were nineteen for which no funds at all had been appropriated after the enabling legislation had been passed, yet which required $140 million to develop and operate. Against a need of $1.8 billion dollars for physical developments, the Park Service was limited to a request for less than $40 million in fiscal 1972.

Land acquisition problems are equally critical. Acquisition of in-holdings (in areas established before 1960) is estimated to cost $177 million; acquisition of lands in the newly authorized parks is estimated at $124 million; if legislation is passed to authorize the major park proposals now before Congress, the acquisition costs will be in the neighborhood of $450 million, for a total cost of more than $750 million. With land costs rising at the rate of 20 per cent each year, the Park Service receives about $70 million annually for land acquisition.

Developing an over-all master plan for a national park is one of the most demanding activities of the Park Service, requiring a variety of talents both within and from outside the organization. The master plan ultimately brings together into one unified document scientific research and planning studies that may require many years to produce. For the 1972 fiscal year alone, the Park Service will prepare more than fifty master plans. To implement individual portions of master plans, to carry out studies of proposed new parks, to restore historic structures and carry out archeological investigations, to produce design studies for roads, parkways, buildings, utilities, campgrounds, the Harpers Ferry Center and the Denver Service Center have several thousand individual projects to complete.

Yet in October, 1971, a new government-wide cutback went into effect. The impact upon the Park Service was to require a further tightening of the belt. The edict required that nearly 375 permanent positions be eliminated, together with more than 350 people from its seasonal work force.

With sincere respect for the intent and the quality of the constructive criticism being offered the Park Service these days to the end of improving its operations, the writer should like to offer a personal observation. The Park Service is some distance removed from being able to manage the parks as well as it really knows how.

One reporter spent six months and traveled 20,000 miles to report on the state of the national park system and to determine whether the condition of the parks was a source of pride or alarm. In his series of sixteen articles for the *Christian Science Monitor*, "Will Success Spoil the National Parks?" which won the Pulitzer Prize for National Reporting in 1969, reporter Robert Cahn observed that overcrowding did exist in the developed areas of the older national parks—at Yosemite, Yellowstone, Grand Canyon, Everglades, Mesa Verde, and Mt. Rainier—but this "only during the peak periods of use." Crime was growing, park rangers were overworked, and many people added to the difficulties by trying to see too much too fast. "Despite all this and more," Cahn concluded, "it is only fair to say that, on the basis of my observations, the national park system appears to be in relatively good physical condition. No disaster situation is evident."

WHAT GOOD IS A PARK?

The abiding purpose of a national park is to bring man and his environment into closer harmony. The ultimate hope that a delicate balance between preservation and use can be maintained will depend upon the ability of the Park Service to promote, and the willingness of the visitor to accept, perception as the highest form of park use.

Every visitor reacts to the beauty of the natural scene or the stirring drama of the historical past, if only passively. Salvation for the parks lies in the hope that the park visitor can be actively stimulated, by the immediacy of his surroundings and the substance of the interpretive programs, to perceive and treasure the natural and historic processes through which the land and all living things have achieved their form and by which they maintain their dependent existence.

Outdoor recreation is not found in the forests or glaciers or historic sites, but in one's reaction to these resources. The mountain men who came up the Missouri to the Great Shining Mountains preferred the wilds to the safety and sobriety of the settlements, and they were not unmoved by the beauty of the land. But of the incredible complexity of the plant and animal communities that made up wilderness America, they were as unaware as the prospectors, cattlemen, and sodbusters who followed. The engendering of a perceptive understanding of these values is perhaps the most important function of the national parks.

Because outdoor recreation has always involved physical activity, invading or even appropriating for personal use a section of the countryside, there has developed among some a philosophy that wilderness that is not personally experienced has little value. In the case of park wilderness this philosophy is translated, "Use it or lose it." The capacity for perception may well separate those who see blank spaces on the map as a profitless waste from those who see it as the most valuable part. Should one be neutral on the prospect of a pipeline being constructed through the Alaskan tundra solely because he never expects to go there himself?

Aldo Leopold, who called upon Americans to develop an ecological conscience a generation before the word "ecology" achieved its current magic, foresaw how relentlessly wilderness would become the objective of recreational use and predicted that unless accompanied by an equal growth in perception, the result would be "qualitative bankruptcy." His oft-quoted conclusion, written in 1938, marvelously defines the single objective of current conservation efforts: "Recreational development is a job, not of building roads into lovely country, but of building receptivity into the still unlovely human mind."

In the end, despite all the brilliant generalizations and skillful rhetoric that have livened the preservation and use dialogue, the effort may prove meaningless. Today all parks, whether isolated wilderness tracts or historic structures in urban settings, are more likely to be altered, even destroyed, by external pressures than by actions within the parks.

Asked the scornful question what good could possibly come from his electricity experiment with the kite, Ben Franklin replied, "What good is a baby?" The argument over preservation and use in the national parks probably comes down to the way in which people individually and collectively respond to the question "What good is a park?"

No organism has yet been discovered that can perpetuate itself in an environment saturated with its own waste products, and there is little reason to suspect that man is an exception. One vote for parks came from the troubled African game warden in Romain Gary's classic novel *The Roots of Heaven*:

It is absolutely essential that man should manage to preserve something other than what helps to make soles for his shoes or sewing machines, that he should leave a margin, a sanctuary, where some of life's beauty can take refuge and where he himself can feel safe from his own cleverness and folly.

Appendix I
Career Opportunities

For young people seeking a career in the general field of conservation and historic preservation work, the National Park Service provides a great variety of career opportunities. Although college training is a requirement for most professional positions, there are also rewarding occupations for technicians.

The largest single occupation group is the ranger force, numbering about 1,100 men and women. This includes a substantial number of persons with specialized backgrounds in history, archeology, and the natural sciences, who are primarily concerned with interpretation. Park ranger candidates are generally college graduates who have passed the Federal Service Entrance Examination.

In the past, rangers were most often selected with college majors in park management, the sciences, or wildlife management, but the Park Service now actively recruits for rangers with training in political science, sociology, and the behavioral sciences—or even dramatic arts, since rangers must deal with people as well as wildlife.

Traditionally, the park ranger has been a generalist, and has received varied assignments in the parks from fire fighting to law enforcement to visitor information to planning and administration. From the entry level, rangers move upward through the ranks to district ranger, park managers, staff specialists in resource management and interpretation, and into upper-level management. Four of the six current regional directors began their Park Service careers as general-duty rangers. The two regional directors located in the East began as park historians, a noble profession.

The entry grade for park rangers is generally at the GS–7 level, with a starting salary of $8,500. After receiving orientation training at one of the training centers, park rangers are assigned first to the National Capital Parks in Washington, D.C., for a year of on-the-job training, following which they are assigned to a park area.

A new occupational group, park aids and technicians, has been recently established to provide technical support for the rangers and other professional disciplines. The park aid position is the first step toward the park technician level. Technicians, operating under direction of park rangers, may lead guided tours or carry out plans to restore historic buildings or work on plant or insect control projects. Applicants who have graduated from high school may qualify for park aids; they begin at the GS–2 level ($4,800). Park technicians generally are required to have two years of college; they begin at GS–4 ($6,200). Both aids and technicians can advance to GS–9 ($13,600).

The Park Service places considerable emphasis upon selecting the best-qualified employees for promotion and transfer. When a park superintendent has a staff vacancy, he asks for a certificate of eligibles to choose from. A special office in Washington screens the records of all eligible employees and sends a list of the best qualified to the superintendent. For all key managerial positions, whether in the parks, the regions, or Washington, the Washington Directorate and the regional directors participate in the screening of eligibles and in the final selection.

"Comers" in the organization are searched out every year, with field areas nominating candidates and management selecting twenty to forty of the best qualified. These are the young people who have displayed drive and savvy and have indicated a capacity to advance rapidly. An individual training plan involving a two-year period of intensive development is designed for each person. Each individual is assigned a counselor to advise on his or her progress.

The objective of the program is to speed up the normal growth process through a combination of formal studies, on-the-job training, special details and assignments, and individualized learning. Periodically the trainees participate in an "assessment laboratory" for the purpose of evaluating their progress and determining their readiness for an assignment in the field as operating managers. These midlevel trainees become the primary source of selection for all midlevel management positions in the National Park Service.

Seasonal Employment

Both the Park Service and the park concessioners augment their permanent staffs during the summer travel season by hiring "seasonals," or temporary employees. The publication *Summary Jobs in the National Parks,* available through Taplinger Publishing Company, 29 East Tenth Street, New York, New York 10003, gives a thorough summary of the qualifications required and types of employment available with the major concessioners, including hours and wages, living accommodations, and terms of employment. This publication includes similar information for positions with the National Park Service itself. A pamphlet, "Seasonal Employment," covering all phases of such employment with the Park Service is available from the Government Printing Office.

Competition for seasonal positions with the Park Service is extremely keen and employment opportunities are therefore limited. A large majority of the positions are filled each year by men and women who have worked for one or more seasons. Among qualified candidates, veterans receive preference. The number of applications far outnumber the positions to be filled.

Appendix II
The National Park System

In November, 1971, the National Park System consisted of 284 separate park areas. National Capital Parks, which includes the more than 700 memorials, monuments, parks, parkways, and green spaces within Washington, D.C., is counted as one park. A booklet, "National Parks and Landmarks," which includes a description of the outstanding features and other pertinent data for each park, is available from the Government Printing Office.

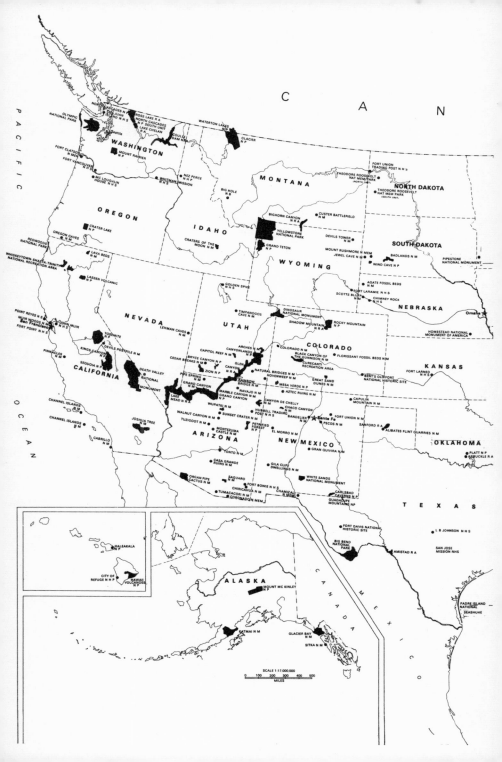

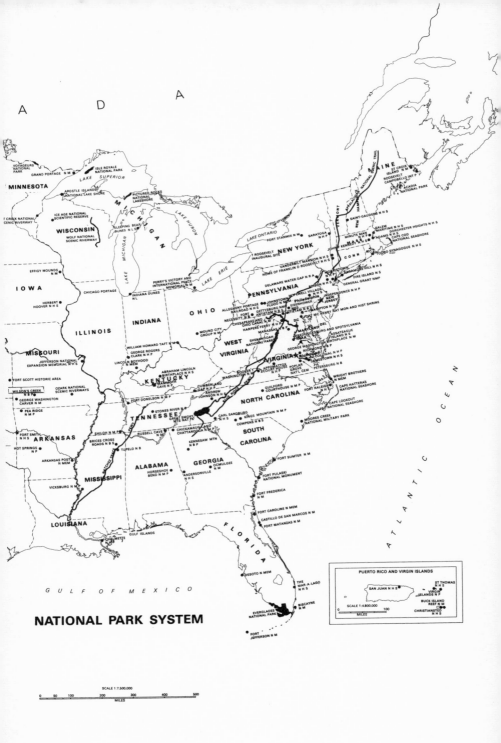

NATIONAL PARK SYSTEM

NATIONAL PARKS

	Established	Gross Area (acres)
Acadia, Maine	1916	41,642
Big Bend, Tex.	1935	708,221
Bryce Canyon, Utah	1923	36,010
Canyonlands, Utah	1964	257,640
Carlsbad Caverns, N. Mex.	1923	46,753
Crater Lake, Oreg.	1902	160,290
Everglades, Fla.	1934	1,400,533
Glacier, Mont.	1910	1,013,101
Grand Canyon, Ariz.	1908	673,575
Grand Teton, Wyo.	1929	310,443
Great Smoky Mountains, Tenn.-N.C.	1926	516,626
Guadalupe Mountains, Tex.	1966	81,077
Haleakala, Hawaii	1916	27,283
Hawaii Volcanoes, Hawaii	1916	229,616
Hot Springs, Ark.	1832	3,535
Isle Royale, Mich.	1931	539,341
Kings Canyon, Calif.	1890	460,331
Lassen Volcanic, Calif.	1907	106,934
Mammoth Cave, Ky.	1926	51,354
Mesa Verde, Colo.	1906	52,074
Mount McKinley, Alaska	1917	1,939,493
Mount Rainier, Wash.	1899	241,992
North Cascades, Wash.	1968	505,000
Olympic, Wash.	1909	896,599
Petrified Forest, Ariz.	1906	94,189
Platt, Okla.	1902	912
Redwood, Calif.	1968	56,201
Rocky Mountain, Colo.	1915	262,191
Sequoia, Calif.	1890	386,863
Shenandoah, Va.	1926	193,537
Virgin Islands, V.I.	1956	14,419
Voyageurs, Minn.	1971	139,128
Wind Cave, S.Dak.	1903	28,059
Yellowstone, Wyo.-Mont.-Idaho	1872	2,221,773
Yosemite, Calif.	1890	761,320
Zion, Utah	1909	147,035
Total number: 36	*Total area:*	14,605,091

NATIONAL HISTORICAL PARKS

Appomattox Court House, Va.	1930	938
Chalmette, La.	1907	142

	Established	Gross Area (acres)
Chesapeake & Ohio Canal, Md.-W.Va.-D.C.	1938	20,239
City of Refuge, Hawaii	1955	181
Colonial, Va.	1930	9,430
Cumberland Gap, Ky.-Tenn.-Va.	1940	20,176
George Rogers Clark, Ind.	1966	23
Harpers Ferry, W.Va.-Md.	1944	1,530
Independence, Pa.	1948	22
Minute Man, Mass.	1959	750
Morristown, N.J.	1933	1,358
Nez Perce, Idaho	1965	3,000
San Juan Island, Wash.	1966	1,752
Saratoga, N.Y.	1938	5,500
Total number: 14	*Total area:*	65,040

NATIONAL MONUMENTS

	Established	Gross Area (acres)
Agate Fossil Beds, Nebr.	1965	3,050
Alibates Flint Quarries and Texas Panhandle Pueblo Culture, Tex.	1965	93
Arches, Utah	1929	82,953
Aztec Ruins, N.Mex.	1923	27
Badlands, S.Dak.	1929	243,508
Bandelier, N.Mex.	1916	29,661
Biscayne, Fla.	1968	95,064
Black Canyon of the Gunnison, Colo.	1933	13,667
Booker T. Washington,Va.	1956	218
Buck Island Reef, V.I.	1961	850
Cabrillo, Calif.	1913	123
Canyon de Chelly, Ariz.	1931	83,840
Capitol Reef, Utah	1937	254,242
Capulin Mountain, N.Mex.	1916	775
Casa Grande Ruins, Ariz.	1892	473
Castillo de San Marcos, Fla.	1924	20
Castle Clinton, N.Y.	1946	1
Cedar Breaks, Utah	1933	6,155
Chaco Canyon, N.Mex.	1907	21,509
Channel Islands, Calif.	1938	18,167
Chiricahua, Ariz.	1924	10,646
Colorado, Colo.	1911	17,669
Craters of the Moon, Idaho	1924	53,545
Custer Battlefield, Mont.	1879	765
Death Valley, Calif.-Nev.	1933	1,907,760
Devils Postpile, Calif.	1911	798

	Established	Gross Area (acres)
Devils Tower, Wyo.	1906	1,347
Dinosaur, Utah-Colo.	1915	206,663
Effigy Mounds, Iowa	1949	1,468
El Morro, N. Mex.	1906	1,279
Florrisant Fossil Beds, Colo.	1969	5,992
Fort Frederica, Ga.	1936	250
Fort Jefferson, Fla.	1935	47,125
Fort McHenry, Md.	1925	43
Fort Matanzas, Fla.	1924	299
Fort Pulaski, Ga.	1924	5,517
Fort Stanwix, N.Y.	1935	18
Fort Sumter, S.C.	1948	34
Fort Union, N.Mex.	1954	721
George Washington Birthplace, Va.	1930	394
George Washington Carver, Mo.	1943	210
Gila Cliff Dwellings, N.Mex.	1907	533
Glacier Bay, Alaska	1925	2,803,840
Gran Quivira, N.Mex.	1909	611
Grand Canyon, Ariz.	1932	198,280
Grand Portage, Minn.	1951	710
Great Sand Dunes, Colo.	1932	36,740
Homestead, Nebr.	1936	195
Hovenweep, Utah-Colo.	1923	505
Jewel Cave, S.Dak.	1908	1,275
Joshua Tree, Calif.	1936	558,184
Katmai, Alaska	1918	2,792,137
Lava Beds, Calif.	1925	46,239
Lehman Caves, Nev.	1922	640
Marble Canyon, Ariz.	1969	32,665
Montezuma Castle, Ariz.	1906	842
Mound City Group, Ohio	1923	68
Muir Woods, Calif.	1908	503
Natural Bridges, Utah	1908	7,600
Navajo, Ariz.	1909	360
Ocmulgee, Ga.	1934	683
Oregon Caves, Oreg.	1909	480
Organ Pipe Cactus, Ariz.	1937	330,874
Pecos, N.Mex.	1965	341
Perry's Victory and International Peace Memorial, Ohio	1936	21
Pinnacles, Calif.	1908	14,498
Pipe Spring, Ariz.	1923	40
Pipestone, Minn.	1937	282

	Established	Gross Area (acres)
Rainbow Bridge, Utah	1910	160
Russell Cave, Ala.	1961	310
Saguaro, Ariz.	1933	79,084
Saint Croix Island, Maine	1949	57
Scotts Bluff, Nebr.	1919	3,084
Sitka, Alaska	1910	54
Statue of Liberty, N.Y.-N.J.	1924	58
Sunset Crater, Ariz.	1930	3,040
Timpanogos Cave, Utah	1922	250
Tonto, Ariz.	1907	1,120
Tumacacori, Ariz.	1908	10
Tuzigoot, Ariz.	1939	43
Walnut Canyon, Ariz.	1915	1,879
White Sands, N.Mex.	1933	146,535
Wupatki, Ariz.	1924	35,233
Yucca House, Colo.	1919	10
Total number: 84	*Total area:*	10,217,011

NATIONAL MILITARY PARKS

Chickamauga and Chattanooga, Ga.-Tenn.	1890	8,113
Fort Donelson, Tenn.	1928	600
Fredericksburg and Spotsylvania, Va.	1927	3,672
Gettysburg, Pa.	1895	3,409
Guilford Courthouse, N.C.	1917	233
Horseshoe Bend, Ala.	1956	2,040
Kings Mountain, S.C.	1931	3,950
Moores Creek, N.C.	1926	50
Pea Ridge, Ark.	1956	4,279
Shiloh, Tenn.	1894	3,702
Vicksburg, Miss.	1899	1,741
Total number: 11	*Total area:*	31,788

NATIONAL MEMORIAL PARK

Theodore Roosevelt, N.Dak.	1947	70,436
Total number: 1	*Total area:*	70,436

NATIONAL BATTLEFIELDS

Big Hole, Mont.	1910	656
Fort Necessity, Pa.	1931	500
Petersburg, Va.	1926	2,731

	Established	Gross Area (acres)
Stones River, Tenn.	1927	331
Tupelo, Miss.	1929	2
Wilson's Creek, Mo.	1960	1,728
Total number: 6	*Total area:*	5,947

NATIONAL BATTLEFIELD PARKS

Kennesaw Mountain, Ga.	1917	3,683
Manassas, Va.	1940	2,727
Richmond, Va.	1936	742
Total number: 3	*Total area:*	7,152

NATIONAL BATTLEFIELD SITES

Antietam, Md.	1890	783
Brices Cross Roads, Miss.	1929	1
Cowpens, S.C.	1929	1
Total number: 3	*Total area:*	785

NATIONAL HISTORIC SITES

Abraham Lincoln Birthplace, Ky.	1910	117
Adams, Mass.	1946	5
Allegheny Portage Railroad, Pa.	1964	767
Andersonville, Ga.	1970	495
Andrew Johnson, Tenn.	1935	17
Ansley Wilcox House, N.Y.	1966	1
Bent's Old Fort, Colo.	1960	178
Carl Sandburg Home, N.C.	1968	247
Chicago Portage, Ill.	1952	91
Chimney Rock, Nebr.	1956	83
Christiansted, V.I.	1952	27
Dorchester Heights, Mass.	1951	5
Edison, N.J.	1955	20
Eisenhower, Pa.	1967	493
Ford's Theatre, D.C.	1866	1
Fort Bowie, Ariz.	1964	1,060
Fort Davis, Tex.	1961	460
Fort Laramie, Wyo.	1938	563
Fort Larned, Kans.	1964	681
Fort Point, Calif.	1970	96
Fort Raleigh, N.C.	1941	160
Fort Scott, Kans.	1965	7

	Established	Gross Area (acres)
Fort Smith, Ark.	1961	19
Fort Union Trading Post, N.Dak.-Mont.	1966	380
Fort Vancouver, Wash.	1948	220
Gloria Dei Church, Pa.	1942	3
Golden Spike, Utah	1957	2,172
Hampton, Md.	1948	45
Herbert Hoover, Iowa	1965	148
Home of Franklin D. Roosevelt, N.Y.	1944	188
Hopewell Village, Pa.	1938	848
Hubbell Trading Post, Ariz.	1965	160
Jamestown, Va.	1940	21
Jefferson National Expansion Memorial, Mo.	1935	91
John Fitzgerald Kennedy, Mass.	1967	1
John Muir, Calif.	1964	9
Lincoln Home, Ill.	1971	12
Lyndon B. Johnson, Tex.	1969	8
McLoughlin House, Oreg.	1941	1
Pennsylvania Avenue, D.C.	1965	0
Sagamore Hill, N.Y.	1962	85
Saint Paul's Church, N.Y.	1943	6
Saint Thomas, V.I.	1960	2
Saint-Gaudens, N.H.	1964	86
Salem Maritime, Mass.	1938	11
San Jose Mission, Tex.	1941	4
San Juan, Puerto Rico	1949	48
Saugus Iron Works, Mass.	1968	9
The Mar-A-Lago, Fla.	1969	17
Theodore Roosevelt Birthplace, N.Y.	1962	1
Touro Synagogue, R.I.	1946	1
Vanderbilt Mansion, N.Y.	1940	212
Whitman Mission, Wash.	1936	98
William Howard Taft, Ohio	1969	1
Total number: 54	*Total area:*	10,476

NATIONAL MEMORIALS

Arkansas Post, Ark.	1960	305
Chamizal, Tex.	1966	55
Coronado, Ariz.	1952	2,834
Curtis-Lee Mansion, Va.	1925	3
DeSoto, Fla.	1948	30
Federal Hall, N.Y.	1939	1
Fort Caroline, Fla.	1950	128

	Established	*Gross Area (acres)*
Fort Clatsop, Oreg.	1958	125
Frederick Douglass Home, D.C.	1962	8
General Grant, N.Y.	1958	1
Hamilton Grange, N.Y.	1962	1
Johnstown Flood, Pa.	1964	54
Lincoln Boyhood, Ind.	1962	200
Lincoln Memorial, D.C.	1911	164
Mount Rushmore, S.Dak.	1925	1,278
Roger Williams, R.I.	1965	5
Thomas Jefferson, D.C.	1934	18
Washington Monument, D.C.	1848	106
Wright Brothers, N.C.	1927	431
Total number: 19	*Total area:*	5,747

NATIONAL CEMETERIES

Antietam, Md.	1870	11
Battleground, D.C.	1867	1
Fort Donelson, Tenn.	1867	15
Fredericksburg, Va.	1865	12
Gettsyburg, Pa.	1870	21
Poplar Grove, Va.	1866	9
Shiloh, Tenn.	1866	10
Stones River, Tenn.	1865	20
Vicksburg, Miss.	1865	118
Yorktown, Va.	1866	3
Total number: 10	*Total area:*	220

NATIONAL SEASHORES

Assateague Island, Md.-Va.	1965	39,630
Cape Cod, Mass.	1961	44,600
Cape Hatteras, N.C.	1937	28,500
Cape Lookout, N.C.	1966	24,500
Fire Island, N.Y.	1964	19,311
Gulf Islands, Fla.-Miss.	1971	20,430
Padre Island, Tex.	1962	133,918
Point Reyes, Calif.	1962	64,546
Total number: 8	*Total area:*	375,435

NATIONAL PARKWAYS

Baltimore-Washington, Md.	1950	2,431
Blue Ridge, Va.-N.C.	1936	94,749

	Established	Gross Area (acres)
George Washington Memorial, Va.-Md.	1930	7,142
Natchez Trace, Miss.-Tenn.-Ala.	1938	45,298
Suitland, Md.-D.C.	1949	731
Total number: 5	Total area:	150,350

NATIONAL LAKESHORES

Apostle Islands, Wis.	1970	42,826
Indiana Dunes, Ind.	1966	8,721
Pictured Rocks, Mich.	1966	67,000
Sleeping Bear Dunes, Mich.	1970	71,068
Total number: 4	Total area:	189,615

NATIONAL SCENIC RIVERWAYS

Ozark, Mo.	1964	72,101
Saint Croix, Minn.-Wis.	1968	67,747
Wolf, Wis.	1968	5,516
Total number: 3	Total area:	145,364

NATIONAL CAPITAL PARKS*

National Capital Parks, D.C.-Va.-Md.	1790	7,054
Total number: 1	Total area:	7,054

WHITE HOUSE

White House, D.C.	1790	18
Total number: 1	Total area:	18

PARKS (Other)

Catoctin Mountain, Md.	1936	5,769
Piscataway, Md.	1961	1,059
Prince William Forest, Va.	1936	18,572
Theodore Roosevelt Island, D.C.	1932	88
Wolf Trap Farm, Va.	1966	118
Total number: 5	Total area:	25,605

NATIONAL RECREATION AREAS

Amistad, Tex.	1965	65,000

*Comprises 706 units within the District of Columbia.

	Established	*Gross Area (acres)*
Arbuckle, Okla.	1965	8,851
Bighorn Canyon, Wyo.-Mont.	1964	122,623
Coulee Dam, Wash.	1946	100,059
Curecanti, Colo.	1965	41,103
Delaware Water Gap, Pa.-N.J.	1965	68,826
Glen Canyon, Ariz.-Utah	1958	1,196,545
Lake Chelan, Wash.	1968	62,000
Lake Mead, Ariz.-Nev.	1936	1,936,978
Ross Lake, Wash.	1968	107,000
Sanford, Tex.	1965	41,097
Shadow Mountain, Colo.	1952	18,240
Whiskeytown-Shasta-Trinity, Calif.	1962	41,987
Total number: 13	*Total area:*	3,810,309

APPENDIXES

	Established	*Gross Area*
Roosevelt, Campobello, Canada	1964	2,722
Total number: 1	*Total area:*	2,722

NATIONAL SCIENTIFIC RESERVE

Ice Age, Wis.	1964	32,500
Total number: 1	*Total area:*	32,500

NATIONAL SCENIC TRAIL

Appalachian Trail, Maine-N.H.-N.Y.-N.J.-Vt.-Mass.-Conn.-Pa.-Md.-Va.-W.Va.-Tenn.-Ga.-N.C.	1968	50,000
Total number: 1	*Total area:*	50,000

GRAND TOTAL
284 Areas
29,808,666 Acres

Bibliography

BOOKS

ABBEY, EDWARD. *Desert Solitaire: A Season in the Wilderness.* New York: Simon & Schuster, 1968.

ADAMS, ANSEL. *These We Inherit: The Parklands of America.* San Francisco: The Sierra Club, 1962.

ALBRIGHT, HORACE M., and TAYLOR, FRANK J. *"Oh Ranger!": A Book About the National Parks.* New York: Dodd, Mead, 1947.

CHITTENDEN, HIRAM M. *Yellowstone National Park: Historical and Descriptive.* (5th ed., rev.) Palo Alto, Calif.: Stanford University Press, 1949.

HOSMER, CHARLES B. *Presence of the Past: A History of the Preservation Movement in the United States Before Williamsburg.* New York: Putnam's, 1965.

ISE, JOHN. *Our National Park Policy: A Critical History.* Baltimore: Johns Hopkins Press, 1961.

JONES, HOLWAY R. *John Muir and the Sierra Club: The Battle for Yosemite.* San Francisco: Sierra Club, 1965.

LEOPOLD, ALDO. *A Sand County Almanac, and Sketches Here and There.* New York: Oxford University Press, 1950.

NASH, RODERICK. *Wilderness and the American Mind.* New Haven, Conn.: Yale University Press, 1967.

———, ed. *The American Environment: Readings in the History of Conservation.* Reading, Mass.: Addison-Wesley, 1968.

OLSEN, JACK. *Night of the Grizzlies.* New York: Putnam's, 1971.

One Third of the Nation's Land. A Report to the President and to the Congress by the Public Land Law Review Commission. Washington, D.C.: Government Printing Office, 1970.

261

OUTDOOR RECREATION RESOURCES REVIEW COMMISSION. *Outdoor Recreation for America: A Report to the President and the Congress.* Washington, D.C.: Government Printing Office, 1962.

ROOSEVELT, NICHOLAS. *Conservation: Now or Never.* New York: Dodd, Mead, 1970.

SHANKLAND, ROBERT. *Steve Mather of the National Parks.* New York: Knopf, 1970 (rev. and enl. ed.).

STEGNER, WALLACE, ed. *This Is Dinosaur.* New York: Knopf, 1955.

SWAIN, DONALD. *Wilderness Defender: Horace M. Albright and Conservation.* Chicago: University of Chicago Press, 1970.

TILDEN, FREEMAN. *Interpreting Our Heritage.* (Rev. ed.) Chapel Hill: University of North Carolina Press, 1967.

————. *The National Parks.* (Rev. ed.) New York: Knopf, 1968.

TREFETHEN, JAMES B. *Crusade for Wildlife.* Harrisburg, Pa.: Stackpole, 1961.

UDALL, STEWART L. *The Quiet Crisis.* New York: Holt, Rinehart & Winston, 1963.

United Nations List of National Parks and Equivalent Reserves. Prepared for the United Nations Economic and Social Council by the International Union for the Conservation of Nature and Natural Resources. Brussels: Hayez, 1971.

ARTICLES AND PAMPHLETS

ALBRIGHT, HORACE M. "Origins of National Park Service Administration of Historic Sites." Philadelphia: Eastern National Park and Monuments Association, 1971.

CAHN, ROBERT. "Will Success Spoil the National Parks?" Boston: Christian Science Publishing Society, 1968.

DARLING, F. FRASER, and EICHHORN, NOEL D. "Man and Nature in the National Parks." Washington: Conservation Foundation, 1969.

DEVOTO, BERNARD. "Let's Close the National Parks," *Harper's Magazine,* October, 1953.

HOPE, JACK. "Hassles in the Park," *Natural History,* May, 1971. An account of the July 4th riot in Yosemite in 1970.

KOEHLER, ROBERT E. "Our Park Service Serves Architecture Well," *AIA Journal,* January, 1971.

LEE, RONALD F. "Public Use of the National Park System." Washington, D.C.: Department of the Interior, 1968.

MARCUSE, PETER. "Is the National Parks Movement Anti-urban?" *Parks and Recreation Magazine,* July, 1971.

MITCHELL, JOHN. "The Bitter Struggle for a National Park," *American Heritage,* April, 1970.

"The National Parks," a special issue of *American West,* containing

"Six Chapters in the History of an American Idea." Palo Alto, Calif.: American West, 1969.

"National Parks and Landmarks" (areas administered by the National Park Service), National Park Service. Washington, D.C.: Government Printing Office, 1970.

"Park Concession Policy." Hearings Before the Subcommittee on National Parks of the Committee on Interior and Insular Affairs: House of Representatives. Washington, D.C.: Government Printing Office, 1964.

"Park Road Standards," National Park Service. Washington, D.C.: Government Printing Office, 1968.

REICH, CHARLES A. "Bureaucracy and the Forests." Santa Barbara, Calif.: Center for the Study of Democratic Institutions, 1962.

Index